Financial Terms Dictionary - Laws & Regulations Explai

Financial Terms Dictionary

Laws & Regulations Explained

Published July 01, 2017

Revision 1.1

© 2014-2017 Evolving Wealth - Thomas Herold - All rights reserved

Financial Terms Dictionary

Copyright And Trademark Notices

This book is copyright 2017 Thomas Herold (the "Author"). All Rights Reserved. Published in the United States of America. The legal notices, disclosures, and disclaimers at the front of this eBook are Copyright (c) 2017 Thomas Herold and licensed for use by the Author.

All rights reserved. All trademarks and service marks are the properties of their respective owners. All references to these properties are made solely for editorial purposes. Except for marks actually owned by the Author, the Author (as both author and as publisher) does not make any commercial claims to their use, and is not affiliated with them in any way.

Unless otherwise expressly noted, none of the individuals or business entities mentioned herein have endorsed the contents of this book.

Limits of Liability and Disclaimer of Warranties

The materials in this book are provided "as is" and without warranties of any kind either express or implied. The Author disclaims all warranties, express or implied, including, but not limited to, implied warranties of merchantability and fitness for a particular purpose.

The Author does not warrant that defects will be corrected, or that that the site or the server that makes this eBook available are free of viruses or other harmful components. The Author does not warrant or make any representations regarding the use or the results of the use of the materials in this book in terms of their correctness, accuracy, reliability, or otherwise. Applicable law may not allow the exclusion of implied warranties, so the above exclusion may not apply to you.

Under no circumstances, including, but not limited to, negligence, shall the Author be liable for any special or consequential damages that result from the use of, or the inability to use this eBook, even if the Author or his authorised representative has been advised of the possibility of such damages.

Applicable law may not allow the limitation or exclusion of liability or incidental or consequential damages, so the above limitation or exclusion may not apply to you. In no event shall the Author's total liability to you for all damages, losses, and causes of action (whether in contract, tort, including but not limited to, negligence or otherwise) exceed the amount paid by you, if any, for this eBook.

Facts and information are believed to be accurate at the time they were placed in this book. All data provided in this book is to be used for information purposes only. The information contained within is not intended to provide specific legal, financial or tax advice, or any other advice whatsoever, for any individual or company and should not be relied upon in that regard. The services described are only offered in jurisdictions where they may be legally offered. Information provided is not all-inclusive, and is limited to information that is made available and such information should not be relied upon as all-inclusive or accurate.

You are advised to do your own due diligence when it comes to making business decisions and should use caution and seek the advice of qualified professionals. You should check with your accountant, lawyer, or professional advisor, before acting on this or any information. You may not consider any examples, documents, or other content in this eBook or otherwise provided by the Author to be the equivalent of professional advice.

The Author assumes no responsibility for any losses or damages resulting from your use of any link, information, or opportunity contained in this book or within any other information disclosed by the author in any form whatsoever.

About the Author

Thomas Herold is a successful entrepreneur and personal development coach. After a career with one of the largest electronic companies in the world, he realised that a regular job would never fully satisfy his need for connection on a deep level. The only way to live his full potential was to start building his own business and find new ways to be in service to others.

For over 25 years he has helped many people - including himself - build their dream businesses. Toward that goal, he focuses on education, simplified and enhanced by modern technology. He is the author of 15 books with over 200,000 copies distributed worldwide.

Other than his passion for creating businesses, Thomas has spent over 20 years in the self-development field. Placing emphasis on the exploration of consciousness and building practical applications that allow people to express their purpose and passion in life, Thomas's work in this area has provided ample and happy proof that this approach works.

He believes that every person has at least one gift and that, when this gift is developed and nourished, it will serve as a fountainhead of personal happiness and help contribute to a better, more sustainable world.

For the past twelve years Thomas has studied the monetary system and has experienced some profound insights on how money and wealth are related. He has recently committed to sharing this financial knowledge in a new venture - the Financial Terms Dictionary, a hub of financial term descriptions designed to help people get started on their own money makeover and get a financial education in the process.

Thomas's ultimate vision for the Financial Terms Dictionary is to empower people to adopt a wealthy mindset and to create abundance for themselves and others. His ability to explain complex information in simple terms makes him an outstanding teacher and coach.

For more information please visit: Financial Terms Dictionary

Financial Dictionary Series

There are 12 books in this financial dictionaries series available. Click the links below to see an overview and available formats. There is also a premium edition available, which covers over 900 financial terms!

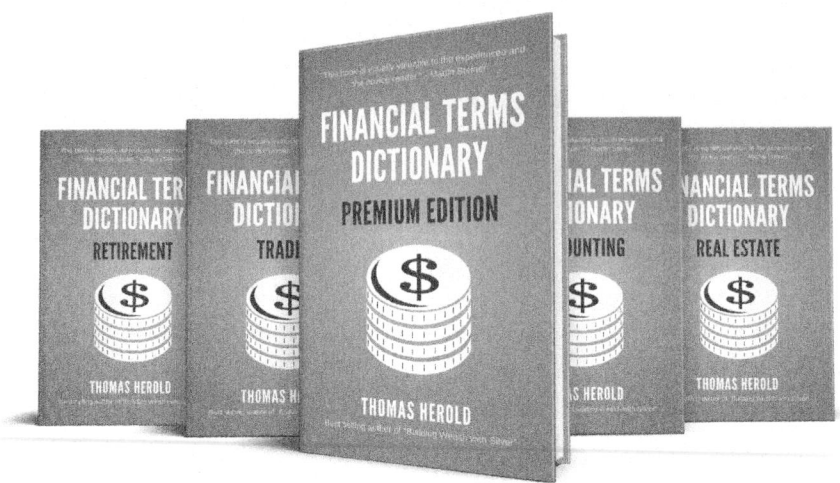

Standard Editions
Financial Terms Dictionary - Accounting Edition
Financial Terms Dictionary - Banking Edition
Financial Terms Dictionary - Corporate Finance Edition
Financial Terms Dictionary - Economics Edition
Financial Terms Dictionary - Investment Edition
Financial Terms Dictionary - Laws & Regulations Edition
Financial Terms Dictionary - Real Estate Edition
Financial Terms Dictionary - Retirement Edition
Financial Terms Dictionary - Trading Edition
Financial Terms Dictionary - Acronyms Edition

Basic & Premium Editions
Financial Terms Dictionary - Basic Edition
Financial Terms Dictionary - Premium Edition

Financial Terms Dictionary - Laws & Regulations Explained

Table Of Contents

1035 Exchange 11
403(b) Plan 13
457(b) Plan 15
501(c) 17
Adjustable Rate Mortgage (ARM) 19
Affidavit 21
Asset Protection 23
Assets Under Management (AUM) 25
Audit 27
Austerity 29
Automated Underwriting 31
Bank Stress Tests 33
Bankruptcy 35
Bretton Woods Agreement 37
Bretton Woods Committee 39
British Bankers Association (BBA) 41
Bureau of Engraving and Printing (BEP) 43
Certificate of Occupancy 45
Certificate of Title 47
Certified Public Accountant (CPA) 49
CFA Institute 51
Chain of Title 53
Chapter 11 Bankruptcy 55
Chapter 7 Bankruptcy 57
Charge Off 59
Commodity Futures Modernization Act (CFMA) 61
Congressional Budget Office (CBO) 63
Constructive Eviction 65
Consumer Data Industry Association 67
Consumer Financial Protection Bureau (CFPB) 69
Council of Economic Advisers (CEA) 71
Credit Report 73
Credit Score 75
Debt Relief Order 77
Deed in Lieu of Foreclosure 79

Financial Terms Dictionary - Laws & Regulations Explained

Defeasance Clause 81
Defined Benefit Plan 83
Department of Justice 85
Department of the Treasury 87
Dodd-Frank Act 89
Due Process Oversight Committee (DPOC) 91
Earned Income Tax Credit (EITC) 93
Environmental Impact Statement (EIS) 95
Environmental Protection Agency (EPA) 97
Equal Credit Opportunity Act (ECOA) 99
European Monetary System (EMS) 101
European Stability Mechanism (ESM) 103
Exchange Rate Mechanism (ERM) 105
Fair Credit Billing Act 107
Fair Housing Act 109
Federal Deposit Insurance Corporation (FDIC) 111
Federal Housing Finance Agency (FHFA) 113
Federal Open Market Committee 115
Federal Reserve Act of 1913 117
Federal Trade Commission (FTC) 119
Financial Industry Regulatory Authority (FINRA) 121
Financial Stability Oversight Council 123
Generally Accepted Accounting Principles (GAAP) 125
Glass Steagall Act 127
HM Treasury 129
Home Affordable Modification Program (HAMP) 131
Import Quotas 133
Internal Revenue Service (IRS) 135
International Accounting Standards Board (IASB) 137
International Bank Account Number (IBAN) 139
International Financial Reporting Standards (IFRS) 141
Keogh Plan 143
Leasehold Estate 145
Liability Insurance 147
Limited Liability Company (LLC) 149
Maastricht Treaty 151
National Association of Securities Dealers (NASDAQ) 153
National Bank Act 155

Nonprofit Organizations 157
Office of Financial Research (OFR) 159
Office of Price Administration 161
Orderly Liquidation Authority 163
OTC Bulletin Board (OTCBB) 165
Payroll Tax 167
Pension Benefit Guaranty Corporation (PBGC) 169
Power of Attorney 171
Promissory Note 173
Protective Tariff 175
Public Company Accounting Oversight Board (PCAOB) 177
Repayment Penalty 179
Required Minimum Distribution (RMD) 181
Sarbanes-Oxley Act of 2002 183
Securities Exchange Act of 1933 185
Securities Exchange Act of 1934 187
Self Directed IRA 189
SEP IRA 191
Sherman Clayton Antitrust Acts 193
Simple IRA 195
Solo 401(k) Plan 197
Tariff Programs 199
Tax Sheltered Annuities 403(b) 201
Term Auction Facility (TAF) 203
Title Deed 205
Trans Pacific Partnership (TPP) 207
Transatlantic Trade Investment Partnership (TTIP) 209
Treasury Inflation Protected Securities (TIPS) 211
Value-Added Tax (VAT) 213
War Production Board (WPB) 215
World Trade Organization (WTO) 217
Zoning Laws 219
American Bankers Association (ABA) 221
American Stock Exchange (AMEX) 223
Appraised Value 224
Capital Gains 226
Capital Loss 228
Corporation 230

Economic Embargo	232
Economic Sanctions	234
Equifax	236
European Central Bank (ECB)	238
Federal Reserve Bank	240
FICO Score	242
Fiscal Policy	244
Foreclosure	246
Fractional Banking System	248
Franchise	250
Intellectual Property	252
IRA Custodian	254
Land Law	256
Legal Tender	258
Lien	260
Money Laundering	262
Oversight	264
Ponzi Scheme	267
Price Controls	269
Price Gouging	271
Progressive Taxes	273
Proportional Taxes	275
Regressive Taxes	277

Financial Terms Dictionary - Laws & Regulations Explained

1035 Exchange

A 1035 Exchange is an exchange process that permits individuals to replace their existing life insurance policy or annuity contract with a similar new contract or policy. Thanks to a provision in the tax code, this can be affected without suffering any negative tax repercussions as part of the trade off exchange. The Internal Revenue Service permits those who hold these kinds of contracts to update their old policies and annuities with those more modern ones that include better benefits, superior investment choices, and lower fees.

The 1035 Exchange is also called a Section 1035 Exchange after the tax code section for which it is named. It literally permits policyholders to transfer their funds out of an endowment, life insurance policy, or annuity into a newer similar vehicle. The way it works is to allow holders to defer their gains. When all of the received proceeds of the original contract become transferred to the newer contract (as there are simultaneously not any loans outstanding on the prior policy), no tax becomes due at point of exchange. Should these proceeds be received and not exchanged according to the 1035 Exchange rules, then all gains obtained out of the first contract become taxable like ordinary income, and not as capital gains.

Gains do not refer to all money received. Instead they are the result of subtracting the gross cash value from the premium tax basis. This basis refers to the original dollar amount put into the contract itself minus the premiums paid for extra benefits or any distributions which qualify as tax free.

In order for this 1035 Exchange to make sense, it has to benefit the policy holder either economically or personally. It is also important for holders to never terminate their in place insurance policies until the newer policy has been fully issued and becomes effective. The holders need to contemplate any health changes since the original policy started. It might cost extra premiums in order for the newer policy to cover them. They might even receive a denial of coverage if the changes in health are too drastic. Similarly, if the holder is well advanced in age, the premium rate may increase.

Some policies also have surrender charges that must be considered. There may be different guarantees, provisions, and interest crediting in the newer policy as well. Most importantly, benefits of the newer policy have to be carefully reviewed. These may change negatively in some cases.

There are rare cases where simply surrendering an existing insurance policy or annuity is more advantageous than engaging in a 1035 Exchange. These primarily occur when the existing contract offers no gain. Sometimes outstanding loans on the initial policy also decrease the benefits of an exchange. In other cases, the original policy may have a "market rate adjustment" type of provision. This would cause the exchange proceeds to be less than those offered in a surrender.

It is usually the case that such a 1035 Exchange will be slower and more involved than simply surrendering the holder's original policy. It can even require a few months much of the time. This is why the conditions that affect the practicality of the exchange include financial conditions of the initial policy carrier, the country's economic climate at the time, and the intentions of the policy holder.

The IRS only deems certain exchanges to be considered "like kind" and allowable. These include life insurance for life insurance, life insurance for non-qualified annuity, life insurance for endowment, endowment for non-qualified annuity, endowment for endowment, and non-qualified annuity for non-qualified annuity. They also will allow multiple numbers of existing contracts to be changed into a single newer contract. It does not work in reverse. A single existing contract can not be exchanged in for multiple newer contracts, per the IRS rules and regulations.

403(b) Plan

403(b) plans were created for employees of schools, churches, and tax exempt organizations. Individuals who are eligible may establish and maintain their own 403(b) accounts. Their employers can and often do make contributions to the employees' accounts. Individuals are able to open one of three different types of 403(b)s.

The first is an annuity plan that an insurance company establishes. These types of plans are sometimes called TDAs tax deferred annuities or TSAs tax sheltered annuities. A second plan type is an account which a retirement custodian offers and manages. With these 403(b)s, the account holders may only choose from mutual funds and regulated investment companies that the custodian allows. The final type is a retirement income account. These accounts accept a combination of mutual funds or annuities for the investment choices.

Employers have some control over these accounts. They are able to decide which financial institution will hold the employees' 403(b) accounts. This determines the kind of plan that the employees are able to set up and fund. Employers receive several advantages from choosing to offer a 403(b).

The benefits which they get to offer their employees are worthwhile. This helps to ensure valuable employees stay with the organization. They also enjoy sharing the funding costs between themselves and their employees. Employers may also choose for the 403(b) to only accept employee contributions if they do not wish to participate financially in the account.

Employees also experience several benefits from these types of retirement vehicles. They may contribute tax deferred dollars from their income. They may also contribute taxed dollars to the accounts. In these Roth 403(b)s, all of their earnings accrue tax free for the entire life of the account. Deferred tax payments until retirement typically allow for the employees to pay fewer taxes as they are often in a more advantageous tax bracket at retirement point. Employees may also obtain loans from their 403(b) accounts as they need them.

A variety of non profit organizations may choose to establish such a 403(b) plan for their employees. This includes any 501(c)(3) tax exempt

Financial Terms Dictionary - Laws & Regulations Explained

organization, co-op hospital service organizations, public school systems, ministers at churches, Native American public school systems, and (USUHS) Uniformed Services for the University of the Health Sciences.

Such 403(b) plans can obtain a variety of contribution types. Employees may have elective deferral contributions taken out of each paycheck. These are taken out in a pretax dollars arrangement. Employees also have the ability to contribute taxed dollars to the accounts. They have these deducted from their payrolls as well.

Employers may also choose to make contributions which are either discretionary or fixed amounts as they desire. Employees and employers may make contributions to Roth 403(b) accounts. These 403(b) accounts may also receive any combination of the previously mentioned contribution types, which demonstrates their flexibility.

Employees have generous annual contribution limits with these plans. In 2016, they may contribute up to $18,000 (or $24,000 if they are over 50 years old and catching up on contributions for retirement). For 2016, employers may also deposit as much as $53,000 (up to 100% of the employee compensation) as an annual contribution.

Regarding distributions, the rules are comparable to the other types of retirement savings vehicles. Distributions of deferred taxed dollars become taxable like regular income when the employee receives them. If these are taken before the employee turns 59 ½, then the withdrawn dollars are assessed the standard 10% penalty for early withdrawals. There are some exceptions to this penalty for which an employee may qualify. One of these exceptions is if the employee terminates the job even before reaching the age of retirement.

Financial Terms Dictionary - Laws & Regulations Explained

457(b) Plan

A 457(b) plan is a retirement savings vehicle. It derives its name from the Internal Revenue Service code that regulates the plans in its section 457(b). Many times this retirement account name is simply shortened to 457 Plan.

There are many similarities between these 457 Plans and tax deferred, employer provided retirement vehicles including 403(b) and 401(k) plans. All of these retirement vehicles are defined contribution plans. People who participate in these 457 Plans set up payroll deductions so that a portion of their income is put into this investment account that is tax free.

The government established these 457 Plans in 1978. They were set up to be another defined contribution account that would help two particular kinds of employers. They are intended for both government employers and non government employers which are tax exempt as with hospitals and charities.

Despite this fact, a few different rules apply for the government plans as opposed to the non government plans. The principle difference revolves around funding. Government 457 Plans have to be funded by the employer in question. The non government 457 Plans are practically all funded by employees. The vast majority of 457(b) plans that private not for profit companies use they only offer to well paid employees usually in upper level management.

With 457 Plans, there must be both a plan administrator and a plan provider. Each plan provides its own limited choices for investment options which are particular to the plan.

Rollover rules are different for these 457 Plans as well. The non government versions can not be transferred over to qualified retirement plans which include IRA and 401(k)s. Instead they can only be rolled over to other tax exempt 457 Plans. The rules are different with government sponsored employer plans. These may be transferred into another employer's 401(k), 403(b), or 457(b) plan as well as to an IRA account. The new plan must permit account holders to make such transfers.

Financial Terms Dictionary - Laws & Regulations Explained

Withdrawals are easier for government sponsored plans as well. Individuals may do early withdrawals before they reach the 59 ½ year old age of retirement and not have to suffer the 10% early withdrawal penalty. The full withdrawn amount would be taxed as regular income. Employees who are switching jobs may also keep the money where it is assuming the plan permits this.

Rollover rules on 457(b) plans are pretty standard. If funds are dispersed to the account owner, he or she has a maximum of 60 days to finish the rollover process. Beyond this time, the IRS considers this money to have been distributed and to be taxable. Owners are also restricted to doing a single rollover in a calendar year with these retirement vehicles.

The date on which the owners receive their 457 Plan distribution is when the one year rule commences. While the money is in the 60 day process of being rolled over, it may not be invested. Direct rollovers avoid the dangers of the 60 day rule. An account holder never obtains a distribution check (as with indirect rollovers) in this type of transfer. Instead, the plan provider will directly transfer all money to the new IRA or retirement plan.

Investment choices in 457 Plans are more limited than with Self Directed IRAs or Solo 401(k) plans. The plan provider will restrict choices to ones that fit their plan. If they permit them, owners may invest their funds in individual bonds and stocks, fixed or indexed annuities, exchange traded funds, and mutual funds.

Gold bullion can not be purchased by these plans. Paper gold investments such as stocks of gold mining firms, mutual funds containing gold mining companies, or gold ETFs like GLD and mining ETFs may be purchased instead.

Financial Terms Dictionary - Laws & Regulations Explained

501(c)

501(c) designations refer to incorporations of entities which are established as charitable not for profit corporations. These charitable operations are companies which are founded in order to offer the benefits of a community service instead of attempting to make profits for their founders or managers.

When such an outfit is incorporated it becomes legal. This gives it responsibility for the actions it carries out within its community. This legal status is critical for the founder. It takes away much of the legal responsibility of the individual who starts up the company. Any people who set up these 501(c) companies do so with the goal of having all legal liability for any damages removed from them. Instead, the responsibilities transfer over to the 501(c) itself so that the founder's own personal assets are protected from any lawsuits or creditors.

Every state has its own particular set of rules for creating a 501(c) company. This is why participants are encouraged to seek out qualified financial and legal advice before they incorporate under this status. The expenses involved in establishing such a corporation are different depending on how large the corporation proves to be. The larger the outfit, the more expensive it is to establish.

The 501(c) status refers to the Internal Revenue Service code section that pertains to the charitable company rules. The document itself is a very dense and difficult read. This helps to explain how the not for profits earned such a non creative and cumbersome name associated with this type of company.

These 501(c)s do not have to pay any income tax to the federal, state, or local governments. The trade off for such a benefit is that they are not allowed to participate in election campaigns with a goal of helping a single candidate to be chosen versus another one. The companies are also forbidden to provide any material or financial benefits to the owners or officers of the organization itself. Such rules apply to the not for profit for its entire life span. This means that companies can not switch their status back to and from 501(c). Any not for profit organization that is no longer such an outfit must be disbanded.

Financial Terms Dictionary - Laws & Regulations Explained

This type of corporate designation proves to be a critical method for individuals who wish to establish organizations to help their overall community. It protects them from personal risks to their assets in the process. It also permits charity outfits to expand to a big enough company that they can affect major changes. These operations can grow far larger than the person who started them and can also outlive him or her.

The Internal Revenue Service has a variety of rules that individuals must observe in order to properly organize and operate under the 501(c) designation. Not a penny of the earnings may go into the hands of an individual or shareholder. The outfit must also not endeavor to sway any federal, state, or local legislation as a mainstay of its daily activities. They similarly may not be involved in political campaigns either for or against any candidates in the election. These organizations must be entirely charitable organizations in order to qualify for this tax exempt status.

Such operations also may not be created or run to benefit any persons' private interests. For any not for profit that participates in excess benefit transactions with groups or people who have significant influence in the operation, they may suffer from the government levying an excise tax against the manager or individual who agreed to such a transaction in the first place.

Adjustable Rate Mortgage (ARM)

Adjustable Rate Mortgages, also known by their acronym ARM's, are those mortgages whose interest rates change from time to time. These changes commonly occur based on an index. As a result of changing interest rates, payments will rise and fall along with them.

Adjustable Rate Mortgages involve a number of different elements. These include margins, indexes, discounts, negative amortization, caps on payments and rates, recalculating of your loan, and payment options. When considering an adjustable rate mortgage, you should always understand both the most that your monthly payments might go up, as well as your ability to make these higher payments in the future.

Initial payments and rates are important to understand with these ARM's. They stay in effect for only certain time frames that run from merely a month to as long as five years or longer. With some of these ARM's, these initial payments and rates will vary tremendously from those that are in effect later in the life of the loan. Your payments and rates can change significantly even when interest rates remain level. A way to determine how much this will vary on a particular ARM loan is to compare the annual percentage rate and the initial rate. Should this APR prove to be much greater than the initial rate, then likely the payments and rates will similarly turn out to be significantly greater when the loan adjusts.

It is important to understand that the majority of Adjustable Rate Mortgages' monthly payments and interest rates will vary by the month, the quarter, the year, the three year period, and the five year time frame. The time between these changes in rate is referred to as the adjustment period. Loans that feature one year periods are called one year ARM's, as an example.

These Adjustable Rate Mortgages' interest rates are comprised of two portions of index and margin. The index actually follows interest rates themselves. Your payments are impacted by limits on how far the rate can rise or fall. As the index rises, so will your interest rates and payments generally. As the index declines, your monthly payments could similarly fall, assuming that your ARM is one that adjusts down. ARM rates can be based on a number of different indexes, including LIBOR the London Interbank

Financial Terms Dictionary - Laws & Regulations Explained

Offered rate, COFI the Cost of Funds Index, and a CMT one year constant maturity Treasury security. Other lenders use their own proprietary model.

Margin proves to be the premium to the rate that a lender itself adds. This is commonly a couple of percentage points that are added directly to the index rate amount. These amounts vary from one lender to the next, and are commonly fixed during the loan term. The fully indexed rate is comprised of index plus margin. When the loan's initial rate turns out to be lower than the fully indexed rate, this is referred to as a discounted index rate. So an index that sat at five percent and had a three percent margin tacked on would be a fully indexed rate of eight percent.

Financial Terms Dictionary - Laws & Regulations Explained

Affidavit

An Affidavit is a declaration in writing which includes a sworn oath or positive confirmation that written contents are factual and true. These declarations and statements could be made related to court cases. They also could be made to support an important document as with mortgage applications or tax returns.

Though many people may not be aware of it, a great number of forms prove to be affidavits. This is because they have a line that states the individuals have filled in the form to the best of their knowledge. The line must also mention that deliberately entering information that is incorrect will lead to perjury charges. If a person is found guilty of perjury charges, it can lead to significant time spent in jail.

The word affidavit is originally taken from the Latin. The Latin roots signifies that individuals have pledged their faith with complete knowledge of the law. It is interesting that affidavits are always voluntarily undertaken documents. This means that no parties in a court case are able to make a person give such statement under oath. Courts can force individuals to give deposition accounts. Depositions differ from an affidavit. They may both be statements that are written, but depositions will be cross examined in a court.

Affidavits must involve knowledge that is personally known by the individual who declares them. This means that persons who do not include information of which they were unaware will not be punished or deemed to be in perjury. Personal knowledge can cover a person's opinion too. In such cases, the statement must be unequivocally stated to be opinion instead of a known fact. Any individual is allowed to provide an affidavit if he or she maintains the necessary mental ability to comprehend how serious the oath given actually is. This is why guardians of mentally ill patients are able to provide such an affidavit on their behalf.

These documents are generally formally witnessed by a qualified official such as a notary public or an account clerk. Notaries are agents who receive a small fee in exchange for witnessing the signing of legal documents for individuals, as with mortgage forms or real estate transactions. This witness signing the document means that the person pledges that the information is accurate and realizes how important this oath is. Documents like these can be utilized in court as evidence. They can also be submitted alongside supporting materials with various kinds of transactions, including for social services.

Individuals who sign affidavits should be extremely careful that they read the documents several times, especially if another individual is recording them. This is because the documents are oaths which are legally binding. The statements contained within must be correctly and clearly related. When the signor recognizes errors in the document, as with facts on a mortgage application, these need to be corrected in advance of signing. This is more important than the inconvenience it will cause the officials who have written down the information and who are witnessing the signing and oath that accompanies it.

Asset Protection

Asset Protection and planning refers to strategies and practices for protecting personal wealth. It happens through deliberate and involved planning processes that safeguard individuals' assets from the potential claims of any creditors. Both businesses and individuals alike can employ these specific techniques to reduce the ability of creditors to seize personal or business property within the legal boundaries of creditor debtor law.

What makes Asset Protection so powerful is that it is able to insulate a variety of assets and all legally. It does not require any of the shady or illegal activities inherent in concealing assets, illegal money transferring, bankruptcy fraud, or tax evasion. The asset experts will warn their clients that efficient protection of assets starts in advance of a liability, incident, or claim occurring. The reason is that it is generally over late to begin arranging such protection afterward. There are a wide variety of normal means for protecting such personal or business assets. Among the most popular are family limited partnerships, accounts receivable financing, and asset protection trusts.

In the heavily litigious society of the United States, Asset Protection involves protecting property from those who might win a judgment in court. There are a variety of lawsuits that could threaten a person's or business' assets. Among these are car accident claims, unintentional negligent acts, and even foreclosure on property lawsuits where the mortgage is no longer paid. The ultimate goal in Asset Protection is to take any nonexempt from creditors assets and move them to a position where they become exempt assets beyond the reach of any claims of the various creditors.

Asset Protection which an individual or business does when a lawsuit is already underway or even imminent to be filed will likely be reversed by the courts. This way they can seize the hidden assets that were deliberately transferred to protect them from an imminent court case judgment. This is the ultimate reason why effective protection of assets has to start well in advance of the first hints of litigious activity or creditor claims.

Two principal goals must be combined in order to effectively construct an efficient and ironclad Asset Protection plan. These include achieving both long term and short term goals and reaching estate planning goals. The financial goals component involves clearly understanding present and future income sources, the amount of resources needed for retirement, and any resources which will remain to leave to any heirs via estate planning. This helps people to come up with highly detailed financial plans.

After this has been done, individuals will want to examine carefully any present assets to decide if they are effectively exempted from any and all sundry creditors. The ones that are not should be clearly repositioned so that they are exempt. This also involves planning to position future assets so that they are similarly effectively protected.

The next step is to come up with a complete and all inclusive estate plan. It should encompass all forms of asset protection and relevant planning via advanced techniques of estate planning. Among these are irrevocable trusts for the individuals, their children, spouses, and beneficiaries as well as family limited liability companies.

The most common mistake that people or businesses make with this Asset Protection planning is waiting until it is too late to safeguard the assets. The other mistake is assuming that such planning can be done rapidly or as a short term fix for a longer term problem. Protecting assets is ultimately longer term planning that must be done carefully and ahead of potential creditor claims on assets or pending lawsuits.

Assets Under Management (AUM)

Assets under management (AUM) refer to the aggregate market value of all assets which an investment management firm or other financial institution (such as a bank) manages for its investor clients. The exact definition of AUM varies from one company to another. Each of them has their own distinctive proprietary formula for figuring up this all important statistic.

There are financial institutions, management companies, hedge funds, and banks that include the client bank deposits, cash, and mutual funds within their calculations. Still others choose to limit this figure to the funds which are under actual discretionary management using the sole choices of the fund manager. In this case, the investor gives over total investment responsibility and control to the management firm and fund manager in question.

Assets under management describe the amount of investment money which such an investment management firm actually controls. These investments are kept within a hedge fund or mutual fund. They are usually actively managed by a brokerage company, venture capital firm, or portfolio manager.

Assets under management express the amount of cash in the fund. It can also reveal the total amount of assets which they manage for their total client base. Alternatively it can be used to refer to the complete amount of assets the company manages for only one particular client. This would include all of the money which the manager is able to utilize in making transactions. As an example, if investors have placed $50,000 within their investment portfolios, the manager of the fund is allowed to purchase and sell whichever shares he so chooses by applying the funds of the investors without having to obtain their consent in advance.

The actual AUM fluctuates daily on every given market trading day. This depends on the investor money flow from one asset fund to another. The performance of assets also changes the Assets under management figure as well. The change in fund value or company investments will therefore alter the total AUM.

Every regulatory regime makes its own rules regarding how large a

Financial Terms Dictionary - Laws & Regulations Explained

company must be to be closely regulated. Within the United States, after a given investment management firm possesses in excess of $30 million under management, they are required by law to register their company with the supreme oversight agency the SEC Securities and Exchange Commission. A given investor's AUM total will decide on what level of service they will receive from their brokerage firm or financial advisor. A great number of companies maintain minimum AUM amounts for certain kinds of investments. This has much to do with qualification levels of the investor in question. Some forms of investments also involve minimum purchase agreement requirements.

Figuring up the total Assets under management requires one of several calculations. With superior investment performance, the figure will rise in every case. As new customers join a firm or additional assets are obtained, this will also increase the AUM. The figure will drop as performance of the investments diminishes, with clients leaving the firm, redemptions, withdrawals, and fund closures. Because AUM includes all investor capital, it may also be comprised of the executives' assets with the firm.

The total currency amount of Assets under management matters immensely to a management company because of the management fees which they derive from these figures. It is true that an investment company garners a certain percentage in management fees based upon these assets. They are also able to employ their AUM numbers as a type of marketing tool to bring in still more investors and assets to the fund. Investors get a true feel for the size of the financial management company and its operations compared to the various competitors within the industry when they consider the figure. This still does not reveal full details about the potential of the investment company and its various investment choices and strategies.

Financial Terms Dictionary - Laws & Regulations Explained

Audit

An audit refers to a third party evaluation and review of a business or individual's financial statements. The goal is to ensure that the financial records are both accurate and reflective of the transactions for the entity they represent. Such a review can be carried out by an external auditing firm or by accounting employees within an organization itself.

There is also the possibility for the Internal Revenue Service itself to conduct audits in order to confirm the veracity of a business or individual's tax payer returns and transactions. As the IRS engages in such audits, this usually creates a dark cloud over the victim organization or individual. This is because such IRS audits come with a negative connotation. It is as if the government suspects the taxpayers in question have engaged in illegal activities with their taxes or income declarations.

For those audits which an external company performs on behalf of corporations, these are often very useful in taking away the tendency towards personal bias. It means that the final picture of the corporation should be more complete, unbiased, and accurate. Such audits are often seeking any inadvertent material error in the corporations' statements or activities. They reassure shareholders of the company that the financial statements are accurate. As third parties undertake audits, the bias of the internal accountant who would otherwise be engaging in the auditing tasks is eliminated.

This could be regarding a company subsidiary or division, the entire corporation or one system within it, or the financial books of the business. There is also no pressure that a member of management will think negatively of the employee for producing less than stellar outcomes from the audit when the corporation engages and retains an external accounting firm.

The majority of publicly traded firms become audited one time each year. Enormous corporations can be audited even every month. There are companies in industries where their oversight organization requires legally that the firm receive routine audits so as to eliminate any temptation to deliberately misrepresent financial information. Such misrepresentation is literally called fraud. Still other large corporations look at audits and auditors

Financial Terms Dictionary - Laws & Regulations Explained

as a valuable tool to ascertain how effective their financial reports and associated internal controls of them actually are.

Two different types of auditors exist in the realm of external audits. These are statutory auditors and external cost auditors. The statutory varieties independently labor to consider the quality of the financial statements and reports. The external cost auditors consider and review the cost sheets and statements to make certain they do not contain any errors, misrepresentations, or fraudulent facts or figures. Each of the two different kinds of auditing personnel work with a range of varying standards that are different than those which the corporation hiring them would engage in otherwise.

Such internal auditors will be hired by the firm or other organization on whose behalf they are engaging in the audit in the first place. They do their fiduciary best to deliver reliable and accurate information and certification to the management of the company, the board of directors, and shareholders regarding the books and all internal operating systems and procedures of the company in question.

Other auditors will be consultants. They will still utilize the standards of the corporation which they are auditing instead of an independent set of standards, even though they are not internal employees of the organization. Such consultants are brought in when the corporation or other organization lacks the necessary resources to perform their own internal operational audits.

Auditors must meet certain specified standards which their jurisdictional governments lay out when they conduct these audits. The American Institute of Certified Public Accountants has its respected external audit standards which they call the GAAS Generally Accepted Auditing Standards. Internationally, the International Auditing and Assurance Board maintain their International Standards on Auditing. The U.S. also has a regulatory body dating back to 2002 called the PCAOB, or Public Company Accounting Oversight Board.

Austerity

Austerity proves to be an unpopular group of government economic policies which a country engages in usually unwillingly in order to reign in public deficits and to reduce government owed debts. These drastic measures turn out to be the response from the government in question to their public debt which becomes so big that the default possibilities on debt service payments become a serious risk.

Such default risk can get out of hand rather fast. This happens when a nation, corporation, or even person falls further and further into debt, lenders retaliate by exacting a greater interest rate on subsequent loans, and force the downward vicious spiral to become all the worse as it costs more to raise capital.

Austerity became necessary after the global financial crisis and meltdown which erupted in 2007 bankrupted numerous especially western developed governments because they were gathering lower tax revenues. This exposed government spending and debt levels which were ultimately unsustainable.

There were a few European countries including Greece, Spain, and the United Kingdom that tried out austerity because they needed to reduce their budget outlays. It became practically forced on them by the economic conditions brought on by the ensuing recession throughout Europe. In this economic contraction, many eurozone members could no longer effectively service their rising debts since they had no control over the euro currency to print more of it and devalue their currency as they needed to do.

There are three principal kinds of such austerity measures. The first one focuses on creating higher tax and fee revenues. Many times this is to encourage additional government outlays and spending. The end goal of such a plan is to encourage growth by seizing the rewards of higher taxation and then spending it to lubricate the stalling economy.

A second form is often referred to as the Angela Merkel model in honor of the long time chancellor of Germany. This kind concentrates on increasing taxes at the same time as it reduces expenditures on any services deemed to be less essential than others. The final form is a reduced taxation and simultaneous reduced spending effort. This is the means that most free market enthusiasts espouse.

The majority of economists can actually agree on one thing, which is that increasing taxes will boost ultimate revenue collection. Many different struggling European nations adopted this form of austerity to solve their budgetary problems. Greece boosted its national value added tax VAT rate to 23 percent back in 2010 as well as adding another 10 percent import duties on vehicles. For those with higher income brackets, the Greek government in Athens increased their income tax rates. Besides this a few new taxes were implemented and assessed on property holdings and values.

Besides increasing taxes and boosting revenues, governments can also reduce the amount of spending which they pursue. This is often regarded as the more effective way of lessening the deficit, though it is far more painful for the lower classes of society as well as the poor which lose access to important basic government services such as high quality health care and welfare and rent subsidies as a result. Cutting spending can take a wide range of forms. There are subsidies, grants, redistribution of wealth, government services, entitlement programs, national defense, government employee benefits, and foreign aid given to poor countries. Reducing spending is true, albeit often quite painful, austerity.

There are a wide variety of historical examples of such austerity measures. The most successful one in the modern era in response to a recession happened within the U.S. in the years of 1920 and 1921. President Warren Harding drastically reduced the federal budget by nearly 50 percent. He simultaneously reduced taxes on all income brackets and cut the debt by over 30 percent. Greece is another much sadder case of this form of spending cuts and tax increases. While they have managed to cut the national deficit and debt through these programs and policies, the country has been in and out of painful and deep recessions for most of the past decade as a direct result.

Automated Underwriting

Automated underwriting proves to be one of the biggest changes that has come to the mortgage lending business in the last several years. The process uses computers to handle the process of underwriting mortgage loans. There are numerous benefits to the concept. Among them are lower closing costs, quicker loan approvals, fewer requirements for documentation, and approval for applications which human underwriters denied in the past.

Underwriting itself is the means whereby the underwriters approve or deny mortgage loans. They do this by considering the property, the ability to pay back the loan, and the credit worthiness of the individuals applying. For most of mortgage loan history, people exclusively handled these activities. In recent years, programs have demonstrated that computers are able to perform these jobs quicker, with greater accuracy, and generally better.

There are now automated underwriting systems that handle much of this work load. Both Freddie Mac and Fannie Mae have created their own such systems to evaluate mortgage loans. They are the two biggest investors in mortgages within the United States. Freddie Mac has a system called Loan Prospector. Fannie Mae developed Desktop Underwriter to perform these same functions. Both computer systems display their abilities via a predictive model. They take the specific mortgage applications and compute a quantitative risk factor for them.

Automated underwriting systems are easy to apply through. The lender or mortgage broker queries the applicant for information. He or she enters this data into the underwriting system. The system pulls a credit report to accompany it. The system next creates a Findings Report using the credit report and application information. The Findings Report reveals the determination on the loan application approval. It provides the list of documents that will be required in order to verify the data of the application.

Consumers benefit from these systems. The approvals they issue represent binding commitments from either Freddie Mac or Fannie Mae. If the information put in is correct and can be documented, then the consumers can enjoy the confidence of knowing that their loan will be issued.

Financial Terms Dictionary - Laws & Regulations Explained

Borrowers no longer have to come up with voluminous amounts of application documents and complete major paperwork thanks to these systems. The new automated underwriting systems commonly only require a single pay stub instead of the two months that human underwriters typically wanted.

Approval time spans are significantly shorter now with these computers. The Findings Report appears in only minutes after the lender enters the information into the system. Less documentation also means that the time frames are reduced.

Consumers receive the benefit of the savings from these systems. Appraisal fees are typically $100 less. Credit report costs come down by $50 or more. Loan origination fees may be less as well.

The greatest single benefit of the new systems is that with automated underwriting, consumers who used to be refused loans are many times approved now. Consumers with excellent credit but fewer down payment resources especially benefit from this system. In the past they would not have been approved, but the system model assigns less importance to the full down payment amount that human underwriters did.

One helpful characteristic of these automated underwriting systems revolves around property identification. Human underwriters often required the property for which they were applying for a mortgage to be stated on the application. The new systems do not have such a requirement. This benefits consumers who are still shopping for a house. Once they are approved by the system, they gain a powerful tool for negotiating deals with the sellers of properties.

Financial Terms Dictionary - Laws & Regulations Explained

Bank Stress Tests

Bank stress tests are special analyses that a government authority or company runs to determine the strength of a bank to resist difficult economic times. They conduct such tests using economic conditions that are unfavorable to learn if the banks possess sufficient capital to survive the effects of negative financial environments. In the United States, the law requires that banks which claim at least $50 billion worth of assets must perform their own internal stress tests. Their risk management department is responsible for overseeing these. The Federal Reserve conducts these stress tests on such banks as well.

The idea behind these bank stress tests is to look at several critical risks which can afflict the banks and banking system. They are supposed to evaluate the financial condition of the bank being tested in one or more crisis scenarios with regards to liquidity risk, market risk, and credit risk. The tests simulate fictitious potential crises using a number of different factors that the International Monetary Fund and Federal Reserve determine.

This mostly came about after the worldwide financial crisis and Great Recession of 2007-2009. As many banks had failed or nearly collapsed, government and international bodies became more concerned about checking on the financial strength of banks in potential crisis scenarios.

These bank stress tests were effectively set up and used on a widespread basis after this worst collapse since the Great Depression of the 1930s. The financial crisis had left in its wake a number of financial institutions, investment banks, and commercial banks that had insufficient capital. The stress tests were established to deal with this threat before it became severely problematic again.

There are two main types of bank stress tests that exist. The Federal Reserve runs its own yearly oversight stress tests of the U.S. banks that have at least $50 billion in assets on their balance sheets. The primary purpose of such a stress test is to learn if the banks possess sufficient capital to weather the storm of challenging economic conditions.

The company operated stress tests are done twice a year by law. They

Financial Terms Dictionary - Laws & Regulations Explained

must be strictly reported according to the deadlines set by the Fed. Results must be turned in to the Federal Reserve board by no later than January 5th and July 5th.

In either of the stress tests, the banks receive a typical set of circumstances to evaluate their performance. It might be a 30% free fall in the prices of housing, a 5% to 10% decline in the stock market, and a 10% or higher unemployment rate. The banks must then take their future nine quarters of financial forecasts to ascertain if their capital levels are sufficient to endure the hypothetical crisis.

These bank stress tests have broader repercussions. Banks must make public their results by publishing them after they undergo the tests. The pubic and investors then learn how the bank in question would survive in a significant crisis situation. Laws and regulations passed since the financial crisis require that companies which are unable to pass the stress tests must cut their share buyback programs and dividend payments so that they can preserve the capital they have.

There are cases where banks receive a conditional passing grade on a stress test. This result states that the bank nearly failed its test. It puts them at risk of not being allowed to engage in more capital distributions going forward. Conditional passing means that a bank has to turn in a plan of action to address the capital shortfall.

These failures cause a bank to look bad to not only investors but the banking public. There have been a number of banks that failed such stress tests. Foreign banks like Germany's Deutsche Bank and Spain's Santander have failed to pass such tests on a number of occasions.

Financial Terms Dictionary - Laws & Regulations Explained

Bankruptcy

Bankruptcy is a term that refers to the elimination or restructuring of a person or company's debt. Three principal different types of bankruptcy filing are available. These are the personal bankruptcy options of Chapter 7 and Chapter 13 filings, and the business bankruptcy restructuring option of Chapter 11.

Individuals avail themselves of Chapter 7 or Chapter 13 bankruptcy filings when their financial situations warrant significant help. With a Chapter 7 filing, all of an individual's debt is erased through discharge. This provides a new start for the debtor. Due to changes in laws made back in October 2005, not every person is able to obtain this type of total debt relief any longer. As a result of this new bankruptcy law, a means test came into being that prospective bankruptcy filers must successfully pass if they are to prove eligibility for this kind of bankruptcy relief.

The net effect of this new test is that consumers find it much more difficult to qualify for total debt elimination under Chapter 7. Besides the means test, the cost of bankruptcy attorneys has now risen dramatically by upwards of a hundred percent as a result of the new laws. Before these laws went into effect, Chapter 7 filings represented around seventy percent of all personal filings for bankruptcy. Chapter 7 offered the individual the advantage of simply walking away from debts that they might be capable of paying back with sufficient time and some interest rate help.

Chapter 13 Bankruptcy filings prove to be much like debt restructuring procedures. In these proceedings, a person's creditors are made to agree to the repayment of principal and zero interest on debts over a longer span of time. The individual gets to keep all of her or his assets in this form of filing. The most common motivation for Chapter 13 proves to be a desire to stop a foreclosure on a home. Individuals are able to achieve this by halting foreclosure proceedings and catch up on back mortgage payments. Once a court examines the debtor's budget, it will sign off on the plan for repayment proposed by the person. Depending on the level of an individual's income, he or she may have no choice but to file a Chapter 13 filling, as a result to the 2005 law changes.

Companies and corporations that are in financial distress may avail themselves of bankruptcy protection as well. Chapter 11 allows for such businesses to have protection from their creditors while they restructure their debt. Some individuals who have a higher income level will take advantage of this form of filing as well, since it does not place income restrictions on the entity filing. It has been instrumental in saving many large and well known companies over the years, including K-Mart, that actually emerged strong enough from the Chapter 11 bankruptcy to buy out higher end rival Sears afterward.

Financial Terms Dictionary - Laws & Regulations Explained

Bretton Woods Agreement

The Bretton Woods agreement represents the outcomes of a three week conference that the United Nations held to set up a new monetary system at the end of World War II. The U.N. organized this meeting called the United Nations Monetary and Financial Conference for July 1 to July 22 of 1944. They held it at Bretton Woods in New Jersey, which gave its name to the deal that ultimately resulted from the conference. The agreement itself proved to be a famed framework that set up a new exchange rate system.

Three significant outcomes resulted from this conference. Two of them are still a major part of the world financial system today. First the group agreed on the Bretton Woods Agreement which set up a new foreign exchange system. Besides this, the United Nations authorized forming the International Monetary Fund and also the International Bank for Reconstruction and Development.

A new foreign exchange system had been called for in the wake of World War II. The international economic system had been destroyed by the already more than five years of fierce global fighting. Allied nations decided even before they successfully concluded the war they needed to come up with a new currency and a plan to rebuild the devastated nations and world economy.

The conference saw 730 delegates attend from all of the 44 Allied countries. They met at the Mount Washington Hotel and spent three weeks coming up with the new currency system and financial institutions. On the last day of the conference on July 22, they signed the Bretton Woods agreement.

The new system rested on several key proposals. One of these involved currency convertibility. All currencies had to be converted for trade purposes and to settle current account transactions. The U.S. sat in a position of commanding strength as it controlled fully two thirds of all the gold in the world.

This gave it the basis to call for a new system of pegging foreign exchange to both gold and the U.S. Dollar. The final agreement had the currencies pegged to gold, but more countries added the U.S. dollar as it became clearer over the subsequent years that it was the world's new reserve currency.

Naturally not everyone felt satisfied with these outcomes to the agreement. Soviet Union (Russia and surrounding republics) representatives came to the conference and participated. They accused the institutions that the conference had created of being mere branches of Wall Street.

As a result, they refused to ratify the final important agreements. Many nations including those of Western Europe, South America, Canada, Australia, the U.S., and eventually Japan after the war did sign on to the agreements and these new institutions began operating in 1945 after enough nations ratified them.

Meanwhile, countries began to exchange their currencies at rates based on the set quantity of gold they held. Whenever an imbalance of payments would occur as a result of the artificial currency pegging system, the International Monetary Fund had the powers to intervene and adjust as necessary. This encouraged foreign trade and global economic growth. It caused expansion in the majority of the developed world following the war.

Besides the International Monetary Fund, the conference also created the International Bank for Reconstruction and Development that eventually evolved into the World Bank. These two organizations still thrive today and promote financial stability and international trade. They encourage worldwide monetary cooperation and economic growth that is sustainable. They also help to reduce poverty and push for higher employment.

Europe and other damaged parts of the world engaged in a long era of rebuilding and development after the war ended with the aid of these institutions. The Bretton Woods system itself became abandoned in 1971 when the U.S. unilaterally left the gold standard. It was replaced by today's free floating currency exchange system.

Financial Terms Dictionary - Laws & Regulations Explained

Bretton Woods Committee

The Bretton Woods agreement failed in 1973 with President Richard Nixon unilaterally abandoning the gold standard. Other countries soon followed suit, first with Switzerland and other European nations and eventually the rest of the world.

The death of the Bretton Woods agreement did not end dreams of restoring a semblance of order and low volatility to the since-then troubled currency markets. One man who was already in government service as Chairman of the Fed in the wake of the agreement's collapse was Paul Volcker. It was he who first seriously called for a new Bretton Woods Agreement back in 2014.

The old defunct 1944 based agreement had set up the U.S. dollar to be the global currency by linking and tying up its value to gold. This had produced thirty years of unprecedented stability in global currency markets and exchange rates. Volcker remembered the consequences of abandoning the agreement personally.

He observed that in the years since the agreement had ended, continuously recurring currency crises had plagued the world economy. Among these were the Mexican, Latin American, and Asian currency crises. In 2008, the global financial crisis and Great Recession had also rocked the world. This amounted to four major currency crises in only 35 years.

Paul Volcker argued convincingly that a new Bretton Woods Agreement would lead to an internationally coordinated financial and monetary system. This would provide much needed stability for the continuously troubled global economy. Such a renewed system would create rules to guide and foster better world monetary policy. He even foresaw the potential for a new global reserve currency that would take over from the U.S. dollar. This system would lead to a balanced equilibrium in various nations' balance of payments. In this way, countries around the world would be able to maintain sufficient foreign exchange reserves.

Paul Volcker made all of these suggestions and observations as he chaired the Bretton Woods Committee meeting in 2014. As the Chair Emeritus, he leads the body of worldwide leaders who wish to rebuild cooperation among

Financial Terms Dictionary - Laws & Regulations Explained

the various international financial institutions. Among these are the European-based International Monetary Fund, the U.S.-based World Bank, international major and important central banks, various national Treasuries, and influential private banks.

The Bretton Woods Committee arose in 1983 around the ten year anniversary of the failure of the Bretton Woods Agreement. Two former U.S. Treasury officials suggested that it be established, democrat Secretary Henry Fowler and republican Deputy Secretary Charls Walker. Both men recognized the urgent need for a concerted, overt effort to make sure that leading global citizens spoke up regarding the critical importance of the IFI International Financial Institutions. The yearly meetings have continued without fail since 1983, with the 2016 meeting representing the 33rd year of the annual meetings.

Bretton Woods Committee members are comprised of around 200 different leaders from the heads of finance, business, academics, and not for profit sectors of economies. This includes numerous former presidents, industry CEOs, lawmakers, and cabinet level officials. They all have one belief in common that it is essential to maintain international levels of economic cooperation which is most effectively achieved via strong and efficient IFIs. Through their work on the Bretton Woods Committee, they spearhead worldwide endeavors to encourage economic growth, to foster financial stability around the world, and to reduce poverty wherever they find it.

The Bretton Woods Committee today puts on regular conferences, educational opportunities, and seminars. A great number of these activities were developed in order to address a large segment of the public. Other events are more exclusive and provide the Bretton Woods Committee membership with the chance to give their support, insight, and constructive criticisms to the IFIs management teams.

The Bretton Woods Committee has a track record of successfully working with all U.S. administrations to remind the elected leaders of yesterday and today that the twin ideas of enduring national security and worldwide economic prosperity are inseparably linked and improved by continuous movement forward on multinational issues.

British Bankers Association (BBA)

The British Bankers Association turns out to be the members' representative for the biggest international banking cluster in the world. This main trade association for the British banking sector boasts over 200 member banks headquartered in both the U.K. and more than 50 other countries that run operations in over 180 jurisdictions around the globe. As such fully 80% of all the systemically critical banks on earth carry membership with the BBA. This is the voice of UK banking.

The BBA claims the greatest and most comprehensive policy resources for those banks operating in the UK. They represent membership not only to the government of the U.K., but also throughout Europe and globally. Besides this impressive membership roster, their network also is comprised of more than 80 of the foremost professional and financial services organizations in the world.

The BBA's members collectively manage over £7 trillion (British pounds) of British bank assets. The members employ almost half a million people throughout the country. Their contributions to the British economy every year are more than £60 billion. Members loan in excess of £150 billion out to business based in the U.K.

The British Bankers Association works to encourage both initiatives and policies that promote the interests of not only banks but also the overall public. They have three principal priorities in their work. The first is to help out customers. This includes both businesses and consumers. The second is to encourage growth. By this they intend to support Britain as the world's global financial center. Finally they are interested in improving standards in the industry on both an ethical and professional level.

The BBA works with two strategic aims in mind. The first is to encourage a superior and improving banking sector for the overall U.K. They do this by working alongside banks and other beneficiaries to increase trust in the banking industry, by raising standards, by encouraging growth, and by assisting customers. They promise to facilitate public approval and overall awareness of the important position banks play in the economy. They are also aspiring to build appreciation for the advantages of hosting an internationally critical banking sector.

Financial Terms Dictionary - Laws & Regulations Explained

Chief among their public relations tasks are to encourage acknowledgement of the substantial improvements the sector has gone through since the global financial crisis. The BBA's goal is to be understood as an agent of positive change that makes a better banking industry by its non members and members alike. They strive to be a trusted partner of both banking regulators and the government. They also take the initiative to impact international and national debates on banking issues.

Their second strategic aim is to be the banking industry's trade association that is world class. They are the principal trade association for the foremost sector of the British economy as well as the main trade group for the foremost banking cluster in the world. This is why they aim to be best in class in their operations.

Before September in 2012, the BBA both compiled and published the LIBOR London Interbank Offered Rate, the most important interest rate in the world. They lost their role in managing the rate after the Barclays scandal erupted that showed the bank had been consistently manipulating the rate for a number of years. As lobby organization for the rate submitting banks, the Bank of England decided the BBA's conflict of interest was too great.

Nowadays the BBA puts on training and events throughout Britain. These include training classes, briefings, and forums besides their annual industry dinners and conferences. They also publish a monthly report that covers figures on high street banking. This is used in their Annual Abstract of Banking Statistics that they produce every August. BBA furthermore runs the GOLD Global Operational Loss Database for members. This serves as a helpful tool in helping to manage risk from operations.

Financial Terms Dictionary - Laws & Regulations Explained

Bureau of Engraving and Printing (BEP)

The Bureau of Engraving and Printing is the Treasury Department entity that actually makes the United States' currency. Their mission centers on creating and producing American currency notes which are trusted around the world. They have a vision to be considered the world standard for securities printing. This is so that they can deliver the public and their customers with the best products that are exceptionally well designed and manufactured.

The main activities of the BEP are to print up billions of Federal Reserve notes (or dollars) every single year. They then deliver these to the Federal Reserve System for distribution into the economy. It is the Federal Reserve that exists to be the American central bank. They bear the responsibility to be certain that sufficient coins and bills currency are in active circulation. The BEP handles all of the U.S. printed bills but does not make any coins. United States coins are always minted at the U.S. Mint.

When various federal agencies have concerns or questions about document security, they turn to the BEP for help and advice. The BEP also engages in research and development for improving their utilization of automation processes in production. They are always seeking out technologies to deter counterfeiters of U.S. currency and security documents as well.

It is no understatement to say that currency creation at the BEP offices has changed drastically from its origins in 1862. In those early years, they used the basement in the Treasury building. Here a handful of individuals worked with hand cranked machines to print and separate notes. Today's BEP does not engage in an easy process or job.

Nowadays making the currency bills takes greatly skilled and expertly trained craftspeople who work with specially designed equipment. They utilize both sophisticated and world leading technology alongside the time tested old world printing methods. Producing the currency takes numerous specific steps. This starts with designing, engraving, and making the plates. The specially sourced paper is then plate printed and inspected. Bills are numbered and re-inspected again before being packaged and shipped to their customer the Federal Reserve Bank.

Financial Terms Dictionary - Laws & Regulations Explained

The Bureau of Engraving and Printing also offers redemption of mutilated currency services and the sale of shredded currency. BEP will redeem such mutilated currency for free for the public. If the bills are so damaged that the value can not be conclusively determined, they can be sent on to the BEP so that their trained experts can examine them. After their determination is made, they will redeem the currency for full face value.

They accept currency that has been mutilated by water, fire, chemicals, or explosives; deterioration or petrification from burying; or insect, animal, or rodent damage. Bills missing security features are also treated as mutilated. For them to consider these bills without supporting documentation and explanations for what happened, at least half of the note has to be identifiable as American currency and remain.

If less than 50% is present, Treasury will require proof that the rest of the currency has been destroyed. Each year the department examines 30,000 mutilated currency claims and redeems them for more than $30 million.

The BEP also sells bags of shredded currency as novelty souvenir items. The Fort Worth and Washington, D.C. BEP visitor centers offer them in pre-packed small amounts for those who just want to have some. The D.C. visitor center and online store of the BEP also sell larger five pound bags of such shredded currency. In order to obtain larger quantities, individuals must get permission from the Treasury department and obtain them from one of the Federal Reserve Banks.

Certificate of Occupancy

A certificate of occupancy is a local government issued document. These papers give permission for tenants or residents to occupy a new building or even a residence. The reason that local governments mandate such certificates is because of building codes. The certificate proves that a building inspector has certified the building to be safe so that it can be occupied. It means that the structure complies with all present building codes.

Local governments will inspect and then issue such a certificate of occupancy any time that a construction company puts up a new building in the local government's jurisdiction as defined by the city limits. Even buildings that are opened outside of city limits can requires these before people can use them. In these cases, it might be the parish or county government that would issue the certificate. Local government will give these after they are satisfied with the results of the inspection. Inspectors look at all of the basic elements in the building including wiring, construction basics, plumbing, and other features to ensure they meet up to date code standards. Then they can sign off on a building being safe to inhabit.

Upgrades and additions to building that already exist can also require a new certificate of occupancy. In these cases, the owner of the building will have to apply to the local government for a new certificate after he has finished the changes and improvements. Inspectors will also check over all features of the structure to make sure that both existing and new parts meet the codes, as they would with a new building. After they finish such an inspection, the building department will have to sign off before the government agency can issue the certificate.

The owners of the building are not generally the parties responsible for requesting an inspection. Professional contractors and renovators will contact the responsible government entity so that the department can schedule the inspection. They also go through any necessary arrangements to make sure the certificate of occupancy becomes issued. The builder or contractor will receive the certificate first. They will provide copies of the document to the building owner. They keep copies in the construction company files too.

Other copies will be delivered to appropriate parties as well. One of these would be a lender. Should the building owner wish to use the property as collateral for an application on a loan, he will likely have to furnish a certificate of occupancy copy to the lender along with the application. A great number of lenders will refuse to make the loan until they have a proper copy of the certificate of occupancy on file.

In the event that a building fails an inspection, a certificate of occupancy will not be issued at first. Whatever modifications the inspector insisted on will have to be made. The building has to be brought up to current code before they can request another inspection. After successfully passing a second or later inspection, the certificate will then be issued by the appropriate department.

Financial Terms Dictionary - Laws & Regulations Explained

Certificate of Title

A certificate of title represents a document which states who the owners or owner of real estate or personal property actually are. It is issued by a municipal or state government. This certificate gives evidence of any ownership rights.

In general a title insurance company will issue a certificate of title opinion on a house or piece of property. This is their statement of opinion regarding the status of a title. They draft this opinion after carefully looking through public records pertaining to the property.

Such a certificate of title opinion will not necessarily assure the buyer of a clean title. It will list out any encumbrance on the property. Encumbrances are often items that keep the property from being freely sold. These could include easements or liens. The title companies will issue such certificates to financial institutions which are making the loan. Many of these lenders must have such documents in hand before they will approve a mortgage loan for a house or piece of property.

Certificates of title are extremely important with real estate. This is why a title company will issue their opinion that the person selling the property actually owns it. Personal property is easier to give to another person than is land. Where land is concerned, a person might be living on a given property and yet not own it. This makes the certificate opinion from the title company critical. It promises that the company has performed the complete background check regarding who owns the land and so has the right to sell it.

This certificate of title is a statement of fact when a state or municipal government actually issues it. These documents contain a good deal of useful information on them. All of them will have the name and address of the owner of the property. They also have information that identifies the property itself in some specific way.

If the certificate pertains to a real estate property, then it will have the location of or address for the land in question. If it is instead for a car or other vehicle, it will have the license plate number and possibly the vehicle identification number. These certificates will also state what the encumbrance is on the property if there is any. If there is a lien on a vehicle or mortgage on the house or land, this will be noted.

State agencies will also issue certificates of title on a variety of vehicles. This covers such things as buses, trucks, motorcycles, trailers, motor homes, boats and watercraft, and airplanes. When a lender makes a loan on such a vehicle, it is able to keep the title in its possession until the debt has been paid in full. They then release the lien at this point and send back the title certificate to the actual owner.

Certificates of title should not be confused with deeds though they share certain common characteristics. Each of these two documents offers a proof of ownership for the property in question. The certificate of title has sufficient information to specifically identify the property itself and any relevant encumbrances. Deeds have additional information on the real property. This includes any conditions for the ownership as well as more detailed information on and about the property. Deeds are critical elements in any transfer of real estate.

Certified Public Accountant (CPA)

CPA's, or certified public accountants, are accountants who have taken and successfully completed a series of demanding exams that are given by the American Institute of Certified Public Accountants. Many states also have their own state level exams that have to be passed along with the national one.

CPA'a are accountants in every sense of the word, but not every accountant is qualified as a CPA. Because of the difficulties in becoming a CPA, there are many accountants who either never attempt or never succeed in successfully passing the Certified Public Accountant exam. This does not mean such an accountant is not qualified to practice accounting tasks, only that he or she will not be allowed to do tasks that require specific CPA credentials.

Such Certified Public Accountants do a number of varying tasks and jobs. Many will provide advice and simple income tax preparing for various clients who might be comprised of corporations, small companies, or individuals. Besides this, Certified Public Accountants practice many other tasks that include auditing, keeping the records of businesses, and consulting for business entities.

Keeping a CPA license is not accomplished through automatic renewal. Certified Public Accountants are required to engage in a full one hundred and twenty hours of courses on continuing education in every three year period. This is so that they will be on top of any and all changes going on in the field of their chosen profession.

The opportunities for Certified Public Accountants are many and varied. The FBI seeks to hire them routinely, preferring applicant candidates with either such a CPA background or alternatively an attorney background. Numerous state and Federal government agencies offer CPA's opportunities by providing CPA positions. Businesses ranging from small companies to large corporations also seek them out. With these firms, CPA's can occupy positions ranging from controllers, to CFO or Chief Financial Officers, to CEO's or Chief Executive Officers.

Among the most significant parts that CPA's can play proves to be one of a consultant. As a consultant, Certified Public Accountants can be looking into possible means of saving small businesses or even enormous corporations money on expenses or putting together specific financial plans that permit a corporation or business to appear more appealing to investors or possible buyers. Certified Public Accountants are sworn to a particular code of ethical conduct. They are required to provide their clients with honest and reliable advice that is also ethical.

Certified Public Accountants who do not stay within the bounds of their ethical code can lead to the total financial failure of a firm. This turned out to be the case in recent years at Enron, the energy trading and producing giant. Not only were Enron corporate executives charged for illegal accounting activities, but also a number of CPA's from nationally renowned accounting firm Arthur Anderson were charged with unethical practices of accounting.

CFA Institute

The CFA Institute stands for the Chartered Financial Analyst institute. This global organization was formerly called the AIMR Association for Investment Management and Research. This institute is made up of over 70,000 individual members (from 137 different member societies located in 60 countries) who have the CFA Chartered Financial Analyst designation or who instead agree to be bound up by the organization's rules. The principal mandate of the group lies in setting forth and ensuring that there is a lofty standard for the members of the investment and financial advisory universe.

The CFA Institute boasts an active membership in nearly all nations of the world, 150 countries and territories specifically. Their board of governors is steered by 20 individual board members. The majority of these become elected by the votes of the members of the institute for three-year long terms. The institute counts important offices in the United States, the United Kingdom, and Hong Kong. It also staffs satellite offices in Mumbai, India, and Charlottesville, Virginia in the United States. It crafts and releases such important industry guidelines as the financial industry's GIPS Global Investment Performance Standards.

Ultimately, the aims of the CFA Institute are to encourage and foster the greatest possible standards in education, ethics, and excellence in the profession for the worldwide investment industry. As such, the Institute itself works to help out financial professionals via offering professional development, education, and also networking possibilities and opportunities. It also concentrates on becoming the world leader in best practices for the industry, highest investment ethics, and integrity for the capital markets of the globe.

The CFA Institute developed its famed Code of Ethics and Standards of Professional Conduct. This is the worldwide benchmark for investment professionals throughout the globe, whatever their particular roles in the industry may prove to be. The members of the Institute as well as the CFA charter holders and candidates for this designation must abide by the gold standard document so long as they are practicing. The Institute similarly strives to influence and direct the public policy and practices of the industry in such a way as to make sure the interests of the investors come first.

Financial Terms Dictionary - Laws & Regulations Explained

The CFA Institute does a lot of great work in the industry, but the educational programs are among the most important. These programs lead to designations of various kinds. The most important, widely recognized, and popular of these accreditations is the CFA Chartered Financial Analyst. The program itself offers an important foundation in investment analysis and portfolio management skills.

In fact, this CFA designation proves to be the preferred professional accreditation for more than 31,000 different investment companies around the world. Attaining this designation mandates that the prospective candidates successfully complete three consecutive exams which deal with professional and ethical standards, economics, quantitative methods, corporate finance, financial reporting, equity, derivatives, fixed income, portfolio management, and alternative investments.

The CFA Institute also purveys its CIPM, the impressive Certificate in Investment Performance Measurement. This designation provides candidates with risk evaluation and investment performance credentials that are based on actual practice. These various skill sets are considered to be useful and relevant on a global scale. In this program, the participants learn useful subjects such as measurement, attribution, appraisals, selection of managers, reporting standards, and ethics.

Another program of the CFA Institute is called the Claritas Program. This course addresses the important elements of ethics, finance, and investment roles. It is also interesting for being a self study program which was specifically designed to help those individuals who already work for financial services and investment firms. This includes professionals in marketing and sales, information technology, and/or human resources.

Financial Terms Dictionary - Laws & Regulations Explained

Chain of Title

A chain of title refers to the consecutive historical transfers in a title on a particular piece of real estate property. These chains start with the current owner of the property and trace their way back to the property's first owner. Reconstructing such a chain can be extremely important when a lender needs complete ownership documentation. Such title documents are generally kept by registry offices with local and municipal governments.

The field of real estate places tremendous importance on such a chain of title. Because it can be difficult to construct them, companies have come up with systems to track ownership and registration of real estate property. One of these is the Torrens Title system.

Insurance companies in the United States will provide title insurance on a property. They do this using the chain of title on real estate that the owners are transferring. These chains are so important that many title insurance companies will keep their own private title operations to track such titles so they do not have to rely on only official government records. In cases where it is difficult to come up with a complete chain, abstracts of title can be utilized. Attorneys will sometimes certify these.

Lack of a clear chain of title has caused significant problems during the Great Recession of 2008. These problems began when many lending companies made the choice in 1995 to use an electronic registry to hold the title. The best known company in this arena was MERS Mortgage Electronic Registration Systems. The banks tried to use this system so they could sell and purchase mortgages without needing to register ownership changes with the appropriate local governments. Without clear title chains, the banks were often not able to come up with the original titles needed to force foreclosures and evictions as individuals defaulted on their mortgages. A number of states throughout the U.S. sued the banks over these actions.

The chain of title is also utilized in intellectual property areas. With the film industry, they refer to documentation that demonstrates the ownership rights of a particular movie. These chains can be used in other creative endeavors in the movie business. If many individuals contributed to the creative work, authorship is owned by a large number of the writers. Film distributors and buyers must carefully examine these chains of title to know the proprietary rights or rights under license of the owner. This is also important with books and encyclopedias.

Documents on chains of title for films can include a number of other intellectual properties. Trademarks can be included. Musical copyrights often form part of these chains as well. Talent agreements are an important part of these. They provide the talent's legal release to utilize their images, works, appearance, and personal rights in movies. This covers everyone from directors to actors to choreographers and cinematographers. There are even insurance policies that cover omissions and errors of movie producers who do not obtain sufficient chains of title.

Specific organizations compile these reports for copyright property on behalf of the movie studios. To do so, they consult with the U.S. Copyright Office regarding author claimants, screening searches, and registration renewal searches. This detailed work requires that records from the Copyright Office dating back to 1870 and extending to the present be consulted. There are also other databases and trade publications which have to be reviewed for possible ownership claims.

Chapter 11 Bankruptcy

Chapter 11 Bankruptcy proves to be a specific type of bankruptcy. This kind has to do with the business assets, debts, and affairs being reorganized. The business reorganization filing was named for the Section 11 of the United States' Bankruptcy Code. Corporations commonly file it that need some time to rearrange the terms of their debts and their business operations. It gives them a fresh start on repaying their debt obligations. Naturally the indebted company will have to stick to the terms of the reorganization plan. This proves to be the most highly complex type of bankruptcy filing possible. Companies have been advised to only entertain it once they have contemplated their other options and analyzed the repercussions of such a filing.

This Chapter 11 bankruptcy rarely makes the news unless it is a nationally known or famous corporation which is filing. Among the major corporations that have filed such a Chapter 11 bankruptcy are United Airlines, General Motors, K-Mart, and Lehman Brothers. The first three successfully emerged from it and became as great or stronger than they were before falling into hard times financially. In reality, the vast majority of these cases are unknown to the general public. As an example, in the year 2010, nearly 14,000 separate corporations filed for Chapter 11.

The point of this Chapter 11 Bankruptcy is to assist a corporation in restructuring both obligations and debts. The goal is not to close down the business. In fact it rarely leads to the corporation closing. Instead, corporations like K-mart, General Motors, and tens of thousands of others were able to survive and once again thrive thanks to the useful process of protection from creditors and reorganization of business debts.

It is typically LLCs Limited Liability Companies, partnerships, and corporations that make application for Chapter 11 Bankruptcy. There are cases where individuals who are positively saddled with debt and who are not able to be approved for a Chapter 13 or Chapter 7 filing can be qualified for Chapter 11 instead. The time table for successfully completing Chapter 11 bankruptcy ranges from several months to as long as two years.

Businesses that are in the middle of their Chapter 11 cases are encouraged to keep operating. The debtor in possession will typically run the business

Financial Terms Dictionary - Laws & Regulations Explained

normally. Where there are cases that have gross incompetence, dishonest dealings, or even fraud involved, typically trustees come in to take over the business and its daily operations while the bankruptcy proceedings are ongoing.

Corporations in the midst of these filings will not be permitted to engage in specific decisions without first having to consult with the courts to proceed. They may not terminate or sign rental agreements, sell any assets beyond regular inventory, or expand existing business operations or alternatively cease them. The bankruptcy court retains full control regarding any hiring and paying of lawyers as well as signing contracts with either unions or vendors. Lastly, such indebted organizations and entities may not sign for a loan that will pay once the bankruptcy process finishes.

After the business or person files their chapter 11 bankruptcy, it gains the right to offer a first reorganization plan. Such plans often include renegotiating owed debts and reducing the company size in order to slash expenses. There are some scenarios where the plan will require every asset to be liquidated in order to pay off the creditors, as with Lehman Brothers.

When plans are fair and workable, courts will approve them. This moves the reorganization process ahead. For plans to be accepted, they also have to maintain the creditors' best interests for the future repayment of debts owed to them. When the debtor can not or will not put forward a plan of their own for reorganization, then the creditors are invited to offer one in the indebted company or person's place.

Chapter 7 Bankruptcy

Chapter 7 bankruptcy is a form of protection from creditors. Unlike Chapter 13 bankruptcy, it does not have any repayment plan. In the Chapter 7 a bankruptcy trustee determines what eligible assets the debtor individual or company has. The trustee then collects these available assets, sells them, and distributes proceeds to the creditors against their debts. This is all done under the rules of the Bankruptcy Code.

Debtors are permitted to keep specific property that is exempt, such as their house. Other property that the debtor holds will be mortgaged or have liens put against it to pledge it to the various creditors until it is liquidated. Debtors who file chapter 7 will likely forfeit property in partial payment of debts.

Chapter 7 bankruptcy is available to corporations, partnerships, and individuals who pass a means test. The relief can be granted whether or not the debtor is ruled to be insolvent.

Chapter 7 bankruptcy cases start when debtors file their petitions with their particular area's bankruptcy court. For businesses, they use the address where the main office is located. Debtors are required to give the court information that includes schedules of current expenditures and income and liabilities and assets.

They are also required to furnish a financial affairs statement and a schedule of contracts and leases which are not expired. The debtors will also have to deliver the trustee tax return copies from the most current tax year along with any tax returns which they file while the case is ongoing.

Debtors who are individuals also have to furnish their court with other documents. They are required to file a credit counseling certificate and any repayment plan created there. They must also file proof of income from employers 60 days before their original filing, a monthly income statement along with expected increases in either, and notice of interest they have in tuition or state education accounts. Husbands and wives are allowed to file individually or jointly. They must abide by the requirements for individual debtors either way.

Financial Terms Dictionary - Laws & Regulations Explained

The courts are required to charge debtors who file $335 in filing, administrative, and trustee fees. Debtors typically pay these when they file to the clerk of court. The court can give permission for individuals to pay by installments instead. When the income of debtor's proves to be less than 150% of the amount of the poverty level, the court can choose to drop the fee requirements.

Debtors will have to provide a great amount of information in order to complete their Chapter 7 filing and receive a discharge of debts. They have to list out each of their creditors along with the amounts they owe then and the type of claim. Debtors have to furnish a list of all property the own. They must also give the information on the amount, source, and frequency of income they have to the court.

Finally, they will be required to provide an in depth list of all monthly living expenses that includes housing, utilities, food, transportation, clothing, medicine, and taxes. This helps the court to determine if the debtor is able to set up a repayment plan instead of discharging the debts.

From 21 to 40 days after the debtor files the petition with the courts, the trustee hosts a creditors' meeting. The debtor will have to cooperate with the trustee on any requests for additional financial documents or records. At this meeting, the trustee will ask questions to make sure the debtor is fully aware of the consequences of debt discharge by the bankruptcy court. Sometimes trustees will deliver this in written form to the debtor before or at the meeting. Assuming the trustee makes the recommendation for discharge, the Federal bankruptcy court judge will discharge the debts when the process is completed.

Charge Off

A charge off refers to an expense item found on a corporation's income statement. This could be one of two things. It might be connected with a debt that the reporting firm has decided is not realistically collectable. They would then write this off from the corporate balance sheet. It might also be a likely one time only expense which is called an extraordinary event. The company incurs this, and it impacts the earnings negatively. This then leads to a portion of the corporate assets' becoming written down in value. Because the assets have become impaired, the write down occurs.

Where bad debt costs crop up, this is related to a company not being able to collects bills owed for at least a portion of its accounts receivable, also called AR. These events unfortunately happen sometimes, and firms can do little about them. They might attempt to sell off the likely bad debts to an interested collection agency. The company would then record a sale on the books, yet it would not be marked down as an expense item. Otherwise, they might simply charge off the amount which is uncollectable on the income statement by calling it an expense.

In order for debts to be considered to be bad debts, they have to be run up in the typical operations of the business. Such a debt could be incurred by either a person or another company. These charge offs for the bad debts more typically happen as companies extend credit (to other entities) that is unsecured. Examples of this would be signature-only loans or credit cards.

One time expenses which are charged off are another story altogether. Sometimes a firm will consent to an extraordinary charge off in a given period of accounting. This would impact the current period earnings, yet they feel it will not likely happen again in the near future. The end result is ultimately that the company will commonly offer its EPS earnings per share numbers both without and with the charge off in question reflected. This allows them to show the company shareholders that the expense is unusual and uncommon. They might also call this a one off charge.

Such charge offs could involve the buying of a major asset. This could be a significant piece of equipment or a brand new production facility. These expenses would not be repeated too often. There might also be charges that are associated with an unusual event. Examples of this are paying deductibles for insured items that became damaged in a natural disaster. There could also be a flood or a fire for which the firm has to pay the costs to cover the damage.

There might also be maintenance types of expenses that are not normal. These might include replacing a roof. It is true that maintenance issues like these can be predicted to a degree. Because the exact date of service and amount of charge can not easily be quantified. Since such maintenance issues are only necessary every few decades, they are extraordinary items indeed.
Charge offs could also pertain to individuals who have seen one of their personal debts charged off. Such an event does not mean that a creditor has specifically cancelled the debt. Borrowers will still have to pay off the balance in theory. When credit card payments become late, they go into late payment status. After a payment is 180 days late, the creditor companies will at last charge off the debt. They might then send it out for collection agencies or file lawsuits if the laws of the state where the debtor resides allow.

Financial Terms Dictionary - Laws & Regulations Explained

Commodity Futures Modernization Act (CFMA)

In the year 2000, the U.S. Government passed the Commodity Futures Modernization Act. The act did several things. First it reaffirmed the regulatory authority of the Commodity Futures Trading Commission over all American futures markets. This authority became extended for a period of five years with this act.

A second and more significant result of the act came about as the government allowed Single Stock Futures to be traded for the first time in the United States. Other countries already allowed their investors to trade these particular types of futures when Congress passed this act. In America up to this point where the CFMA passed, it was illegal for investors to participate. Yet investors were eager to gain the leverage that these futures delivered.

Single Stock Futures are popular precisely because they do allow significant exposure to equity markets. A single stock future is a special kind of futures contract. The instrument allows a buyer to trade a certain number of shares in a single company at a price that they agree on now for a particular date in the future. The price is known as the strike price or futures price. The future date that the two parties set is the delivery date.

Buyers of these contracts are long the future in the stock. Sellers of the contract are short the stock in question. The buyer makes money if the price of the underlying stock increases, while the seller makes money if the value of the underlying stock declines. There is no cost to open the contract besides commissions and fees.

Single Stock Futures trade typically in contracts of 100 shares. Buying the contract does not cause any dividend or voting rights to transfer from the seller to the buyer. Futures trade using margin and provide tremendous leverage. There are no short selling rules applied to them as there are to stocks themselves.

Other countries adopted the Single Stock Futures trading ahead of the United States. The American market was not allowed to trade them before the passage of the Commodity Futures Modernization Act of 2000. This was because there was conflict between the two regulatory agencies the

Financial Terms Dictionary - Laws & Regulations Explained

U.S. Securities and Exchange Commission and the Commodity Futures Trading Commission. The two could not work out which agency would regulate these new Single Stock Futures products and trading.

When the government passed the CFMA of 2000 into law, they agreed to a compromise. Both of these agencies decided to share the jurisdiction under a plan that allowed the Single Stock Futures to finally start trading on November 8 of 2002. This allowed the United States based traders to catch up with other countries who were already trading these instruments.

The Commodity Futures Modernization Act brought the United States into a global market of the Single Stock Futures that included Great Britain, Spain, South Africa, India, and other countries. The South African market has traditionally been the largest of the single stock futures marketplaces. Their average numbers of contracts amount to 700,000 each day.

Though the CFMA allowed single stock futures to be traded, this did not establish a marketplace for them on which they could be traded in the U.S. Two different companies began trading them initially. One of these closed. The remaining company trading these types of futures in the U.S. is now known as the One Chicago. This is a joint venture of the main Chicago commodities and futures exchanges the Chicago Mercantile Exchange, the Chicago Board Options Exchange, and the Chicago Board of Trade.

Congressional Budget Office (CBO)

The Congressional Budget Office was created by Congress in 1975. Since that time, it has continuously developed and published its own independent analyses for economic and budget related issues. Its goal is to support the process of making Congressional budgets. Ever year the agency puts together literally hundreds of estimates for costs of proposed legislation as well as dozens of routine reports.

The CBO is religiously non partisan so that it can engage in unbiased and objective analysis. It only hires staff based on their professional abilities and does not consider their political affiliations. CBO never engages in recommending policies. It is concerned with all of its reports and price estimates explaining its analytical methodology.

The CBO produces Baseline Budget and Economic Projections. It does this regularly to come up with predictions for economic and budget outcomes. These estimates assume that the present conditions for revenues and spending will continue. Such baseline projections extend for 10 year time frames as utilized in the process of Congressional budget making.

Long Term Budget Projections are another item that the Congressional Budget Office offers Congress. These extend well beyond the usual 10 year budget forecasts to cover the next 30 years. They reveal the impacts of economic developments, demographic trends, and increasing health care expenses for federal deficits, spending, and revenues.

With the Cost Estimate analyses, the Congressional Budget Office delivers estimates in writing for the expenses created by every bill which the committees in Congress approve. They reveal the ways the bill will impact revenues or spending for the coming five to 10 years.

The CBO also develops Analytic Reports which consider specific elements of the tax code, programs of federal spending, and economic and budget constraints. Such reports pertain to a number of elements of federal policy. This includes economic growth, health care, social insurance, taxes, income security, the environment, energy, national security, education, financial issues, infrastructure, and other areas.

Financial Terms Dictionary - Laws & Regulations Explained

Once the President submits his Presidential Budget, CBO get involved. It re-estimates the impacts of it. The office does this by using its particular methods for economic estimating and forecasting.

From time to time, the CBO comes up with a volume on Budget Options. This reference work provides a number of ways that the government could reduce its budget deficits. The options are varied and come from a number of sources. They include raising additional revenues and lowering spending.

The Congressional Budget Office also produces Sequestration Reports. They must put out estimates of funding caps on discretionary programs in every fiscal year that goes through 2021. They consider these numbers to determine if cancelling the pre-allocation of budgeted resources is necessary.

The CBO knows what it should study because of its mandates. It's responsibilities are to assist the Senate and House Budget Committees in their jurisdictional affairs. They also are directed to support various other committees of the Congress. This includes especially the Finance, Ways and Means, and Appropriations Committees as well as the leadership of Congress. They are required by law to produce many of the annual reports which they create. The best known of these remains the Budget and Economic Outlook.

Constructive Eviction

Constructive eviction is a backdoor way of evicting a tenant. It is not done through legal means because of a tenant failing to pay rent or seriously breaking the property rules. It is instead the process of a landlord making a rental uninhabitable for the tenant. Though the term sounds positive, it is quite the opposite. Landlords who engage in this type of eviction are failing to carry out their legal obligations.

For constructive eviction to take place, a residential rental property must deteriorate into enough disrepair that it becomes very difficult or near impossible to live in the property. It could also be that the landlord allows a condition to exist that makes inhabiting the home or apartment intolerable. As the condition becomes so severe that the property is no longer fit to live in, the tenant is forced to leave. An uninhabitable property exists in a state that compels the renter to move away, or to be constructively evicted. Because the renter is incapable of completely utilizing and possessing the property, he or she has been evicted technically.

There are a number of way in which a tenant could be a victim of constructive eviction. The landlord might turn off the electricity, gas, or water utilities. The owner might disregard an environmental problem such as toxic mold or flaking off lead paint and not properly clean it. He or she could also not fix leaking roofs. This causes water damage to walls and eventually leads to mold. The owners could block the unit entrance or change the locks. They might do something extreme such as take out sinks or toilets from the property as well. When the conditions deteriorate to the point that tenants abandon the rental then constructive eviction has occurred.

A landlord might engage in this type of unethical behavior because of rental controls. Many cities limit the amount by which rent can be increased. They may also allow the tenant to remain in the rental with an automatically renewing lease so long as they fulfill the contract obligations.

Tenants have the ability to fight back against this type of eviction. This starts with providing the owner a notice in writing of the constructive eviction. The landlord must be given a fair amount of time to address the issue. This may not translate to an instant repair that happens in 24 hours.

Many repairs require more time to have completed. Water and gas leaks are examples of these. Still the repairs have to be done in a time frame that is reasonable.

Renters who find themselves in living conditions that are poor should take pictures. They also should invite independent inspectors to examine the property. These types of inspectors come from the permit or building department, as well as from the area health department.

When landlords are unwilling to address the uninhabitable living conditions in a reasonable time frame after having been given fair written notice, renters have rights. They are usually allowed to leave the property without having to pay rent that would still be owed according to the rental or lease agreement. In general, tenants have to move away from the property while they begin the legal process of terminating the lease and suing the owner for damages.

It is often better to compel the owner to make the necessary repairs or to address the issues that are creating the uninhabitable living conditions on the property in the first place. This is easier in cities and states that have strong legal enforcement of the landlord obligations. New York City and state are an example of places in the United States that make it difficult for owners to practice constructive eviction by requiring that they fulfill their maintenance duties.

Consumer Data Industry Association

Consumer reporting has become a huge business in the United States. It makes sense that they would have a large and important trade association. The Consumer Data Industry Association is this organization that functions as the industry trade association for credit reporting companies in the United States.

While they have over 140 different corporate members, they represent approximately 200 companies in the consumer data business. These companies provide a wide range of services. Among these are risk management, fraud prevention, and mortgage and credit reports in the data reporting business.

Other companies offer additional services that are newer in nature. These cover employment and residential screening services, collection services for companies and individuals, and even check verification and check fraud services. Naturally the major consumer reporting agencies are important pillar members of the CDIA. These include Experian, Equifax, TransUnion, and Innovis.

This Consumer Data Industry Association works to provide education to all parties involved in the learning process of consumer data and information. This includes regulators, legislators, the media, and consumers. Their goal is to teach about the proper utilization of such information.

The members of this association also deliver analytical tools and data to help companies provide safe, fair transactions for their customers. Their products and services encourage competition and make better opportunities for the economy as a whole and their customers.

The products and services produced by the members of the Consumer Data Industry Association are enormously utilized. They are a part of over nine billion transactions that are processed every year. The goal of these companies is to offer better access to consumers. They also strive to create products and services which are centered on the needs of the consumers. Finally, they try to offer innovation in an industry that is constantly changing to keep up with rapidly expanding technology and the times.

The history of the Consumer Data Industry Association goes back to 1906. Its founders established it in Rochester, New York as the National Association of Retail Credit Agencies. The organization arose because American consumers were requiring more credit. At the same time, Americans were moving around like never before. Creditors needed a standardized and consistent form of credit information on these consumers. This way they would be able to assess their history of credit payment.

The CDIA underwent numerous name changes over the decades before settling on their present one as the services provided by their membership gradually evolved. In 1907 they became the National Association of Mercantile Agencies. After World War I this organization changed to the Associated Credit Bureaus of America. Under this identity they created the very first standardized system for credit data reporting following World War II.

In the 1960s they began computerizing the industry to keep better track of credit records. Nearly all credit became accessed through such automation by the end of the 1960s. The agency again changed its name at this time to Associated Credit Bureaus as it had expanded to become international. The government took notice of all this activity and passed the first of the consumer reporting industry regulatory laws the Fair Credit Reporting Act in 1971.

In 1991 they moved the office to Washington, D.C. to be near the regulatory and legislative bodies of the U.S. A final name change came about in 2001 as the group evolved to its present Consumer Data Industry Association. Today the organization is the representative body for all companies that deal with analyzing and managing credit data for consumers. Since the 1990s this has grown beyond credit reports to include background screening and employment reporting.

Financial Terms Dictionary - Laws & Regulations Explained

Consumer Financial Protection Bureau (CFPB)

The CFPB is the Consumer Financial Protection Bureau. Congress created this government agency in 2008 as one of the reactions it took to the devastating financial crisis and Great Recession, the worst financial shocks to the system since the end of the 1930s era Great Depression.

The idea was to erect an organization that would protect consumers from risks and predatory practices of Wall Street and the mega banks which already had been determined as "too big to fail." The Dodd-Frank Wall Street Reform and Consumer Protection Act actually set up this new entity the CFPB.

The role of this new twenty-first century organization is to assist consumers in the financial markets through creating rules that are more efficient and fair, by continuously and equitably enforcing the rules, and by helping consumers to be able to gain additional command over their own economic futures and affairs.

The Consumer Financial Protection Bureau's goal is to ensure that the various financial markets function fairly and appropriately for providers, consumers, and the all around national economy. To this effect they strive to safeguard consumers from deceptive, predatory, abusive, and unfair activities in the marketplaces. They enforce action on any companies which break the laws. The CFPB provides people with the tools and information they require to make decisions that are smart for their own situations.

The Consumer Financial Protection Bureau believes in and labors towards a financial market that works fairly. This means that the terms, risks, and prices of any deals must be transparent and obvious in advance so that all consumers are able to know their choices and fairly and effectively comparison shop. They work to see that all corporations abide by the identical consumer protection rules. Each company must fairly compete to provide high quality goods and services.

To see this vision become reality, the Consumer Financial Protection Bureau strives to empower, enforce, and educate. Empowering means that they develop tools, answer commonly posed queries, and offer helpful tips for consumers who are interested in making their way through the various financial options to shop around for the deal that best meets their needs. They pride themselves on their effective enforcement of the rules against predatory operations and actions that break the law.

The CFPB has obtained and returned literally billions of dollars in damages to customers who were wronged. Education means that the CFPB fosters consumer abilities and educational opportunities from a young age extending on to retirement. They inform financial companies of their legal and ethical responsibilities and publish research to help out consumers.

The Consumer Financial Protection Bureau operates in several core functions. They acknowledge that the government created them to offer one accountability agency to enforce the laws for federal consumer finance and to safeguard consumers in the financial arena. This used to be the purview of a number of different agencies. Among the CFPB's core functions are receiving complaints from consumers, enforcing the discrimination laws in consumer finance, and creating and enforcing rules to rid the market of abusive, deceptive, and predatory actions by companies.

They also foster financial education among consumers, regulate and oversee the financial markets for upcoming risks for consumers, and do research on consumer's experiences in utilizing financial services and products. They do this to try to locate problems lurking in the financial marketplace so that more fair ultimate outcomes can be achieved for American consumers everywhere.

As of 2016, Richard Cordray is the Consumer Financial Protection Bureau's first director. Before he assumed this important responsibility, he served in the role as head of the Bureau's Office of Enforcement.

Financial Terms Dictionary - Laws & Regulations Explained

Council of Economic Advisers (CEA)

The President's Council of Economic Advisors proves to be an agency of the President's Executive Office. They give the President unbiased and non partisan economic advice for coming up with both international and national economic policies. This council is made up of three people of whom one is the chair. They use analysis of empirical evidence based on economic research to come up with their regular recommendations to the President. They gather the most esteemed information they can to help the President in putting together the critical national economic policy and annual report.

In 2016 the Chairman of this CEA was Jason Furman. The two members of the group were Jay Shambaugh and Sandra Black. Distinguished one time chairs of the group include former Chairmen of the Federal Reserve Alan Greenspan and Ben Bernanke and 2016 Federal Reserve Chairperson Janet Yellen. This council receives significant support from a number of staff members. Among their support personnel are staff economists and senior economists, research assistants, and a statistical back office.

Congress established this Council of Economic Advisors for the President with its 1946 Employment Act. In this act, the legislation called for three members whom the President would appoint. The Senate was to advise on selection and give consent on the final selection of these members. Members chosen for the CEA are to be recognized for their experience, training, and accomplishments in the field of economics.

Their purpose in greater detail is to consider and explain the economic developments to the President and to review the activities and programs the government establishes for economic appropriateness. They are also expected to create and recommend policies to encourage production, better employment, and higher purchasing power in a freely competitive economy. One of the three members the President is to appoint as Chairman for the council.

The council specifically has five different duties in the performance of their role. They have to help with and give advice for the Economic Report that the President's office prepares annually. They are instructed to collect information that is timely and accepted on the economic trends and developments in the U.S. They can then analyze and understand if the trends are interfering with attaining the stated Presidential policy. The group has to put all of this information together and turn it in to the President.

A third role is to consider the activities and programs of the government. The CEA is supposed to ascertain which of these activities and programs are helping to advance the policy and which are hurting it so they can let the President know.

They must also create and recommend policies for the President that help to develop and encourage competitive free enterprise. These policies should help to reduce and stop economic fluctuations and to improve national production, employment, and purchasing power.

Finally, the Council of Economic Advisors was set up to create and provide a range of reports and studies that have bearing on national economic legislation and policies. These are to be drawn up as the President requests them.

Every month the CEA prepares a report for the Joint Economic Committee of Congress. This is known as the *Economic Indicators*. In this publication there is information on income, gross domestic product, business activity, production, employment, prices, credit, money, security markets, international statistics, and the finances of the Federal government.

They also produce reports and fact sheets on a nearly every month basis that address a wide variety of economic issues. These reports and the speeches and testimony of the members of the Council of Economic Advisors are all available to the public on their official website.

Financial Terms Dictionary - Laws & Regulations Explained

Credit Report

A credit report is an individual or business' credit history. This includes their record of borrowing and repaying money in the past. It similarly covers data pertaining to any late payments made or bankruptcies that have been declared. In some countries, credit reports are also referred to as credit reputations.

When an American like you completes a credit application for a bank, a credit card company, or a retail store, this information is directly sent on to one of the three main credit bureaus. These are Experian, Trans Union, and Equifax. These credit bureaus then match up your name, identification, address, and phone number on the application for such credit with the data that they keep in their bureau's files. Because of this match up process, it is essential that lenders, creditors, and other parties always provide exactly correct information to the credit bureaus.

Such information in these files at the three major credit bureaus is then utilized by lenders like credit card companies in order to decide if you are deserving of having credit issued to you by the creditor. Another way of putting this is that they decide how likely that you will be to pay back these debts. Such willingness to pay back a debt is usually indicated by the timeliness of prior payments to other lenders. Such lenders will prefer to see the debt obligations of individual consumers, such as yourself, paid on time every month.

The second element considered in a lender offering loans or credit to individuals like you is based on your actual income. Higher incomes generally lead to greater amounts of credit being accessible. Still, lenders look at both willingness, as shown in the credit report and prior payment history, along with ability, as shown by income, in deciding whether or not to extend you credit.

Credit reports have become even more significant in light of risk based pricing. Practically all lenders of the financial services industry rely on credit reports to determine what the annual percentage rate and grace period of repayment of a loan or offer of credit will be. Other obligations of the contract are similarly based on this credit report.

In the past, a great deal of discussion has gone on considering the information contained in the credit reports. Scientific studies done on the issue have determined that for the most part, this credit report information is extremely accurate. Such credit bureaus also have their own authorized studies of fifty-two million credit reports that show that the information contained therein is right a vast majority of the time.

Congress has heard testimony from the Consumer Data Industry Association that in fewer than two percent of credit report issue cases have there been data which had to be erased because it was wrong. In the few cases where these did exist, more than seventy percent of such disputes are handled in fourteen days or less. More than ninety-five percent of consumers with disputes report being satisfied with the resolution.

Credit Score

Credit Score refers to a number generated by the credit bureaus to represent the creditworthiness of an individual. The credit bureaus possess literally from hundreds to thousands of distinct lines worth of information on each person with a credit profile. This makes it extremely difficult for lending institutions to go through it all. Since they lack the man hours to carefully peruse each applicant's credit reports personally, the majority of financial institutions which lend money employ these credit scores rather than tediously read through credit reports on applicants.

These Credit Scores are actually numbers that a computer program generates after crawling through an individual's credit report. Such programs seek out certain fundamentals, patterns, and so-called warning flags in any credit report and history. They then generate a credit score based on what they find. Lenders love these scores since they can be basically interpreted by a consistent set of comparative rules.

Consider the following examples. Lending institutions might automatically approve any application that comes with an associated 720 credit score or higher. Those profiles with 650 to 720 would likely be approved but with a greater interest rate. Applications with credit scores below 650 might simply be rejected. The computer is consistent and fair using these standards, so no one is treated in a discriminatory way relative to any other applicant.

Federal laws require that each individual be granted a free credit report annually from every one of the big three credit bureaus Experian, Trans Union, and Equifax. This does not mean that anyone is required to hand out free credit scores. In fact there is no such thing as a truly free credit score offer. There are scores provided in exchange for signing up for trial membership services in things like credit monitoring services. In general though, individuals pay for their credit scores from each of the major credit bureaus.

The particulars of a Credit Score are interesting. It is always a three digit formatted number that ranges from 300 to 850. These become created using one of a variety of mathematical algorithms that work off of both the individuals' credit profiles and their credit report's particular information. This score is crafted with the intention of predicting risk to the lenders, not to benefit the person it covers. It is particularly concerned with the chances of an individual going delinquent on any credit obligations within the next 24 months after the score has been issued.

It is a common misnomer among many individuals that there is only one credit scoring model in the country. There are countless models that exist. It is only the FICO credit score that matters in nearly all cases though. This is because fully 90 percent of financial institutions within the United States rely on FICO credit scores in making their decisions on to whom they will extend credit and at what interest rate.

The higher the FICO score these algorithms generate, the lower the risk is to the various lenders. What makes matters more confusing is that there is not only one FICO credit score in existence for every adult American. Each of the three major bureaus generates its own particular score. Since 2009, consumers are only able to view two of their credit scores, those from both Trans Union and Equifax. This is because Experian chose to terminate its myFICO.com arrangements in 2009. Experian does not share their proprietary credit scores with consumers any longer.

Five different significant categories make up the FICO Credit Score. These are payment history (35 percent of the total component), Amounts owed (30 percent), length of credit history (15 percent), types of credit used (10 percent), and new credit inquiries and accounts opened (10 percent).

Financial Terms Dictionary - Laws & Regulations Explained

Debt Relief Order

A Debt Relief Order (also known by their acronym DRO) refers to a British legal system type of insolvency method which is relatively new. It was Chapter 4 from the Tribunals, Courts, and Enforcement Act 2007 that actually created these new orders. The advantage that such DROs offer is a less expensive, faster, and simpler means of receiving bankruptcy styled relief in Great Britain.

The DRO works well for those indebted individuals who possess no or very few assets (under 1,000 British pounds without owning a home), and who count tiny disposable income levels (which have to be under 50 pounds sterling each month). Individuals who meet these criteria and several others may pay only a 90 pounds one time fee and then make application for the Debt Relief Order without a court appearance. Participants can even pay this fairly reasonable fee in a period of installments before they file the application for the order. Such DROs took the full force of law for both England and Wales on April 6th of 2009.

There are a range of specific requirements that individuals must meet in order to qualify for such a Debt Relief Order. It must be clear the persons can not pay their debts. They must not owe more than 20,000 pounds in total unsecured bills. Homeowners do not qualify, nor do those who have over 1,000 pounds in total gross assets. They can only keep their car if its value is under 1,000 pounds. The debt holder has to live in Wales or England or at least have been resident or engaged in business in either place within the past three years. They also may not have been issued a DRO in the prior six years.

Besides this the indebted individuals may not be part of any other kind of insolvency proceedings. These include bankruptcies which are not yet discharged, voluntary individual arrangements, present debt relief restrictions, present bankruptcy restrictions, a bankruptcy petition, or an interim order. It is true that these Debt Relief Orders are still insolvency forms that will be publicly listed in the insolvency services website.

In order for Debt Relief Orders to be successfully implemented, there must be a government approved intermediary who handles the event with the relevant authorities. For intermediaries to be approved, they generally have

Financial Terms Dictionary - Laws & Regulations Explained

to be debt advice organization personnel which have experience as debt advisors. Some of these approved organizations include the Consumer Credit Counseling Service, one of the Citizens Advice Bureaus, Baines and Ernst National Debtline, Think Money, Payplan, the Institute of Money Advisers, and members of the entity Advice UK. Any of these approved intermediaries are able to consider the information of the persons applying, discern if they are DRO eligible, and finally make an online application on their behalf. These intermediaries who are approved do not charge fees to submit such applications.

The Official Receivers are able to issue the Debt Relief Orders after they obtain both the fee and the application. No court involvement is necessary if the applicant is eligible. Otherwise they will reject the application out of hand. These Official Receivers also have the authority to rescind these DROs if more relevant information on the debtors' financial conditions appears after the order has been granted. There are also criminal charges and penalties allowed by the British law if the applicants knowingly perjure themselves or provide deliberately misleading information on their financial conditions, assets, debts, and other personal financial costs.

Back in November of 2014, the New Policy Institute released data (research funded by the Trust for London) on the quantities of debt relief orders throughout different parts of the United Kingdom. Unsurprisingly, the total numbers of these DROs for London in the years of 2009 to 2013 proved to be vastly less than the rest of England's average.

Deed in Lieu of Foreclosure

A deed in lieu of foreclosure represents an alternative option to a standard foreclosure on a house. In this deed in lieu arrangement, the owner of the property decides to hand over the property in question to the lender on a completely voluntary basis. In exchange for agreeing to this, the lender cancels out the mortgage loan. The deed to the house becomes transferred from the owner to the lender. As part of this conciliatory arrangement, the mortgage lender guarantees that it will not start the foreclosure process on the owner. If there are any foreclosure actions that have already begun, the lender will also terminate these. It is up to the lender to decide if they will forgive any extra balance that the sale of the home does not cover.

There are some tax issues that can arise with a deed in lieu of foreclosure deal. One potential downside to this type of debt forgiveness involves the consequences of it with the IRS. Federal law in the United States requires creditors to file 1099C forms for tax purposes when they choose to forgive any loan balance that amounts to more than $600. This debt forgiveness is then considered to be income and it becomes a tax liability for the home owner.

Fortunately for many home owners during the financial crisis, Congress passed the Mortgage Forgiveness Debt Relief Act of 2007. This delivered tax relief on a number of loans that banks forgave in the years starting from 2007 till the end of 2013.

The main issue and advantage that a deed in lieu of foreclosure offers centers around this excess balance debt forgiveness. Anyone who enters into such a voluntary agreement should carefully review the contract to learn how the deficiency balance topic will be addressed. Sometimes the documents are not clear on this point.

In this case, the homeowner should take the deed in lieu document to a lawyer who specializes in property law. It is not inexpensive to have a lawyer review such a contract document. The money it can save the home owner in the future for signing a contract he or she does not understand and may suffer significantly from will make the fees seem reasonable by comparison.

There are a number of requirements in order for a deed in lieu of foreclosure to be accepted. First the house would have to be on the seller market for a minimum number of days. Ninety days is usual. There also may not be any liens on the house. The property typically could not be in the process of foreclosure already. Finally, the deed in lieu offer has to be voluntary on the part of the home owner.

Another option that can be pursued in place of this deed in lieu of foreclosure is a short sale. Short sales have the same requirements as do the deed in lieu arrangements with several additional stipulations. The home seller must be suffering from financial hardship. The home itself has to be offered at a reasonable price.

In an alternative short sale, the mortgage lender will consent to receiving a lesser amount from the sale than the remaining mortgage balance that the owner still owes. It is up to the bank and the contract if any additional balance which exists will be forgiven or not. The same tax issues apply if the lender agrees to forgive more than $600.

Defeasance Clause

A defeasance clause refers to a mortgage contract. It is the statement in a mortgage loan that explains what will happen once a borrower has repaid all of the outstanding loan amounts. At that point, the lender usually will be required by law to hand over the title of the property to the owner. These defeasance clauses are not utilized in every part of the country. Instead they are a part of mortgages where they are not issued on a lien basis. When such liens are used instead, lenders keep their interest in the house. This gives them the right and ability to foreclose on the property in case the borrower does not make the payments according to the loan terms and agreement.

When a loan contains a defeasance clause, borrowers should carefully read through it. They must be certain that the lender interest in the house will come to an end after the loan is fully paid off including principle, interest, and other costs. This is the standard and accepted practice in the industry.

As mortgages are set up using a defeasance clause, lenders keep a special form of title called a defeasible title. These conditional titles may be revoked in specific scenarios. It is the defeasance clause itself found in the mortgage contract that determines when the lender will give up the title to the property after the borrower has fulfilled all of the loan obligations. The clause may also detail additional information. This can include penalties for prepayment should the loan come with them.

After the home buyers have completely repaid their loan, they can redeem their property's title. The one time borrower then becomes the home owner with title. Having the title is important for many reasons. It allows owners to refinance the home, sell it, rent it out, pledge it for a line of credit, or keep and live in it indefinitely. These titles are supposed to be free and clear after the interest of the lender terminates. An exception to this might be if the title had other issues hanging over it that had nothing to do with the mortgage loan with which the buyer purchased it. This might be from a tax lien or other problem.

It is the paperwork associated with the mortgage which usually spells out such things as defeasance clauses. Such paperwork should come with terms and conditions that are spelled out in great detail. For example, this contract contains all of the relevant information that pertains to the forecast repayment date, total amount to be paid back throughout the loan, and other issues. Buyers should carefully review all of this for accuracy. If any of it does not appear to be as expected by the borrowers, then they need to talk with the lender before signing any contracts.

There are several different ways that titles can be released by the lender. A defeasance clause may stipulate that the lender needs to release the title at once to the borrower after the loan has been completely paid. In other cases, the borrower might need to file paperwork for the release before the title comes back. The title should be cleared when the loan is paid off in full. Should any problems with this title arise, it can be a serious issue in the future when the owner wants to sell or refinance the house. Clearing up issues and mistakes on a title can take time, so these should be addressed as soon as possible.

Defined Benefit Plan

A defined benefit plan is a pension plan that serves as a vehicle for retirement. These plans give owners who are retiring benefits that are already pre-determined when they are established. These plans turn out to be a win-win situation for all parties.

Employees like the set benefit towards retirement that this provides. Employers also appreciate particular features of the plan. An employer is able to make larger contributions with this type of plan than with a defined contribution plan. Businesses can deduct the amounts they contribute from their tax liabilities. These types of plans are more complicated than the defined contribution plans. This is what sets the two types of plans apart. Defined benefit plans are more expensive to set up and to maintain than are alternative employee benefit plans.

What makes these plans more helpful to employees is the contributor. Employers usually contribute the most to them. Cases exist where employees can make voluntary contributions of their own. Occasionally the plan requires employees to make contributions. Whoever contributes, the benefits delivered by the plan are limited. The IRS sets and changes these limits every few years.

There are numerous distinctive features to these types of plans. An advantage to defined benefit plans is that plan participants can be allowed to take a loan against the value of the plan. Distributions before the participant reaches 62 are usually not allowed while the employee is still working for the company. The employees with the defined benefit plans are allowed to participate in other retirement plans.

Businesses have certain requirements with these plans as well. Companies of all sizes can participate in one. They are able to offer other types of retirement plans as well. Participating companies need to have an actuary who is enrolled in the plan decide how much the funding levels should be. Businesses also may not decrease the plan benefits after they have set them.

There are many advantages to defined benefit plans. Companies can confer significant retirement benefits on employees in a small amount of time. Employees can earn these benefits in a similarly short time frame. Even early retirement does not eliminate the ability to access these benefits. Employers appreciate that they can put more into these plans than with alternatives plans Employees love the predictable dollar benefits that the plans deliver. They also are happy to have a retirement account whose benefits do not depend on investment returns.

The schedule for becoming vested in the money of this benefit account varies. It can be set up for immediate full vesting. Schedules for vesting can stretch to as long as seven years with defined benefit plans as well. Some employers use the flexibility with these accounts to provide an early retirement package. Offering special benefit packages for early retirement is achievable with defined benefit plans.

There are also several downsides to these types of plans. They are the most complicated plan to administer and run. Defined benefit plans are also the most expensive kind of retirement benefit plan that a company can offer.

The IRS penalizes companies that do not make their minimum contribution requirement for a year. They do this using an excise tax when the minimums are not met. Some companies may wish to make larger contributions to the plan than they need to do. They might be motivated by the larger tax breaks. If a company over contributes, than an excise tax also applies.

Department of Justice

The Department of Justice is the largest law office in the world. It is an executive department of the Federal government in the U.S. whose head is appointed by the President. This department holds responsibility for administering justice and enforcing the laws in the United States. This makes the department similar to other nations' interior or justice ministries.

Head of the department is the U.S. Attorney General. The President nominates this individual whom the Senate later reviews, vets, and confirms. The attorney general is also a cabinet member for the President.

The mandate of the DOJ is to defend U.S interests with the law and to enforce the nation's laws. They also are tasked with making sure the public is safeguarded from dangers that are either domestic or foreign. They set out policy for the federal government to help stop and control crime. DOJ also works to punish anyone who breaks the law and to make sure that all Americans receive unbiased, fair justice.

The history of this department goes back to the early founding of the country. A single part time individual filled the federal Office of the Attorney General that the Judiciary Act of 1789 created. Originally the roles of this position were limited to prosecuting lawsuits in the Supreme Court and to advising the President and his department heads on any concerns.

It did not take long for the work load to be too great for any single individual. At this point, the Attorney General hired a few assistants. Still the work expanded and the government chose to retain private attorneys to assist with the increasing number of cases.

Finally following the end of the Civil War in 1870 Congress saw that they were wasting enormous amounts of money by retaining a huge quantity of private attorneys to help with the litigation concerning the U.S. from the war. The Congress then wrote and passed the Act to Establish the Department of Justice. This set up an executive level department of the Federal government. The Attorney General became its head.

The act similarly provided the Attorney General with more help. It created an Office of the Solicitor General. This individual handles U.S. interests in front of the United States Supreme Court. The tasks of the Attorney General were specifically redirected to managing civil suits and criminal prosecutions where the U.S. had interests.

The DOJ has continued to add to the department's structure in ensuing years since the 1870 Act founded it. Today there are also the offices of Associate Attorney General and Deputy Attorney General. Besides this there are numerous offices, divisions, boards, and components that make up the department. From humble beginnings as a single part time position, the DOJ has become the main enforcer of all Federal Laws today and grown into the biggest law office in the globe.

The Department of Justice has an important anti-trust division. This subdivision within the DOJ is responsible for enforcing the nation's anti-trust laws. It also works with the Federal Trade Commission on civil types of anti-trust cases. Together they advise businesses in matters that pertain to offering regulatory forms of guidance.

When businesses are considering buying out or merging with another, they may need to get approval from the anti-trust division. If the deal creates a large and powerful new entity within an industry and threatens the ongoing competition it is especially the case. This is because this group oversees fair competition in industries around the United States.

Department of the Treasury

The Department of the Treasury is an American Federal government department which is tasked with financing the spending of the United States. It bears the responsibility for raising funds by issuing and selling treasury bills, notes, and bonds to banks and investors.

The treasury department has oversight for a number of other important government agencies. Beneath its umbrella and authority are the U.S. Mint, the Internal Revenue Service, the Secret Service, and the Bureau of Alcohol and Tobacco Tax. As such Treasury and its subsidiary government agencies wear many hats which include protecting both the President and Vice President of the U.S.

The Treasury itself has a variety of functions which both it and the bureaus under it perform. Among these are printing postage, bills, and Federal Reserve notes. It also enforces the government tax laws, collects taxes (via the IRS), and manages the Federal government spending accounts and debts. Treasury also must oversee the various U.S. banks alongside the Federal Reserve. Besides this the U.S. Secretary of the Treasury carries the responsibilities for financial policy, international monetary policy, and intervention in the foreign exchange rate of the U.S. dollar.

This cabinet level department in the United States was originally intended to encourage and facilitate economic security and growth in the country. The origins of the department itself go back to the United States First Congress that sat on March 4 of 1789 after the states ratified the Constitution. This makes it among the oldest and most important departments in the country. As a cabinet level post, the American President nominates the U.S. Secretary of the Treasury. It is the responsibility of the U.S. Senate to vet and confirm this nominee.

Once the U.S. Constitution received ratification in 1789, a much stronger centralized Federal government arose. It became necessary for the new government to have a centralized Treasury Department to manage its expenses and income.

The first Treasury Secretary proved to be Alexander Hamilton. He served the country well in this capacity until 1795. Hamilton accomplished numerous important achievements as secretary. He assumed American Revolution debts from the states to the Federal government. Hamilton made provision to pay off the war bonds the new country had issued during the war for independence. His greatest achievement probably lay in the new system he set up to collect Federal government taxes.

The Treasury Department today finances an enormous and increasing portion of the United States' spending by borrowing money. It does this constantly by issuing longer term Treasury Bonds and shorter time frame Treasury Bills. The bonds can take as many as 30 years to reach maturity.

Treasury Bonds and Bills are guaranteed by the full faith and credit of the federal United States government. This makes them extremely popular around the globe. Other government central banks, individuals, corporations, commercial banks, and institutions alike all invest in these interest paying debt instruments.

Government Treasury Bonds and Bills pay extremely low interest rates because they are considered by the major ratings agencies Moody's, Standard & Poor's, and Fitch to be guaranteed safe investments. These U.S. Federal debt issues traded in a world wide market estimated at $12.9 billion at the end of the year 2015.

Once the Department of the Treasury issues these bonds and bills, it is up to the Federal Reserve Bank to work alongside them to manage them. The Federal Reserve Bank utilizes these government debt instruments by buying and selling them from banks. This way they are able to manage the money supply for the United States as they determine the interest rates for the country.

Dodd-Frank Act

The Dodd-Frank Act is fully entitled the Dodd-Frank Wall Street Reform and Consumer Protection Act. This enormous law served to reform the financial world following the financial crisis and Great Recession that began in 2008. President Obama's administration passed it through congress in 2010.

This Dodd-Frank Act legislation is literally thousands of pages long and contains numerous provisions. The regulations of this Dodd-Frank Act law are set for implementation over the course of a number of years. They were meant to reduce the obvious risks for failure in the American financial system. In order to oversee and carry out the numerous parts of the act it addresses, the controversial legislation created a range of new government agencies.

The first of these new agencies is the Financial Stability Oversight Council and Orderly Liquidation Authority. This group is tasked with overseeing major financial firms whose continued financial stability is necessary for the proper and continuous functioning of the U.S. economy.

These companies were negatively referred to as "too big to fail." The agency also handles necessary restructurings or liquidations of such firms in an orderly fashion should they become too unstable. They are charged with preventing these firms from being propped up with tax dollars. This council has great authority. They can even break apart banks which they deem in their judgment to be so big that they pose a risk to the banking system. It may also order higher reserve requirements for such banks. Another new group the Federal Insurance Office is similarly tasked with identifying and overseeing insurance companies which are too important to fail.

The CFPB Consumer Financial Protection Bureau was created to stop predatory forms of mortgage lending by the lenders. They are also responsible for increasing the simplicity of mortgage terms so that consumers can understand what they are signing before they complete the contracts. The group stops mortgage brokers from obtaining larger commissions when they close loans that have higher interest rates and fees.

It states that originators of mortgages may not direct possible borrowers to loans which provide the largest payouts to the loan originators. This group also governs various other kinds of lending to consumers. Their domain includes debt and credit cards and consumer complaints. They insist that lenders provide information in a manner that is simplest for consumers to comprehend. Credit card application simplified terms are an example of their work.

One potent rule that emerged from this Dodd-Frank Act legislation proved to be the so-called Volcker Rule. Named for the former Federal Reserve Chairman Paul Volcker, the rule was intended to reduce the amount of speculative trading, while simultaneously banning proprietary trading, by banking institutions. Banks have complained that these changes in the business model will make it more difficult to stay profitable.

The rule addresses regulating the derivatives like the infamous credit default swaps that majorly contributed to the financial meltdown in 2008. This rule also limits the ability of financial companies to utilize derivatives. The goal is to stop the systemically critical institutions from building up enormous risks that could ruin the banking system and overall economy.

The Dodd-Frank Act further created the new SEC Office of Credit Ratings. This group received the job of watching the credit agencies to ensure that the credit ratings they provide for various entities prove to be both dependable and reliable. Credit rating companies received a lot of blame for the financial crisis for falsely dispensing investment ratings that were misleading and overly positive.

Critics of the Dodd-Frank Act legislation claim the law will hamper economic growth and lead to higher unemployment in the future. Fans of the act insist that over time it will reduce the chances of the economy suffering from another 2008 styled crisis all the while safeguarding consumers from the abuses that eventually led to the crisis.

Due Process Oversight Committee (DPOC)

Within the structure and organization of the IFRS International Financial Reporting Standards, the trustees have various bodies that help them to perform their duties. The Due Process Oversight Committee is the one that carries the responsibility to monitor the procedures for effective due process. They also do this for the IASB International Accounting Standards Board and its Interpretations Committee.

This Due Process Oversight Committee generally holds meetings four times per year on the sidelines of the usually quarterly IFRS Foundation trustees meeting. When they require additional meetings, the DPOC usually handles them via conference call. Each year, they select different international locations for their meeting places. One of their quarterly meetings is usually held in London. In May and June of 2016, the IFRC Trustees and DPOC met in Jakarta and London, respectively. The Trustees and committee met in Beijing in October of 2015, London in June of 2015, Toronto in of April 2015, and Zurich in February of 2015.

There are a number of different responsibilities that the Due Process Oversight Committee carries out for the IFRS and the IASB. These are all spelled out within the Interpretations Committee Due Process Handbook of both the IFRS and the IASB. The first of these is to review the standard setting activities in which the IASB and staff of the IFRS Foundation engage. They do this review of due process activities routinely and with expediency as their mandate requires.

The Due Process Oversight Committee is also responsible for reviewing the Due Process Handbook that governs the committee among other things. They are to suggest updates to it that are in order. These updates would pertain to developing new and reviewing old standards, their various interpretations, and the Taxonomy of the IFRS itself. They do this to make sure that the procedures of the IASB are the best practice possible.

Besides this the Due Process Committee is tasked with reviewing the consultative groups of the IASB. They check who makes up the groups to ensure that the perspectives included are well balanced. They wish to have representation from the various relevant sub-disciplines. It is the committee's aim to ensure that these consultative groups are effective in their duties.

When outside parties request information on any due process issues, this Due Process Committee is the one that has to respond to them. They work with the technical staff of the Director for Trustee Activities to cohesively do so.

The IFRS Foundation bodies are also monitored for effectiveness by the Due Process Oversight Committee. They check up on the activities that involve standard setting at both the Interpretations Committee and the IFRS Advisory Council. Other groups within the IFRS Foundation which address the setting of standards are also followed up on by this Due Process Committee.

Finally, this important oversight committee is responsible for coming up with and issuing its recommendations to the IFRS Trustees about changing the committees. When the Due Process Oversight Committee determines that the makeup of these various committees that deal with due process needs to be changed, they let the Trustees know so that the committees can be appropriately re-balanced.

The Due Process Oversight Committee issues summaries of all of its meetings. These and any other papers and reports which they author are all found on their websites which are sub-pages of the International Financial Reporting Standards and the International Accounting Standards Board.

Earned Income Tax Credit (EITC)

The Earned Income Tax Credit, also known by its acronym EITC or EIC (for Earned Income Credit), is a benefit offered by the Internal Revenue Service to working people who only have lower to moderate levels of income. In order to qualify for it, prospective taxpayers have to measure up to specific requirements in a year in which they file their tax return.

The IRS requires that they file even when they do not owe any taxes, or if they otherwise do not have to file a tax return. A key benefit of the EITC is that it not only lowers the amount in tax receipts these families owe the government, but it can also create a negative tax liability that translates into a personal income tax refund.

Among the requirements necessary to qualify for this Earned Income Tax Credit, individuals have to receive at least some income while working as an employee for a person or business. Alternatively, they are able to qualify by owning or running either a farm or a business. There are also basic additional rules that involve having a qualifying child or children who meet each of the qualifying rules as set out by the IRS.

The Earned Income Tax Credit is intended primarily to help those families who have children, though it can also apply to other couples and individuals who receive lower to moderate levels of income. The actual amount of the benefits from the EITC is based upon the specific income of the filers as well as the actual number of children they have.

For those couples and individuals who claim children which qualify, they must be able to prove age, parental relationship, and shared residency. For the tax year 2013, the income levels that met IRS requirements had to be under $37,870 on up to under $51,567, which varied based on the numbers of children considered to be dependent in the family. Those workers who have no children yet who earn under $14,340 for an individual or $19,680 for married couples were eligible to get a tiny EITC amount in benefits. Those who do not have children which qualify are able to utilize U.S. tax forms including 1040, 1040A, or 1040EZ to apply. When qualifying children are involved, the head of household filer must utilize either the 1040 or 1040A forms alongside an attached Schedule EITC.

Financial Terms Dictionary - Laws & Regulations Explained

In the tax year of 2013, the IRS had established maximum benefit levels which individuals, couple, and families with qualifying children could obtain. For those who had no children which qualified, the maximum was $487. With a single child who qualified, the maximum benefit rose to $3,250. Where there were two children, this amount grew to $5,372. Finally, with three or even more children who were qualified, the maximum amount increased to $6,044. Each year, these numbers are raised according to the inflation index. In tax year 2015, this reduced tax revenues owed to the U.S. federal government by a not-insignificant around $70 billion.

It should not come as a surprise that these Earned Income Tax Credits have been and still remain a significant item for discussion in the ongoing political conversations within the United States. The debate has centered on the question of which approach would help the poor and lower middle class most. One idea is to raise the minimum wage significantly. The other is to boost the maximum amounts of the EITC. Back in the year 2000, The American Economic Association took a random survey of 1,000 of their members to learn their perspective. Over 75 percent of American economists agreed that it made sense to increase the program of the Earned Income Tax Credit.

Environmental Impact Statement (EIS)

The Environmental Impact Statement (EIS) analyzes and succinctly describes any potential proposed actions and the substantial effects these may cause for the environment where they will take place. Such an EIS is always made available to members of the public who wish to learn more about or comment on them. There are five components that every EIS has to contain per the rules.

The opening element to an Environmental Impact Statement is the description of the intended action. This portion will detail why it is needed and what are the benefits it offers. As a second item, they must also contain detailed information describing the setting of the environment and any areas that will be impacted by the action the document proposes.

The third part and substance of the Environmental Impact Statement surrounds a detailed analysis. This analysis has to consider all of the effects on the environment that the action will cause. As a fourth part of the EIS, it must also contain another analysis. This must suggest any practical alternatives to the intended action in question. Each of these alternate actions must be addressed for why they are not superior.

Finally, the EIS has to contain an outline of the means for lessoning the negative impacts on the environment. If possible, it should spell out a way to avoid these harmful effects altogether.

The reason that companies, organizations, or federal agencies prepare an Environmental Impact Statement is to learn what the consequences of their actions will be for the environment and how they can mitigate them. In this case, the word environment refers to the physical and natural environment. It also pertains to the mutual relationship between the environment and individuals. EIS definitions for the word environment involve many different components. These include water, land, air, life forms, structures, site environmental values. They also cover the aspects of culture, social concerns, and the economy.

Impacts from a proposed action are not always negative. They can be positive or sometimes both positive and negative. The idea is to find ways to lesson the impacts, especially the harmful ones. Sometimes the effects can not be effectively lessened. This is why the EIS will also go into detail on any alternatives to the proposed action which might involve fewer negative effects on the environment.

There are a variety of national regulations and federal laws that the American federal government has passed so that impacts on the environment can be calculated. These also mandate that alternative actions must be considered. The statute that stipulates when such an Environmental Impact Statement has to be created is known as NEPA the National Environmental Policy Act of 1969.

This centerpiece legislation was established primarily to govern federal agencies in their actions on the environment. It also relates to company or organizational efforts that will impact the environment. It means that these agencies or parties have to not only detail what the potential action will do. They must also outline what they might reasonably do as an alternative to the suggested course of action.

These laws also require that enough information has to be included so that the Environmental Protection Agency or other reviewing group is able to adequately consider the pros and cons of every alternative action. The group that bears responsibility for the content and format of these Environmental Impact Statements is the CEQ Council for Environmental Quality. It is usually the Federal Environmental Protection Agency or a state's Department of Environmental Conservation that will require such a statement to be put together on a project.

Environmental Protection Agency (EPA)

The Environmental Protection Agency is the United States' environmental enforcement group. It is not a cabinet level department, though its Administrator typically receives cabinet status and rank. The president appoints the administrator after the individual is approved by the Congress. The EPA is headquartered in Washington, D.C. It also operates ten regional offices and 27 laboratories throughout the U.S.

President Richard Nixon originally proposed the EPA and created it by signing an executive order. It started operating December 2nd of 1970. President Nixon's order received ratification from Congress via committee hearings in the Senate and the House of Representatives.

The mission of the Environmental Protection Agency lies in protecting human health and the environment. To do this, it engages in research and environmental assessments. The group also promotes education. It carries the responsibility for enforcing environmental standards as provided in the national laws. The EPA does this by consulting with the federal, state, local, and tribal governments. Some of this enforcement, monitoring, and permitting it delegates out to the fifty states and the recognized Indian tribes.

The powers of the EPA allow it to issue sanctions and levy fines. Whenever possible it works with the government and industries to prevent pollution voluntarily. It also promotes efforts to conserve energy throughout the country.

The Environmental Protection Agency has a number of priorities in its mission. First and foremost it is interested in protecting Americans from substantial risks to their health as well as the environment in which they work, live, and learn. To do this, they carry out the best scientific research so that environmental risk can be effectively reduced on a national level. They also work to enforce the federal laws which safeguard the environment and health fairly and efficiently.

The EPA feels that every individual and group in society should be able to access correct information for taking care of environmental risks and health. This includes businesses, people, communities, and local, state, and tribal governments. They want to see environmental protection treated as a critical priority in all American policies. Energy, economic growth, natural resources, transportation, health, industry, agriculture, and foreign trade should all be taken into consideration when making environmental policy.

Making the protection of the environment help with sustainable and economically productive development is another concern of the Environmental Protection Agency. They make it their business to ensure that the U.S. is leading other nations in protecting the world's environment as well.

The EPA carries out a number of activities in order to see through their mission and goals. The primary one is to develop and enforce the environmental regulations. Congress passes laws that the EPA puts into effect by writing regulations. They set national standards for state and tribal governments to enforce on their own. They also help these groups if they can not achieve the national standards. Enforcing such regulations becomes necessary if they are not able to convince offenders voluntarily.

The EPA gives many grants out to educational groups, state programs, not for profits, and others. Almost half of their budget is devoted to this. These finance everything from cleaning up communities to paying for scientific studies. They also sponsor dozens of partnerships as part of this. Some of these help to recycle solid waste, lower greenhouse emissions, and conserve energy and water.

The group spends a lot of time and effort studying environmental issues. In their over two dozen labs around the country, they find and attempt to solve these problems. They also share the findings with academic circles, the private sector, other government agencies, and foreign countries. The Environmental Protection Agency publishes online and written materials regarding what they learn and their various activities.

Equal Credit Opportunity Act (ECOA)

The Equal Credit Opportunity Act is also known as the ECOA. Congress created this regulation in order to provide all legal American residents with a fair and reasonable opportunity to obtain loans from banks or other financial institutions that make loans.

The act clearly states that such organizations may not discriminate against individual people for any reason that does not directly pertain to their credit history and file. It makes it illegal for lenders and creditors alike to take into consideration such factors as the consumer's color, race, ethnicity, nation of origin, religion, sex, or marital status when they are determining whether or not they will accept the credit or loan application.

Besides this, the law prohibits denying any credit application because of the age of the applicant. This assumes that the person applying has attained the legal minimum age and demonstrates the mental abilities necessary to execute such a contract. Finally, companies making loans may not reject an applicant because he or she receives public assistance funds from the government.

The governmental agency responsible for enforcing this Equal Credit Opportunity Act turns out to be the FTC Federal Trade Commission. As the consumer protection agency for the country, the FTC monitors lending organizations to make sure that they are not in violation of any of these discriminatory rules. Creditors are allowed to ask applicants for such information as their color, race, religion, sex, ethnicity, nation of origin, age, or marital status.

They are not allowed to consider any of these factors when determining whether or not to extend credit or even when deciding the terms of the credit which they are offering. The fact remains that not all people applying for credit will receive it or will obtain it on equal terms. Many factors are taken into consideration by lenders in ascertaining a person's creditworthiness, such as expenses, income, credit history, and levels of debts.

This Equal Credit Opportunity Act specifically protects consumers when they transact with investors or organizations that routinely offer credit. This

Financial Terms Dictionary - Laws & Regulations Explained

includes loan and finance companies, banks, department or retail stores, credit unions, and credit card companies. Every party who is a part of the credit granting or terms setting decisions has to abide by the rules of the ECOA. This includes even the finance arrangers such as real estate brokers.

As a person applies for a mortgage, lenders will routinely inquire about some of the elements of information that are forbidden to be considered in the ultimate application decision. Because of this, applicants do not have to respond to these questions. The only considerations which they are allowed to employ in judging the merits of the individual must be information that is financially relevant, like the person's income, credit score, and present debt levels.

The Equal Credit Opportunity Act will not allow lenders to make approval decisions because of an individual's present or past marital status. They will require that applicants inform them of any child support or alimony payments which they are making. Persons receiving such substantial payments as part of their income should also disclose this so that they can obtain the loan. Companies may refuse to provide a loan because the individual's financial obligations along with child support payments are too high to pay back the loan under the required terms. This does not mean that a person can be turned down for a loan because he or she is or has been divorced.

The penalties for violating the Equal Credit Opportunity Act are severe. Class action lawsuits can be brought against them. Organizations found guilty of ignoring this act can be made to pay damages that amount to either $500,000 or a percent of the applicant's net worth, whichever is less.

Financial Terms Dictionary - Laws & Regulations Explained

European Monetary System (EMS)

In 1979 a few European nations linked their currencies together in an arrangement and system to stabilize exchange rates called the European Monetary System. This system endured until the EMU European Economic and Monetary Union succeeded it.

As an important institution within the European Union, the EMU established the euro. The origin of the EMS lay in an effort to reduce significant changes in exchange rates between the European nations and to reign in inflation. It led to the creation of the European Central Bank in June of 1998 and the euro in January of 1999.

After the failure of the defunct Bretton Woods Agreement in 1972, the Europeans wanted to create a new exchange rate system of their own to help encourage political and economic unity throughout the EU. They came up with the EMS in 1979 as a means of moving towards the common currency of the future.

The EMS eventually formed its successor the European Currency Unit. With the ECU, exchange rates could be formulated by methods that were official. In the first year of the EMS, currency values proved to be uneven. Adjustments had to be made to lower weaker currencies while increasing the stronger currency values. In 1986 they came up with a more stable system of altering national interest rates instead.

Crisis broke out in the EMS in the early years of the 1990s. Germany's reunification created political and economic conditions that made the exchange rate bands less workable. Britain withdrew permanently from EMS in 1992. They became more independent from the central EU this way and banded together with Denmark and Sweden in refusing to become members of the eurozone.

This did not stop other nations within the EU from continuing to push for closer economic integration and a common currency. They formed the European Monetary Institute in 1994 to set up an orderly transition to the ECB that arose in 1998. The main tasks of the new ECB were to come up with one interest rate and monetary policy by laboring alongside the national central banks.

The ECB was not given the role originally of lending money to governments in financial crises or increasing employment rates like the majority of central banks. This would later cause delays and problems in bailing out struggling countries in the financial crisis that began in earnest in 2008.

The end of 1998 saw the majority of nations in the EU cut their interest rates at the same time to encourage economic growth while preparing to implement the Euro currency. This is when they established the EMU to succeed the EMS as the primary economic policy mechanism in the European Union. The adoption and subsequent circulation of the euro by the eurozone countries proved to be a significant step towards the aimed for European political unity. The EMU has helped member nations attempt to work toward lower inflation, less public spending, and lesser government debts.

Hidden weaknesses in the European Monetary System became obvious during the global financial crisis of 2008 and the following years. Member nations like Greece, Portugal, Spain, Ireland, and Cyprus ran up high deficits that later erupted in the European sovereign debt crisis.

Because these countries did not have national currencies to devalue, they could not increase their exports. The EMU forbade them from spending additional money and running higher deficits to help increase employment. EMS policies had expressly forbidden eurozone bailouts to any countries whose economies were in trouble.

After months of arguments from the larger economy members such as Germany and France, the EMU at last came up with bailout policies that allowed aid to be dispensed to peripheral members who were struggling. They set up the European Stability Mechanism as a permanent pool of money to help out economies of struggling EU member states in 2012. This allowed a few of the countries in trouble like Spain, Portugal, and Ireland to make some progress on recoveries.

European Stability Mechanism (ESM)

The European Stability Mechanism is a significant part of the financial stability and safeguard mechanisms in the Euro Zone area. It replaced the EFSF European Financial Stability Facility in 2013. This original EFSF was never intended to be permanent. Instead it was designed as a temporary solution to financial problems within the EU.

The European Stability Mechanism that took over for it was better established to deliver financial help to those Eurozone member countries that found themselves either threatened by or actually experiencing financial difficulties.

These two financial facilities ran concurrently from October of 2012 through June of 2013. Beginning in July of 2013 the EFSF could no longer begin new programs for financial support or help. The program still exists to manage and collect repayments of debts that are outstanding.

Once all of the existing loans that the EFSF program made have been repaid and all funding instruments and guarantors have received full payment for their contributions, then the EFSF will cease to exist entirely. This makes the replacing ESM the only and ongoing internal means for delivering aid in response to new calls for financial assistance from Eurozone member nations.

The European Stability Mechanism proves to be the principal means of resolving crises for nations which participate in the Euro. It obtains its money by issuing debt obligations. This permits it to fund financial aid and loans to the member countries of the Euro area. The European Council actually created the ESM in December of 2010. Participating Euro member states came together and signed a treaty between the governments on February 2 of 2012. October 8 of 2012 was the day they inaugurated the new ESM.

This ESM has great flexibility in funding its distressed member states. As various conditions are met, it is able to deliver loans as part of a program for macroeconomic adjustment. The mechanism is also able to buy member countries' debt in either the secondary or primary markets.

It can help to recapitalize banks of member states by loaning the governments money for this purpose. It can also deliver credit lines as a means of providing financial help as a precaution. In worst case and last resort conditions, the facility is allowed to recapitalize banks and other financial institutions directly. This is limited to times when resolution funds and bail ins are not enough to make the bank financially viable again.

The resources of the ESM are considerable. It has a capital base that has been subscribed in the amount of 704.8 billion. Of this amount, 80.5 billion has been paid in to the facility. The remaining 624.3 billion is classified as callable capital when it is needed. The fund is able to loan out a maximum total of 500 billion.

The ESM is based in Luxembourg. It is governed by public international law as an intergovernmental organization. It has only government shareholders making up its ownership. These are the 19 member countries that make up the Euro area. In 2016, 153 staff members worked under the direction of Klaus Regling the managing director.

European countries which are in trouble have other outside recourses for help besides the ESM. The principal other provider of assistance is the International Monetary Fund. The EU has supported having its own ESM, along with the predecessors the EFSF and the European Financial Stabilization Mechanism because it feared the consequences of some of its member states' problems with debt. Not all of the EZ countries suffered from debt issues. One EZ country failing could have contagious effects and widespread repercussions on the other national economies' health.

Exchange Rate Mechanism (ERM)

Exchange Rate Mechanisms are systems that were established to maintain a certain range of exchange for currencies as measured against other currencies. These ERMs can be run in three different ways. On one extreme they can float freely. This permits the systems to trade without the central banks and governments intervening.

The fixed Exchange rate mechanisms will do whatever it takes to maintain rates pegged at a specific value. In between these two extremes are the managed ERMs. The best known example of one of these is the European Exchange Rate Mechanism known as ERM II. It is in use today for those countries who wish to become a part of the EU monetary union.

The European Economic Community formally introduced the European ERM system to the world on March 13, 1979. It was a part of the EMS European Monetary System. The goal of this new system centered on attaining monetary stability throughout Europe by reducing the variable exchange rates. This was set up to prepare the way for the Economic and Monetary Union. It also paved the way for the Euro single currency introduction that formally occurred on January 1, 1999.

The Europeans changed their system once the Euro became adopted. They introduced ERM II as a way to link together those EU countries who were not a part of the eurozone with the euro. They did this to boost extra eurozone currencies' stability. A second goal was to create a means of evaluating the countries who wished to join the eurozone. In 2016 only a single currency uses the ERM II. This is the Danish krone.

The European ERM ceased to exist in 1999. This was the point after the eurozone country European Currency Units exchange rates became frozen and the Euro began trading against them. ERM II then replaced the initial ERM. At first the Greek drachma remained in the ERM II alongside the Danish currency. This changed when Greece adopted the Euro in 2001. Currencies within the newer system may float in a fairly tight range of plus or minus 15% of their central exchange rate versus the euro. Denmark does better than this. Its Danmarks Nationalbank maintains a 2.25% range versus the central rate of DKK 7.46038.

Financial Terms Dictionary - Laws & Regulations Explained

In order for other countries that wish to join the Euro to participate, they are required to be a part of the ERM II system for minimally two years before they can become members of the eurozone. This means that at some point, a number of currencies for member states that joined the EU will have to be in the system. This includes the Swedish krona, Polish zloty, Hungarian forint, Czech Republic koruna, the Romanian leu, Bulgarian lev, and Croatian kuna. Each of these is supposed to join the system according to their individual treaties of accession.

In the case of Sweden, the situation is more complicated. The country held a referendum on becoming a part of the mechanism to which the citizens voted no. The European Central Bank still expects that Sweden will join the system and eventually adopt the euro. This is because they did not negotiate for an opt out of the currency as did the U.K. and Denmark. The Maastricht Treaty requires that EU member states all eventually join the exchange rate mechanism.

Britain participated in the mechanism from 1990 until September of 1992. On September 16, 1992 the British famously crashed out of the system on what became known as Black Wednesday because of manipulation of the pound by currency speculators led by Hedge Fund Billionaire George Soros.

Financial Terms Dictionary - Laws & Regulations Explained

Fair Credit Billing Act

Congress passed the Fair Credit Billing act back in 1975. They enacted this national law in order to safeguard consumers from unfair or prejudiced billing actions. It created mechanisms for dealing with billing errors that affect credit accounts which are open ended. This includes credit cards and charge card accounts.

There are many different and all too common types of billing errors that the Fair Credit Billing Act specifies and protects against in its statute. Charges which are an incorrect amount are one. It also covers charges showing up on a bill that the consumer did not process. These are often known as unauthorized charges. Consumers can never be responsible for more than $50 of these. The act also covers the costs of any goods that did not come as they were supposed to when the consumer bought them, as well as for those goods that the consumer never received.

Consumers are similarly protected by the Fair Credit Billing Act from errors in calculation. They can not be held responsible for billing statements which the companies send out to the wrong address. Changes of address are required to be submitted by the account holder in writing and received by the creditor more than 19 days before the billing period ends. Consumers are similarly protected against any charges which they request proof of or clarification for on a statement. They may also not be held liable for a creditor improperly showing payments or charges to their credit accounts.

Customers are able to avail themselves of the protections spelled out in the Fair Credit Billing Act. To do so, they have to begin the process by writing the creditor at their business address specified for billing inquiries. They must include their name and address, account numbers, and any information on the billing dispute in question. The letter must be received by the creditor within 60 days or less of the original bill mailing date.

Such a letter should be dispatched by certified mail with return receipt so that the consumer has conclusive proof of when the creditor received it. All relevant copies of receipts and supporting documents need to be included with the letter. The creditor concerned is required by law to acknowledge that they have received the letter of complaint in 30 days or less after they receive it. The creditor then has up to 90 days (as in two billing cycles) to

Financial Terms Dictionary - Laws & Regulations Explained

research and resolve the dispute per the terms of the Fair Credit Billing Act.

The Fair Credit Billing Act also governs what happens when a bill is placed in dispute by a consumer. The person is allowed to not make payments on any charges pertaining to the disputed amount in question. Such a period of withholding only applies throughout the time frame in which the investigation is ongoing. All remaining portions of the bill and relevant interest amounts have to be paid as per the governing credit agreement and terms. The creditor may not engage in any legal action or collection activity against the borrower so long as the investigation phase is ongoing. The account of the borrower is not permitted to be closed or restricted in this phase.

The creditor is also forbidden to make threats against the borrowers' credit ratings when charges are under investigation and in dispute. The dispute itself can be reported to the credit ratings agencies. Creditors are not allowed to discriminate by withholding credit approval from any consumer who uses his or her rights to dispute a credit charge. This means in practice that consumers may not be refused credit because they have filed disputes against charges on a bill.

Fair Housing Act

The Fair Housing Act of 1968 is officially known as Title VIII from the Civil Rights Act of 1968. It makes it illegal to discriminate with regards to renting, selling, or financing homes or apartments. No one may consider color, race, sex, religion, or national origin in these activities.

Congress amended the Fair Housing Act of 1968 with the Fair Housing Amendments Act in 1988. These amendments expanded the rulings of the original act in a number of important ways. No one was permitted to discriminate with housing because of an individual's disability or based on their family status. This meant that home sellers or renters could not disallow families with pregnant women or who had children less than 18 years of age living with them.

To prevent disability discrimination, the act included construction and design accessibility rules for some multifamily homes. Those that were to be occupied initially after March 13, 1991 had to comply with the accessibility provisions for disabled people.

The amendments also created new means of enforcing and administering the rules. HUD Housing and Urban Development attorneys were now able to take cases to administrative law judges for victims of such housing discrimination. The jurisdiction of the Justice Department became expanded and revised in such a way that it could file suits in Federal district courts for discrimination victims.

HUD has been tasked with the principal responsible to administer the Fair Housing Act of 1968 since the government adopted it. Thanks to the amendments in 1988, the department has become substantially more involved in enforcing the provisions. This is because the newly protected families and disabled brought many new complaints. The department also had to move beyond investigating and conciliating. They were tasked with mandatory enforcing the rules.

Any complaint regarding the Fair Housing Act of 1968 that individuals file with HUD becomes investigated. The FHEO Fair Housing and Equal Opportunity office handles this responsibility. When complaints can not be resolved voluntarily, the FHEO decides if there is sufficient evidence for a reasonable case of discrimination in housing practices. If they find reasonable cause, then HUD issues a Determination and Charge of Discrimination to the complaint parties. Hearings are next scheduled in front of a law judge for the HUD administration. Either the complaining party or the accused can terminate this procedure to instead have the matter resolved in Federal courts.

At this point, the Department of Justice assumes HUD's responsibility for the aggrieved party's complaints. They act as counsel that seeks to resolve the charges. The matter then becomes a civil case. In either the case of the HUD law judge hearing or the civil action held in the courts, the U.S. Court of Appeals can review the outcome.

The Fair Housing Act of 1968 proved to be historic as the final major act in the civil rights movement legislation. Despite this, housing remained segregated throughout much of the United States for decades. During the thirty years from 1950 through 1980, America's urban centers' black population grew from 6.1 million up to 15.3 million people.

At the same time, white Americans continuously abandoned the cities in favor of the suburbs. With them went a great number of the jobs that the black population needed to communities where they did not find welcome. The result of this ongoing trend caused urban America to be filled with ghettos. These are the communities inside the American inner cities where many minority populations live. They have been dogged by consistently high crime, unemployment, drug use, and other social problems.

Federal Deposit Insurance Corporation (FDIC)

The U.S. government started The Federal Deposit Insurance Corporation back in 1933. They created it because of the literally thousands of failed banks that went down in the 1920s and 1930s. The FDIC began insuring bank accounts at the beginning of 1934. Since then, no depositors have lost any insured bank account money despite a consistent number of banks failing every year.

The first role of the FDIC is to insure and to increase the public's confidence in the American banking system. They do this in several ways. The FDIC insures minimally $250,000 in bank and thrift accounts. They watch for and take action on any risks to the deposit insurance funds. They also stop the spread of any bank failures when one of the banks does fail.

The Federal Deposit Insurance Corporation only insures deposits. This means that it does not cover mutual funds, stocks, or any other investments that some banks offer to their customers. They offer a standard $250,000 amount for each depositor's account. This single limit amount does not apply to other types of account ownerships and accounts at other banks. To help individuals understand if the insurance provided is enough to cover their various kinds of account, the FDIC provides its Electronic Deposit Insurance Estimator.

Another important role of the FDIC lies in its supervisory position. The outfit oversees over 4,500 different savings and commercial banks to make sure that they are operationally safe and sound. This represents more than half of the banks. Those banks that are set up as state banks may choose to become a member of either the Federal Reserve System or the FDIC. Any banks that are not overseen by the Federal Reserve System are watched over by the FDIC.

Another job of the FDIC is to check on the various banks to make sure they abide by the government's consumer protection laws. These laws include The Fair Credit Reporting Act, the Fair Credit Billing Act, the Fair Debt Collection Practices Act, and the Truth in Lending Act.

Lastly, the FDIC checks banks to make sure the different institutions are abiding by their responsibilities under the Community Reinvestment Act.

This law ensures that banks help the communities where they were started to achieve their needs for credit.

Despite all of these roles, the only one that members of the public really encounter on a personal basis is the FDIC protecting insured depositors. When a bank or thrift goes down, the FDIC immediately reacts to the situation. They come in fast with the group that chartered the bank to close it down. The charter group could be the Office of the Comptroller of the Currency or the state regulator.

The next step is for the FDIC to wind up the failed bank. In their preferred method, they sell both the loans and the deposits of the bank to another banking institution. Customers rarely feel the transition in the majority of the cases. This is the FDIC's goal, to make sure that people do not lose access to their accounts and money.

The FDIC carries out its several mandates through six regional branches. It has more than 7,000 staff members that help it to carry out these goals. The organization is based in its headquarters in the capital Washington, D.C. Besides these locations, they also have various field offices throughout the nation.

The leadership of the FDIC is supplied by the Federal Government. The President appoints the board which the Senate confirms. There are five members of their Board of Directors. No more than three of them may belong to one political party to ensure bipartisanship in the decisions.

Federal Housing Finance Agency (FHFA)

The Federal Housing Finance Agency is a government regulating agency. They are independent and responsible for overseeing several agencies within the secondary mortgage market. These include Freddie Mac, Fannie Mae, and the Federal Home Loan Banks. They work to keep these critical government sponsored organizations, along with the entire American housing financial system, in good health.

As such, the FHFA labors constantly to build up and safeguard the secondary mortgage markets in the United States. They do this through their leadership in and delivering excellent research, dependable data, strong supervision, and pertinent policies. The three government sponsored entities of Freddie Mac, Fannie Mae, and the Federal Home Loan Bank system together deliver over $5.5 trillion in financial institutions and mortgage markets funding throughout the United States.

The FHFA helps to keep this all possible by providing their independent regulation and careful oversight of these vital mortgage markets. Besides this, they are also the conservator of both Freddie Mac and Fannie Mae since the financial crisis and Great Recession that began in 2007-2008 wreaked havoc on the two giant government sponsored agencies along with the housing market they guaranteed.

The Federal Housing Finance Agency is concerned with creating a better market of secondary mortgages for the country's future. To this effect, they are working on a sequence of strategies and initiatives to boost the housing financial system in the future. Among these new ideas is the construction of a new and improved database called the Common Securitization Platform. This will have dual roles. It will take the presently outdated infrastructures and modernize them. It will also allow for the possibilities of other players in the market choosing to utilize this same infrastructure.

The FHFA considers itself to be in a partnership. They strive alongside the entities they regulate to keep home ownership alive and affordable through a variety of programs. These include the HARP Home Affordable Refinance Program and the HAMP Home Affordable Modification Program. The two programs deliver significant and tangible aid to both communities and their homeowners. So far such programs have assisted literally millions of home owning Americans to keep or stay in their houses.

The FHFA does not have a long history. It is a new organization that grew out of the housing market collapse and Great Recession. President Obama signed the Housing and Economic Recovery Act of 2008 to create the Federal Housing Finance Agency back on July 30, 2008.

The ongoing mission of the FHFA is to make certain that the government sponsored enterprises for housing function in a manner that is both economically viable and safe. This is so that they can continue to provide a dependable source of both funds and liquidity for investment in communities and the financing of home purchases. As part of this, they envision a housing financial system that is stable, dependable, and liquid for both the present and the future.

The FHFA values four virtues. They prize excellence in all areas of their work. The organization appreciates respect for their team members, resources, and the information they collect. They value integrity and commit themselves to the greatest possible professional and moral standards. The group also encourages diversity in all of their business dealings and employment arrangements, as well as in the entities which they regulate and for whom they are the conservator.

FHFA is also an important member group of the Financial Stability Oversight Council. Chief among their tasks is to identify financial stability risks in the U.S., to respond to rising threats to the American financial system, and to encourage discipline in the market. They serve on this council with fellow members that include The Federal Reserve governors, CFTC, FDIC, Comptroller of the Currency, SEC, and Treasury Department.

Federal Open Market Committee

The Federal Open Market Committee is a group within the Federal Reserve, the central bank for the United States. This central bank is more commonly known as the Fed. They carry out actions of monetary policy. This impacts the cost and readily available quantity of money and credit. The Fed uses these tools to foster the country's economic goals. Thanks to the Federal Reserve Act of 1913, the Fed gained the authority to set the national monetary policy.

Under the mantle of the Federal Reserve are three different monetary policy tools. These are reserve requirements, the discount rate, and open market operations. It is the Federal Reserve System Board of Governors that carries out the task of setting the reserve requirements and the discount rate. The Federal Open Market Committee handles the Fed's open market operations.

With these three different tools, the Fed is able to influence the supply of and demand for balances that the financial institutions keep inside the Federal Reserve Banks. This is how it affects the federal funds rate. This is the interest rate that banks and other financial institutions are willing to loan money from their Federal Reserve accounts to other such institutions on an overnight basis.

When the federal funds rate changes, this sets off events which impact foreign exchange rates, other types of shorter term interest rates, longer term interest rates, and the quantity of money and credit in the economy. Eventually this affects a number of important economic indicators like economic output, employment, and the costs for goods and services.

Open market operations are the main tool that the Federal Reserve uses to carry out American monetary policy. Specifically they buy and sell government securities like Treasuries and T-Bills. They do this in the open market so that they can contract or expand the quantity of money that exists in the banking system. When they buy securities, it puts money into the banking system. This boosts growth in the economy. When they sell their securities, they withdraw money from the system. This shrinks the economy. Ultimately it is the federal funds rate the Federal Open Market Committee is trying to adjust with these operations.

The Federal Open Market Committee is made up of twelve members in total. These are comprised of the Federal Reserve System Board of Governors' seven members, the Federal Reserve Bank of New York President, and four of the other eleven Presidents of the Reserve Banks. These other Reserve Bank Presidents rotate in and out serving one year terms. Rotating seats have a special order in which they are filled. There are four groups of Banks which each contribute a Bank President to the voting Federal Open Market Committee. The groups are Richmond, Philadelphia, and Boston; Chicago and Cleveland; Dallas, Atlanta, and St. Louis; and San Francisco, Kansas City, and Minneapolis.

Those Reserve Bank Presidents who are not voting members of the committee in a given year still attend all of the committee meetings, make their contributions to the economy and policy choices assessments, and take part in all discussions.

Every year the Federal Open Market Committee engages in eight routinely scheduled meetings. In these meetings, the committee does a number of important activities. It reviews national financial and economic conditions, considers the risks to maintainable economic growth and long term price stability, and decides on its monetary policy appropriate stance.

The FOMC legally is authorized to set its own internal organization. They have a tradition of electing the Board of Governors Chair to be the Chair of the FOMC and selecting the New York Federal Reserve Bank President to be the vice chair. The eight annual meetings occur in Washington D.C.

Federal Reserve Act of 1913

The Federal Reserve Act of 1913 created the Federal Reserve Bank. This proved to be the Act of Congress that set up the Federal Reserve System. This system became the Central Bank organization for the United States. As part of the act, the Federal Reserve acquired the powers to issue the nation's legal tender currency. President Woodrow Wilson actually signed this act, making it law in 1913.

The leadership of the country felt the need to create such a central bank for several reasons. The United States had operated without a central bank going back to the expiration of the Second Bank of the United States' charter. This meant that for about eighty years, the country had existed without any form of central bank.

In time, a number of financial panics had ensued without any central bank to intervene in them. The one that really galvanized congressional and public opinion for having a central bank proved to be the serious financial panic of 1907. As a result of these factors, a number of Americans decided that the nation required serious currency and banking reforms that could handle such panics by offering an available liquid assets' reserve. They also figured such an institution might be capable of managing a consistent expansion and contraction of credit and currency from time to time as appropriate.

The original Federal Reserve Act plan recommended an establishment of an unusual combined public and private entity system. They suggested that minimally eight and as many as twelve regional private Federal Reserve banks should be created. All of them were to have their own boards of directors, regional boundary lines, and branches. This new entity would be led by a Federal Reserve Board comprised of seven members and made up of public officials that the President appointed and the Senate would confirm. An advisory committee known as the Federal Advisory Committee would be created, along with a brand new U.S. currency that would alone be accepted nationally, the Federal Reserve Note. In the final version of the bill, twelve regional Federal Reserve Banks were actually created. The rest of the above provisions became law and subsequently a part of the newly created Federal Reserve System.

Another important decision that Congress settled on with the Federal Reserve Act revolved around the private banks throughout the U.S. Every nationally chartered bank had to join the Federal Reserve System as a part of this act. They were made to buy stock that could not be transferred in their own area's Federal Reserve Bank. It furthermore required that a set dollar total of reserves that did not pay interest had to be deposited to their own regional Federal Reserve Bank. Banks that are only state chartered have the choice, but not the obligation, of joining this system and being regulated by the Fed.

Finally, the act allowed the member banks to receive loans at a discounted rate from the discount windows of their own regional Federal Reserve Bank. They were promised a six percent yearly dividend on their Federal Reserve stock and provided with additional services. The act also gave the Federal Reserve Banks the authority to assume the role of U.S. government fiscal agents.

Financial Terms Dictionary - Laws & Regulations Explained

Federal Trade Commission (FTC)

The FTC Federal Trade Commission proves to be the agency responsible for protecting the American consumers. They strive to stop tricky, fraudulent, and unfair practices in business in the nation's marketplaces. They also disburse valuable information to consumers that helps them to recognize, stop, and sidestep these frauds.

The FTC accepts consumer complaints by phone, email, their website, and through the mail. They take these complaints and enter them into a database that is called the Consumer Sentinel Network. This secure online tool is utilized for investigation purposes by literally hundreds of criminal and civil agencies for law enforcement throughout the United States and overseas.

What the FTC would like to do is to stop these types of deceptive and non-competitive business dealings before they hurt consumers. They are also attempting to improve consumer opportunities so that they are better informed about and comprehend the nature of competition. The agency attempts to perform all of these tasks without putting too many burdens and restrictions on businesses activities that are legitimate.

Congress created the FTC back in 1914. Originally its mandate lay in stopping unfair means of competition in trade and business caused by the trusts. They were a part of the government's stated goal to bust up these trusts. Congress has given them more authority to monitor and fight practices that were against fair competition over the years by passing other laws.

The government enacted another law in 1938 that was broadly addressed to stop any deceptive or unfair practices and acts. They have continued to receive direction and discretion to govern a number of other laws that protect consumers over the subsequent years. Among these are the Pay Per Call Rule, the Telemarketing Sales Rule, and the Equal Credit Opportunity Act. Congress passed another law in 1975 that gave the Federal Trade Commission the ability to come up with rules that regulated trade throughout the industries.

The FTC has a vision for the American economy. They want to see one that has healthy competition between producers. They also desire to see consumers able to obtain correct information. Ultimately the government agency looks for all of this to create low priced and superior quality goods. They encourage innovation, efficiency in business, and choice for consumers.

This agency carries out its vision with three strategic goals. It starts with them protecting consumers by heading off trickery and deception in the business and consumer marketplace. They desire to keep competition going strong. In this role, they stop mergers and business dealings that they believe are against competition. They also work to increase their own performance with consistently improving and excellent managerial, individual, and organizational efforts.

All of these goals and efforts combine to make the FTC one of the government agencies that most impacts each American citizen's economic and personal life. They are the only government entity that possesses a mandate for both competition jurisdiction and consumer protection in large segments of the U.S. economy. They go after aggressive and effectual enforcement of the laws.

The FTC shares its knowledge with international, state, and federal groups and agencies. The group creates research tools at a variety of conferences, workshops, and hearings every year. They also develop and distribute easy to understand educational materials for business and consumer needs in the transforming technological and global market.

The FTC carries out its work through its Bureaus of Economics, Competition, and Consumer Protection. They receive assistance from the Office of General Counsel. Seven regional offices around the country help them to carry out their mandate.

Financial Industry Regulatory Authority (FINRA)

The Financial Industry Regulatory Authority is a congressionally authorized independent and non profit outfit. Congress established them to safeguard the investors of America by ensuring that the stock market industry runs honestly and fairly for all participants.

FINRA is not an agency of the government, even though they have broad disciplinary and enforcement powers. The organization tirelessly works to ensure the integrity of the market and protection for investors by regulating the securities business.

FINRA carries out these duties in a variety of ways. They investigate brokerage firms to make sure they abide by the rules. The not for profit creates and then enforces these rules that govern the actions of more than 3,941 securities companies who have over 641,157 brokers on staff. FINRA also encourages transparency in markets and settles disputes. The group does all of this without taxpayers having to support them via taxes.

The authority works every day to make sure individuals selling securities are tested and licensed. They ensure all advertisements for securities utilized to sell the products are clear and truthful. FINRA holds companies to a high standard for only selling suitable investments to individuals that are appropriate to their needs. They ensure that every investor obtains full disclosure about their investment before they buy it.

The independent agency carried out 1,512 disciplinary actions on registered firms and brokers in 2015. This allowed them to collect fines of over $95 million. They mandated that $96.6 million be given back to investors who where harmed in these and other actions. The group handed over 800 different insider trading or fraud cases to other agencies like the SEC for settling or prosecuting the same year.

Ultimately FINRA's goals are to deter misconduct in the industry. They do this by enforcing rules for everyone. This is not only the rules that they create. The group also enforces the Municipal Securities Rulemaking Board's regulations and federal securities laws as well. They make the qualifying exams and require brokers to come to continuing education classes.

Financial Terms Dictionary - Laws & Regulations Explained

The organization puts hundreds of their own financial examiners in the field to check on the way these brokers carry out their business. Their main concern is for the investors and risks to the markets. They follow up on complaints filed by investors and other suspicious activities.

They also review all advertisements, brochures, websites, and communications to be certain brokers are fairly presenting their products. This amounts to approximately 100,000 different communications and advertisements they examine and approve between broker firms and their investors.

FINRA also disciplines rule breakers. They use their authority, technology, and professional experts to rapidly react to wrongs. The organization has the authority to fine brokers, suspend them, or expel them from the business.

The independent agency also possesses technology that is potent enough for them to be able to review various markets and pick up on possible fraud. They are able to gather data in such a way to keep tabs on insider trading or other practices that give broker firms advantages that are unfair. To this effect they process anywhere from 42 billion to 75 billion transactions daily to have a full picture of U.S. market trading.

The group is also involved in resolving disputes in the securities' business. This pertains to problems between investors and brokers. FINRA handles almost 100% of all mediations and arbitrations that are related to securities. They hear these disputes in 70 different locations. This includes one hearing center in every state, Puerto Rico, and London.

Financial Stability Oversight Council

The Financial Stability Oversight Council is an organization that was created by the Dodd-Frank Act following the financial crisis of 2008. It possesses a clear legal mandate that provides an accountability to look for risks and respond to perceived upcoming threats to the United States' financial stability.

This is the first time that a single organization has held such important responsibility. The group is actually headed by the Secretary of the Treasury. It combines the various experience and knowledge of state regulators, an insurance expert who is both independent and Presidentially appointed, and federal financial regulators.

The Financial Stability Oversight Council was granted first time powers by Congress to restrain and head off dangerous risks within the financial system. This Council can select a financial firm that is not a bank and mark it for intense supervision so that the firm can not threaten to blow up the financial system and its stability. As an aid in determining what qualifies potential risk to the country's financial stability, this FSOC is allowed to obtain information and analysis from and supply information to the recently established OFR Office of Financial Research that is headquartered in the Treasury building.

Before the financial crisis erupted, the financial regulation in the United States focused exclusively on specific markets and institutions. This permitted gaps in supervision to expand amidst inconsistencies in the regulation. Standards weakened as a result. There was no one regulator responsible for watching over and dealing with the various risks to American financial stability. The threats often revolved around various financial firms which functioned at once in numerous interrelated markets. Because of this, critical portions of the financial system remained unregulated. The Dodd-Frank Act dealt with these failures by creating the Financial Stability Oversight Council.

The Financial Stability Oversight Council has many roles. It facilitates and coordinates regulation. They are tasked with sharing information and coordinating action with the agencies involved to deal with examining, making rules, developing policy, reporting, and enforcing their actions.

Financial Terms Dictionary - Laws & Regulations Explained

They are also to encourage gathering and sharing information among their various member organizations. If they are unable to gather enough information, they are to turn to the OFR to obtain information from individual companies they need to evaluate. Gathering and evaluating such information is supposed to eliminate blind spots in the financial system. By doing this they are fostering a more stable and less dangerous overall financial system in the United States.

The Financial Stability Oversight Council is also to select nonbank financial entities that need to be consolidated. Dodd-Frank identified companies that did not receive appropriate supervision and then led to the outbreak of the financial crisis back in 2008. The act provides the Financial Stability Oversight Council the authority which it needs to force supervision on such companies at entirely its own discretion.

The council also has the power to make recommendations for harsher standards for those firms they deem to be the biggest and most interconnected operations which provide increased risks to the system. This includes both banks and non bank financial organizations. As the Council learns about activities and practices that are threatening financial stability in the country, they are able to recommend tougher standards to the appropriate financial regulators.

The extensive powers of this Financial Stability Oversight Council are most clearly shown in their ability to choose to break up companies at will which they perceive to represent a clear and present danger to the nation's financial stability. They can decide if action should be followed to break up these kinds of firms which they deem to be a grave threat to the United States and its financial stability.

Generally Accepted Accounting Principles (GAAP)

Generally Accepted Accounting Principles, more commonly referred to by their acronym GAAP, are the mostly American used set of accounting principles, procedures, and standards. These are utilized by companies to put together their corporate financial statements. Such GAAP proves to be a blend of the most accepted means of reporting and recording accounting data in the United States combined with the American policy board set standards.

Companies must use GAAP in order for their investors to have some common standard of consistency with financial statements they compare when considering the various companies in which to invest their money. These standards include such areas as balance sheet items classification, revenue recognition, and measurements of outstanding shares of stock.

Regulators expect that companies will obey these generally accepted accounting principles rules as they release their financial statements to routinely report their financial information. American investors should be leery of company financial statements that are not properly developed utilizing these guiding principles.

Despite this fact, these accounting procedures are merely a cohesive group of guidelines and standards. Crooked accountants are still able to distort and misrepresent the numbers while using these generally accepted procedures. Although a company may utilize the generally accepted procedures, investors should still carefully go through their financial statements with a healthy degree of skepticism.

The competing accounting standards that most of the rest of the world employs is known as the IFRS International Financial Reporting Standards. There has been a recent move to harmonize the two sets of standards in past years. Because of the global financial crisis and economic collapse of 2008 and its terrible aftermath, globalization, the SEC agreeing to accept international standards, and the Sarbanes-Oxley Act, countries like the United States have been severely pressured to close the gap between GAAP and the IFRS.

Doing so would have major ramifications on accounting throughout the U.S.

It also would affect investors, corporate management teams, accountants, national accounting standard makers, and American stock markets. Bringing these two sets of standards together is impacting CFO and CPA attitudes regarding international accounting. This influences the International Accounting Standards quality as well as the various endeavors that professionals are making on converging the two sets of standards.

There are some problematic inconsistencies with international financial reporting because the financial reporting standards and rules are somewhat different from one country to another. This dilemma has become more of a challenge for those international investors who are attempting to figure out the various differences in global accounting and reporting. As they are thinking about offering substantial investments to overseas companies which are earnestly seeking capital in good faith, it makes it more challenging since companies report according to the standards of the country where they do business.

The IASB International Accounting Standards Board has been sincerely looking for a practical solution to this international complication, confusion, and conflict that inconsistency in accounting standards for financial reporting has created and continues to encourage. The principle difference with GAAP and the IFRS methods lies in the totally different approaches that either one uses regarding the standards.

Generally Accepted Accounting Practices prove to be based on a set of rules. It employs a complicated group of guidelines that set criteria and rules in any given scenario. The International Financial Reporting Standards alternatively utilizes a method based on principles. The IFRS instead starts with the goal of good financial reporting and gives guidance on the particular needs and challenges of a given scenario.

Glass Steagall Act

Congress created and passed the Glass Steagall Act in 1933. This legislation arose because of the effects of the 1929 catastrophic stock market crash. Two congressmen came up with this solution in the Great Depression when many banks were failing. The law made separate all activities which involved commercial banking and investment banking.

Commercial banks had become heavily involved in the stock market. This activity received much of the blame for the stock market and financial crashes. Lawmakers felt that commercial banks had employed money from their depositors in speculation in the stock market.

The reasons this act came forcefully into law had to do with banks' activities. Commercial banks had bought new and unproven stocks to sell to individual customers. It was the greed of banks that led to the new legislation. The goals of banking were mired in conflict of interest. Banks would make loans to corporations in which they already had an investment. These loans were not issued based on good underwriting.

They would then push these investments to their clients. Their goal was to have their customers help support these companies. Such commercial speculation insured that when the companies failed, the banks and their customers all lost huge amounts of money. Finally banks began to collapse in the thousands as a result of this poor and unregulated activity.

The act actually came about because of Senator Carter Glass. Glass had served as Treasury secretary previously. He also founded the U.S. Federal Reserve System. The failing banks motivated him to act on a bill. He became the main driving force of this legislation. His partner on the project was Henry Bascom Stegall.

Stegall served as House Banking and Currency Committee chairman. At first he would not support the bill with Glass. They added an amendment to create insurance for bank deposits. This brought Congressman Stegall's critical support of the act.

The effects of this Glass Steagall Act erected a variety of barriers in the banking industry. A new firewall of regulation arose between investment bank and commercial bank businesses. The two types of banks experienced unprecedented oversight and control over their activities. All banks received one year to choose a specialty in either investment banking or commercial banking.

Those that chose commercial banking were heavily limited in their investment banking activities. Income from securities could not exceed 10% of the commercial bank earnings. Commercial banks were permitted to underwrite bonds the government issued. The ultimate goal was to stop banks from committing their depositors' funds to projects which were poorly underwritten and speculative.

Banks that were too big to fail at the time became significant targets for this act. JP Morgan and Company and rival financial empires were among these. Such outfits had to eliminate many services. This targeted a large and important part of their incomes.

Later on criticism of the Glass Steagall Act arose. This happened as different explanations became popular for the Great Depression. Many different individuals also saw that this act had created problems for financial services. They blamed the law for restricting financial firms to the point that they were not able to compete effectively.

Many opposed the act by the 1980s. Glass Steagall opposition grew into the 1990s. Congress finally repealed the act in 1999. The elimination of this act has been blamed for the Great Recession crisis that started in 2006.

Banks were again able to mix investment and lending activities. Close regulation of commercial banks had been largely eliminated. Because of this, banks again made many risky loans that were either liar loans or not properly documented for income.

Financial Terms Dictionary - Laws & Regulations Explained

HM Treasury

HM Treasury stands for Her Majesty's Treasury. This is the United Kingdom's finance and economic ministry. It keeps control over the public spending and lays out the direction for the economic policy of Great Britain. Among its important mandates is to work towards a sustainable and strong level of economic growth.

The HM Treasury of today dates back to the time of the Norman Conquest in 1066. The kingdoms of the Anglo Saxons also had Treasuries which collected taxes and handled expenditures before this nation altering invasion occurred. The Danegeld was a tribute levied on Anglo Saxons to pay the Vikings to leave or not attack. Britain's first official Treasurer was likely one "Henry the Treasurer."

He held land from King William located near Winchester which proved to be the location for the royal treasuries of both late Anglo Saxon and Norman Britain. Henry is believed to have functioned as William the Conqueror's treasurer. He is mentioned in the Domesday Book, the very first systematic tax assessment of the entire nation which the Treasury carried out at the time.

Eleven Downing Street is the home of HM Treasury. In 1684, Mr. Downing obtained the permission from King Charles II to construct and name his new Downing Street development at St. James Park. These houses were finished in 1686. Even though Number 11 Downing Street did not become the official residence of the head of Treasury the British Chancellor of the Exchequer until 1828, a precedent had been set a generation earlier.

In 1806 and 1807, Lord Henry Petty dwelt there while he held the position as Chancellor of HM Treasury. Chancellors who have since elected to live over their office have experienced a house that is not only historic for Britain, but unique and quite comfortable as a home as well.

HM Treasury bears many important responsibilities today. They handle all aspects of public spending. This includes the pay for pensions and public sectors, spending of the various ministries, welfare policy, capital investment, and the AME annually managed expenditure. They carry out a number of functions in financial services. Among these responsibilities are

Financial Terms Dictionary - Laws & Regulations Explained

to ensure the City of London remains competitive, to guarantee financial stability in the UK, and to regulate banking and other financial services throughout the nation.

Treasury also maintains responsibility for overseeing the various taxes in Britain. This includes indirect, direct, property, business, corporation, and personal taxes. The ministry handles encouraging private sector involvement and investment in national infrastructure and delivers infrastructure projects throughout the public sector. Finally, they must make certain that the growth of the British economy is ultimately both steady and sustainable.

In carrying out these critical responsibilities, HM Treasury has a range of priorities. They work towards strong growth which is sustainable. They attempt to utilize the tax money responsibly. Their goal is to rebalance the national economy while reducing the deficit. They strive to create a fairer and simpler tax system for all.

Treasury looks to develop safer and stronger British banks. They work towards levying the most competitive corporate taxes possible. They help to increase the ease and access to financial services for British consumers. Finally, they seek to better the financial sector's regulation so that it will safeguard both the national economy and members of the British public.

HM Treasury has its headquarters in London. They also maintain regional offices in Edinburgh, Scotland and Norwich, England.

Home Affordable Modification Program (HAMP)

The Home Affordable Modification Program is also known by its acronym HAMP. This stands for a program created by the United States government. They founded it in order to assist those homeowners who were struggling to keep up with their mortgages. For any homeowners who have watched in dismay as their financial conditions deteriorated since they originally purchased their house, they could be able to qualify for loan modifications to make keeping the home possible and affordable.

The program actually helps participants by allowing them to reduce their monthly mortgage payments. This happens as the program approves a lower rate of interest, extends the mortgage's time frame (and term), or alters the type of mortgage to fixed rate from adjustable rate ARM. In some cases, two or even three of these changes may be approved together. The modifications can happen because the United States government backs them.

The Home Affordable Modification Program began as the Departments of Housing and Urban Development HUD combined forces with the Treasury in order to forge a new initiative that they named Making Homes Affordable. Though there were other parts to this ground breaking concept, the HAMP proved to be a key pillar of it. The government recognized in the wake of the Great Recession that many Americans were only one accident, job loss, or illness away from falling hopelessly behind on their mortgages and payments. This is why they decided to come up with their innovative program for modifying mortgages to make them more affordable for those who are in the most need of help.

Becoming eligible for this home modification assistance program requires an applicant be able to successfully meet a particular set of criteria. They must have bought and financed the house before or on January 1st of 2009. They have to be capable of proving a real financial hardship that makes them struggle to meet their monthly mortgage payments. At the same time, they have to show that they are already behind on the monthly payments or even at risk of sliding into foreclosure of their home. In order to successfully qualify, the property can not have been condemned. They may not owe more than $729,750 on the primary residence which is a single family home. Finally, applicants may not show any personal real estate

Financial Terms Dictionary - Laws & Regulations Explained

fraud convictions from any time within the past ten years.

If they meet all of these exacting criteria, then interested parties are able to call their specific mortgage servicer to inquire about any additional requirements that could exist with their particular company. It is also important to inquire if the mortgage servicing company even participates with the Home Affordable Modification Program in the first place. If the provider does participate and the applicant actually meets all of the minimum requirements for participation, then the home owner will need to speak with his or her lender in order to obtain all of the necessary paperwork and forms to enroll.

These forms include first the Request for Mortgage Assistance Form, or RMA. There is also the Income Verification Form as well as the IRS' 4605T-EZ form to complete. It is important to note that the final application does not get submitted to the government, but instead to the mortgage servicer. They will require a tangible proof of financial hardship when the individual submits this application.

There are actually a number of key benefits which this Home Affordable Modification Program delivers for successful applicants. They are able to sidestep foreclosure of the home, reduce their costs for keeping the house, obtain a new start on the mortgage, and better their credit history and rating. The home loan will be made to work for the owners so that they can simply modify the mortgage instead of losing the house.

Though the program is one that has helped a number of Americans, it is not the foolproof answer to irresponsible home buying and borrowing. There have been a number of homeowners who availed themselves of the program in HAMP only to re-default a second time. Some of these have actually forfeited their homes in the foreclosure process. The program has been shown in a recently conducted study that it can help a number of the fully 20 percent of homeowners who are not saving money which they might be able to by taking advantage of either a loan modification program such as this one or through refinancing their home.

Import Quotas

Import quotas are numerical restrictions which a government of one country imposes on the imports of another competing nation. The main purpose of such quotas lies in decreasing imports while simultaneously boosting a country's own inherent domestic production. With the numbers of such imports restricted, the price of these imports will increase. This then fosters the production, purchase, and consumption of more domestically-produced goods and services by a nation's own consumers.

Import quotas prove to be among three of the most common foreign trade policies utilized to discourage imports while encouraging exports. Besides these are export subsidies and tariffs. National governments undertake to enforce these quotas as foreign trade policies. They are enacted with the intention of defending domestic production through limiting foreign competition.

Quotas in general are typically quantity limitations which a group slaps on activities, services, and goods. Employers typically run into hiring quotas for different national groups of people. Sales representatives also face such quotas in their sales activities and endeavors.

This is why import quotas as an extension of this idea are simply the foreign sector amount of imports which a domestic government will permit in a given industry or service sector. By increasing the numbers of domestically-produced goods in an economy while discouraging the numbers of competing imports, a nation's consumers are prompted to buy home-produced goods and services instead of foreign-based and -produced ones.

There are five principal reasons why import quotas are sometimes imposed on foreign imports of goods and services. The political pressure is such that domestic employment has to be protected and encouraged. Many domestic jobs proponents fear the competition of low foreign wages. By decreasing the number of imports from such countries, governments are able to lower the playing field for higher and better paid domestic employees.

Governments can also be concerned about unfair trade practices and infant industry worries. Unfair trade means that the foreign-created imports could be dumped at prices which are lower than possible production costs.

Foreign exporters would do this temporarily in a market in order to reduce the ability of domestic producers to effectively compete and remain in business at the same time. China has been a major practitioner of dumping and unfair trade practices in industries such as steel around the world in the past. Infant industry refers to a comparatively new domestic industry which has not grown up sufficiently in order to benefit from the necessary economies of scale. Import quotas serve to safeguard this infantile industry while it develops and grows from cheaper and more efficient competition overseas.

A final motivating factor for import quotas revolves around the quite complex idea of national security. These quotas could be employed to discourage imports while encouraging domestic production of those goods which are called crucial for the nation's security and ultimate survival of its national economy. The military hardware production industry is one such example of a sector which many nations are eager to protect from less expensive foreign competition.

Economists are divided on the net effect and overall effectiveness of import quotas as they pertain to foreign trade and government policies. They do tend to help out the domestic economy for which they are the most advantageous. Domestic firms which are struggling against competition from stronger foreign competitors are most likely backers of such policies. The national companies see benefits from greater sales and profits, as well as additional income for the owners of the resources and factors of production. The problem with boosting domestic prices by restricting consumers' access to foreign imports is that such foreign trade policies will hurt the domestic consumers by increasing prices in stores and reducing both the ultimate quality and available choices offered.

Internal Revenue Service (IRS)

The Internal Revenue Service is an agency of the United States government. It is an entity that falls under the Department of the Treasury. The IRS' purpose is to collect incomes taxes from businesses and working individuals. Workers generally pay in their incomes taxes to the IRS once a year. There are cases where groups pay taxes quarterly, as with businesses and independent contractors who make more than pre-determined amounts. In practice employers withhold most individuals' taxes are from their paychecks.

For most individuals and small businesses, annual tax payments are due every year on April 15th. They pay these for the preceding year. Submitting these payments and forms is known as filing taxes with the IRS. The agency also permits extensions for filing if the requests are turned in ahead of the due date. Estimated payments have to come with the request for extension.

The Internal Revenue Service figures up taxes for individuals and businesses on a sliding scale. Individuals and entities that earn higher amounts are subsequently placed into higher tax brackets. The more individuals earn, the higher amount they will be required to pay to the IRS.

Any person who earns a yearly salary or who is paid wages by the hour will have taxes estimated and deducted directly from every payroll. This creates a situation where too much or too little money may be deducted throughout the year. Individuals who overpay will receive a refund. Those who underpay will have to make a payment to cover the additional tax if the appropriate amount did not come out of checks during the year.

Income taxes in the U.S. depend on the amount of net income. This is the income that remains once deductions have been calculated and subtracted from the total gross income. Individuals in the poverty bracket are not expected to pay any income taxes. Those people who earn $50,000 will pay around 20% of their net incomes. Over $100,000 earners are more likely to pay near 25% of net income earned. Sometimes those earning millions of dollars per year are able to use tax shelters, business write offs, and accounting strategies to receive substantial tax breaks and actually pay a lower percentage of their net income in taxes. This is why the middle

Financial Terms Dictionary - Laws & Regulations Explained

class in America bears the greatest taxation burden.

The IRS was not the original Federal taxing authority in the United States. President Lincoln began its original predecessor the Bureau of Internal Revenue in 1862 with Congressional approval. They set this agency up to collect a new income tax to assist in paying for the Civil War. This tax was intended and enacted to be temporary at the time.

While the first income tax did become repealed in 1872, the government reinstated it again in 1894. Supreme Court legal challenges kept the income tax in a quasi legal state until the 16th Amendment came into force in 1913 and allowed income taxes to be permanent. Eventually the Bureau of Internal Revenue evolved into the Internal Revenue Service.

The IRS website offers consumers and businesses all of their forms in a convenient, downloadable format. It also features instructional pages to properly complete these tax forms. A frequently asked questions page helps individuals with general queries. For people who need assistance in filing, there are a variety of software programs available that will ask questions and prepare the relevant tax forms for individuals. These programs then file the forms online with the IRS. Another option is to hire and pay a CPA certified public accountant to complete and file their tax forms.

International Accounting Standards Board (IASB)

The International Accounting Standards Board is an independent and private entity which arose back in 2001. The group was originally created to replace the former International Accounting Standards Committee. The IFRS Foundation maintains all oversight of the IASB.

Under their auspices, the IASB creates, publishes, and approves the International Financial Reporting Standards for the global accounting community. There are presently 14 members of the IASB. The IASB group is headquartered in London, Great Britain.

The constitution of the IFRS foundation gives the IASB full control over all technical and operating issues. This includes pursuing and developing the technical agenda after consulting with the public and the appropriate trustees of the foundation. They also approve and deliver interpretations that the IFRS Interpretations Committee recommends. Finally, they prepare and publish the International Financial Reporting Standards and all accompanying related drafts as laid out in the constitution of the IFRC Foundation.

The IASB itself was originally organized under the auspices of the IFRS Foundation. The foundation itself proves to be a non profit company incorporated in Delaware in the United States on March 8, 2001. The IFRS Foundation oversees all of the tasks that the IASB pursues as well as its strategy and structure. At the same time, the IFRS maintains the responsibility for fund raising for the IASB.

Another governing agency within the IFRS Foundation is the DPOC Due Process Oversight Committee. This trustee committee bears responsibility for the function of overseeing the IASB, as per the foundation's constitution. The last governing board is the Monitoring Board. It monitors the trustees of the IFRS foundation. It also participates in nominating the Trustees as well as approving all final appointments that the board makes to the Trustees.

There are several technical groups within the framework of the organization of the IFRS Foundation. The International Accounting Standards Board itself is among these. It bears the sole responsibility for setting all

International Financial Reporting Standards since 2001.

There is also the IFRS Interpretations Committee. Their job is to create interpretations that the IASB actually approves. It also engages in tasks as requested by the IASB since 2001. Finally there are the various working groups. These different task forces are for particular projects that meet a necessary agenda of the group.

There are also numerous advisory groups within the IFRS Foundation that carry out important functions for the IASB. The ASAF Accounting Standards Advisory Forum gives advice regarding the activities for setting technical standards by the IASB. The IFRS Advisory Council provides advice to both the IFRS foundation and the IASB.

There are also a variety of specific policy committees that serve advisory roles to the IASB and the IFRS foundation. These include the Capital Markets Advisory Committee from 2003, the Effects Analyses Consultative Group of 2012, the Emerging Economies Group from 2011, the Financial Crisis Advisory Group that merged with FASB in 2008, the Global Preparers Forum, the IFRS Taxonomy Consultative Group from 2014, the Joint Transition Resource Group for Revenue Recognition of 2014, and the SME Implementation Group from 2010.

One of the important tasks of the IASB has been to help with the project to converge the differing GAAP and IFRS standards. In order to simplify the understanding of different countries' accounting and financial statements, the group is trying to bring the standards into some sort of harmony. This will especially help out investors who must read and compare the financial statements and reports of various international companies.

Financial Terms Dictionary - Laws & Regulations Explained

International Bank Account Number (IBAN)

IBAN is an acronym which stands for the International Bank Account Number. This standardized numbering system for identifying bank accounts around the world with precision was first conceived of and implemented by the banks of Europe. They wanted to make simpler the means of transacting between bank accounts of financial institutions based in different countries.

This internationally agreed to system for identifying the world's banks and bank accounts was critically needed for banking across international borders. European banks found it necessary to come up with a way to effectively process the cross border transactions. They wanted to dramatically lower the dangers of errors in transcription and subsequent transmission problems which sometimes resulted.

It was the ECBS European Committee for Banking Standards that first adopted the IBAN concept. It later evolved into a global standard under the auspices of ISO 13616:1997. This standard became updated with ISO directive 13616:2007 that now utilizes SWIFT as the official registrar. The system originally arose as a means of facilitating payments made throughout the European Union. It has now been put into place by the majority of European nations along with many countries throughout the globe, especially in the states of the Caribbean and Middle East. Sixty-nine different nations utilized the IBAN account numbering system as of February 2016. More sign up all the time.

The IBAN account number is made up of several components. The two letter national code comes first. This is followed up by the two check digits which enable an integrity check of the IBAN number to be sure it is correct. Finally come as many as thirty alphanumeric characters which are also called the BBAN, or Basic Bank Account Number. Each national banking association decides which BBAN will become the standard for their own national bank accounts. In general, the remaining thirty characters include such information as the domestic bank account number, branch location identifier, and additional routing information.

While the IBAN concept has taken hold effectively throughout the continent of Europe, it is not a universal global standard yet, though it is the closest thing to one. The practice of working with such standardized account numbers as these is growing and gaining in popularity in other countries of the world. This is proven by the fact that nearly forty non- European countries now employ the International Bank Account Number system for themselves on only the twentieth anniversary of the concept being introduced originally.

Before the rise of the IBAN, every country utilized its own national standard to identify bank accounts within their own borders. This proved to be confusing in Europe, particularly as the borders between the 27 different EU countries began to blur thanks to the EU. Free movement of people, capital, and goods meant that money was being drawn from and transferred back and forth between the banks and bank accounts of different European states on an increasingly common basis. Sometimes important and even critical routing information was simply missing from transfers and payments.

SWIFT's routing information does not require transaction specific formats which identify both account numbers and transaction types specifically. This is because they leave the transaction partners to agree on these. SWIFT codes also lack check digits, meaning transcription errors can not be detected nor can banks validate the routing data before they submit the payments without these two digits. Continuous costly routing errors were creating delays on payments and transfers as the receiving and sending banks were also working with intermediary banks for routing.

The ISO International Organization for Standardization overcame these problems in 1997 by creating the IBAN in association with the European Committee for Banking Standards. Because the ECBS simplified and better standardized the original format proposed by the ISO, an update was issued with ISO 13616:2003 and then again in ISO 13616-1:2007.

As of 2017, the United States' banks do not employ IBANs themselves. Instead, they utilize either Fedwire identifiers for the banks or the ABA Routing Number.

Financial Terms Dictionary - Laws & Regulations Explained

International Financial Reporting Standards (IFRS)

The International Financial Reporting Standards prove to be the principally used set of accounting regulations in the world. Their main rival is the United States' based GAAP Generally Accepted Accounting Procedures. These IFRS turn out to be a single collection of accounting standards. They were created and are maintained still by the IASB International Accounting Standards Board based in London.

The IASB developed these IFRS standards with the goal of them being effectively utilized on a consistent basis throughout the globe. They were written with developed, developing, and emerging market economies and nations all in mind. These standards provide both investors and other consumers of business financial statements with the necessary tools to make like comparisons between various companies. Thanks to the IFRS, investors can effectively compare and contrast the financial performances of various publicly traded corporations on a consistent basis against their global peers.

This is a high standard for the IFRS. It of course requires more and more countries sign on to these accounting standards in order for the objective to be effectively and eventually met. This vision of a single set of worldwide accounting standards is well supported by numerous globally active organizations. Among these are the International Monetary Fund, the World Bank, the G20, the Basel Committee, the IFAC, and the IOSCO.

Thanks to the tireless efforts of the IASB and the IFRS foundation along with the support of these other active international organizations, the IFRS account standards have now been made law in over 100 countries. These include all of the 27 core countries in the European Union plus Great Britain as well as over two thirds of the member nations comprising the G20. This makes sense as the G20 and other critical worldwide bodies have always encouraged the important task of the IASB and its goals of achieving a universally recognized set of international accounting standards that everyone can rely on and understand.

Since the year 2001, the International Accounting Standards Board has created and continued to improve and promote the International Financial Reporting Standards. The IASB turns out to be the body that sets the

Financial Terms Dictionary - Laws & Regulations Explained

standards for the IFRS Foundation. This foundation is an organization that serves the public good. It has been well recognized for the award winning examples of its organizational transparency as well as the participation of all of its stakeholders and other participants.

The 150 members strong staff based in London hail from around 30 individual countries. The IASB operates under the auspices of a 14 member Board of Directors that is appointed and monitored by 22 different trustees coming from around the globe. These trustees themselves are further accountable to a public authority monitoring board. This way all of the various members of the leadership at the IASB are accountable to someone else.

The work of the IASB via the IFRS allows international accountants to more consistently deliver a standard means of detailing the financial performances of companies and other financial entities. This benefits investors, companies, and regulators. The standards of accounting that the IASB creates and the IFRS represents give the preparers of financial statements a complete set of principles and rules to follow when they are compiling the financial accounts of these organizations. This makes for an international standardization throughout the global markets.

It all works because the various corporations traded on public stock exchanges are required by law to prepare and produce financial statements that follow the appropriate IFRS accounting standards as do their business rivals and peers. The IFRS foundation maintains an online database of profiles on 143 countries and jurisdictions to show whether or not they accept and utilize these standards.

Keogh Plan

Keogh Plans are like 401(k) plans intended for small businesses. They are distinguished from them by having higher limits than the 401(k)s do. These tax deferred pension plans can be established by businesses that are not incorporated or individuals who are self employed.

These types of plans can be one of three types. There are money purchase plans preferred by those who are high income earners. Profit sharing plans provide yearly flexibility that is dependent on the company profits. Defined benefit plans feature higher yearly minimums.

Keogh Plans are also referred to as HR(10) plans. They are permitted to invest in the same investments as IRAs and 401(k)s. This includes stocks and bonds, annuities, and certificates of deposit. The reasons these plans are so popular for sole proprietors and small business owners has to do with their higher contribution limits. A downside to them revolves around their greater maintenance costs and more burdensome administration than SEP Simplified Employee Pension plans feature.

These Keogh Plans derive their name from the creator of the concept Eugene Keogh. He put together the 1962 Self Employed Individuals Tax Retirement Act which became named for him. The plans received a name change after the Economic Growth and Tax Relief Reconciliation Act passed in 2001. This act so altered these plans that the IRS code dropped the reference name of Keogh.

They simply call them HR(10) plans now. These retirement accounts are still utilized, but have lost many followers to the solo 401(k) and the SEP IRA. The HR(10) plans still find a good fit with professionals who are highly compensated as with lawyers or dentists who are self employed. Otherwise these plans generally do not serve retirement savers better than the competing plans.

The HR(10) plans come in two different principal breakdowns. These are defined contribution and defined benefit plans. With defined contribution plans, self employed persons can decide the amount of contribution they will make every year. This can be done either through money purchase or profit sharing plans.

Financial Terms Dictionary - Laws & Regulations Explained

Money purchase requires that the profits percentage to go in the Keogh be decided at the beginning of the year. If the employed person makes profits, these contributions must be made without changes or a penalty will be assessed by the IRS. The amounts owners contribute to their profit sharing plans may be changed every year. As much as 25% of income can be deducted and contributed every year. The limit on this amount is $53,000 for 2015 and 2016.

Defined benefit plans operate much as traditional pensions would. Business owners determine a pension goal for themselves then fund it. As much as $210,000 may be contributed in a year (up to 100% of all compensation) for the years 2015 and 2016. Business owners make all contributions in both types of Keogh plans as pre-tax. This means they these contributions come out of the taxable salary before taxes are figured.

Keoghs plans are also similar to typical 401(k)s in the way that invested monies are able to be tax deferred until retirement. This may start as early as 59 ½ years old but can not be delayed until any later than 70 years of age. Any withdrawals taken before these years are federally and potentially state taxed as regular income and also penalized at 10%. Exceptions to the penalty rules exist if certain physical or financial health issues come up for the account owner before retirement.

In order to maintain a Keogh Plan, a great amount of paperwork has to be filed each year. This includes the Form 5500 from the IRS. It requires a financial professional or tax accountant's help.

Leasehold Estate

A Leasehold Estate relates to an official and legal interest that permits a company or individuals to assume temporary ownership of the land of another individual or company. They are able to use this land for business purposes, agricultural applications, or even as a dwelling. Property could include timber land, mineral land, oil land, farm land, or business and/or residence property. With such leasehold estates, landlords possess the title of the property at the same time as the tenant holds the rights to utilize said property. These estates range wildly in the format for the agreement and how it is set up, the amount of time the status exists, and the kind of property which is being leased.

A Leasehold Estate can be established orally or as a written agreement. Those agreements which are intended to endure over a year might have to be composed in a written document per the laws of the relevant state which has jurisdiction. These agreements provide either explicit or implicit permission for all the receiving end parties, who are called the lessees, to assume control of the said property of the other party, who is referred to as the lessor.

There are other various kinds of property agreements which exist. What separates leasehold agreements from these competing formats, such as purchase agreements, is the actual termination date. Every party which is involved with a leasehold agreement comprehends that the agreed upon ownership interests will eventually conclude. This is to say that they are not intended to last in perpetuity. Another distinctive feature of such estates lies with the lessee's right to possess the said property in question. Various other kinds of property agreements, like licenses or easements, actually provide the holder with the permanent rights to utilize the property as they see fit.

Leasehold Estates are quite specific. They comprise both land and any property on the land in question at a given address. Land in this sense of the word does not simply mean the physical land, but also includes any buildings which lie on the property. It also applies to any and all natural resources which occupy the land in question. These estates could also include other forms of personal property, like machinery or fixtures which are so permanently a part of the land that they become considered to be part and parcel of the property. Such fixtures could comprise things like fencing, lighting, wells, or windmills.

Estates are types of personal property. Applicable state laws commonly govern the legal definition of personal property. This means that they could supersede clauses within the Leasehold Estate agreement. An example of this is found in the state of California. The leasehold which pertains to agricultural purposes may not be extended past a maximum time frame of 51 years total.

This is why such leasehold agreements are established with a pre-determined and limited number of years in mind. This is articulated in the tenancy of years. Such a specified length of lease is determined by both lessor and lessee. The only exception is when state laws set the time span directly. It is possible to terminate such a leasehold tenancy ahead of the articulated time. The lessee must decide to surrender his or her possession of the property at the same time as the lessor agrees to resume control over his property and rights.

Four different classifications of these Leasehold Estates exist. They are fixed term, periodic, at will, and at sufferance. Fixed term tenancy refers to the number of years of the tenancy. It is states as an interest which is established to endure a particular amount of time.

Periodic tenancy relates to a set out amount of time, as with week to week, month to month, or even year to year. The leasehold can be ended by either tenant or landlord simply giving a notice to vacate the property. Usually a 30 days notice in writing must be provided to the owner of the property.

Tenancy at will refers to the lack of structure with these kinds of leasehold agreements. No date is given for the end of tenancy in such a form of leasehold estate. Tenancy at sufferance happens as a tenant decides to overstay the date of termination as spelled out in the applicable agreement. Landlords in these cases possess the legal rights to simply evict the tenant if they wish.

Liability Insurance

Liability insurance is a commercial insurance product that protects businesses and other enterprises from accidents and injuries that occur on their premises. Accidents in a business can cause various types of injuries that create financial, physical, or psychological problems for customers. Business owners are ultimately at risk of law suits and claims from any individuals who deal with the business in any capacity. These issues can range from business contracts that are unfulfilled to medical injuries that require money for treatment.

Business liability insurance practically helps businesses to survive difficult scenarios in this way. It provides for the expenses involved in the legal defense and damages that the business owner may be required to cover. The maximum amount that can be paid out by the insurance company is the policy limit of the liability insurance policy. Owners of the business would then be responsible for any claims beyond these limits if there were any remaining. In general, business liability coverage limitations are sufficient to cover expenses in the claims and lawsuits.

There are a variety of different scenarios where this type of insurance proves to be useful for a business. Operations and premises are a first potential area of business liability. This covers accidents such as slips and falls in a business. It would pay for hospital bills that the customer incurred because of the accident. It could also be used to pay for legal bills that resulted from a negligence lawsuit.

Completed operations and products are another area of concern. A job that the business performed or the products which it sold may turn out to be flawed. This could lead to financial and other repercussions for the injured customer. Liability insurance would take care of the legal defense costs. If the business loses the case, it will also cover the financial damages for which the company is responsible.

Data breaches and cyber liability are a growing area of concern for countless businesses with online presences. Any business with a computer is potentially at risk for this type of cyber crime. Customers' names, addresses, phone numbers, and sensitive credit card information can all be stolen this way.

Financial Terms Dictionary - Laws & Regulations Explained

Important sensitive business information can also be taken. Fixing the problems in the hacked computers and websites is the easy part. Making sure the customers and even business itself do not become victims is the complicated issue. Cyber liability insurance provides hacked businesses with important security and risk management services for the business and its customers at no charge. It also aids with needed forensic and legal help to track down the source of the breach and to prosecute where possible.

Another area that liability insurance assists business owners with is employment practices. Businesses that operate in a segment which has significant turnover will have hired and lost numerous full or part time employees. Any employees that have been let go can file legal action against their former employer without warning. Employment practices liability insurance protects business owners as well as officers, directors, and employees from these suits. It deals with lawsuits involving discrimination, harassment, wrongful termination, and other offenses while employed.

Business liability insurance is also important for another reason. Many individuals structure their businesses as partnerships or sole proprietorships. It may be that the business income and assets are insufficient to pay for all of the expenses of a lawsuit and associated claim. If they do not have business liability insurance any other expenses can be taken from their own personal income and assets. Owners of companies who are unprotected may also be sued for personal liability in certain cases. This is why every business should have the full coverage of business liability insurance.

Limited Liability Company (LLC)

A limited liability company is often referred to by its acronym LLC. These business setups combine the best in both worlds of proprietorships and corporations. They offer the sole proprietorship or partnerships' advantages of pass through taxation. At the same time, an LLC provides the same limited liability for the owners which a corporation receives.

With a limited liability company, the owners will file their business losses or profits with their individual tax returns. This is because an LLC is not considered to be its own taxable structure. When lawsuits against the company are involved, it is only business assets that are at risk of seizure.

Creditors and lawsuit parties are not usually able to get to the LLC owners' personal assets, like cars or houses. This is not absolute protection. If the owners of the LLC engage in unethical, illegal, or irresponsible behavior, then they can forfeit this level of security.

Setting up a limited liability company is harder than establishing either a sole proprietorship or partnership. Once this hurdle is cleared, it is much easier to run the LLC than it is a corporation. Officers of corporations are not completely protected from actions they undertake in the business.

LLC owners must be careful not to behave like the entity is a mere extension of their own individual activities. Should the owners not act as if the LLC is its own separate business concern, then courts can determine that the business LLC does not really exist. In these cases, the judge could decide that individuals are masquerading their business affairs and conducing business as a personal venture. They can became liable then for these actions if this determination is made.

Taxes are another major reason that individuals opt to set up a limited liability company. As pass through entities, the income from their business passes on through the entity directly to the members of the LLC. This means that they must report all financial gains or losses from the enterprise directly on their own tax returns. They do not have to file separate business tax returns. The IRS does require that LLC owners make an estimated quarterly tax payment four times per year.

Financial Terms Dictionary - Laws & Regulations Explained

LLCs which are owned by more than one individual do have to file the informational return Form 1065 every year with the IRS. This form clearly states every owner's share of the limited liability company profits or losses. The IRS goes over these to be certain that the owners are all appropriately reporting their share of the earnings.

Limited liability company management is specific in how it has to be conducted. There are two forms of this. Member management involves an equal participation of the owners in the operating of the business. This is the way that the majority of smaller LLC owners run them.

The alternative form of management is called manager management. In this type of business operation, the collective owners of the LLC must choose someone to handle the daily responsibilities of managing the company. This could be an owner or several of the owners. It could also be someone who is not a part of the LLC ownership who professionally manages the business on their behalf. In this arrangement, the owners who are not managing are only tasked with sharing in the profits or losses of the business. This is often the case with family members or friends who invest in a limited liability company.

Maastricht Treaty

The Maastricht Treaty is the main treaty of the European Union. It was originally known as the TEU Treaty on European Union. This agreement was signed in Maastricht, the Netherlands on February 7, 1992. Members of the European Community debated it in their individual countries and then signed it. The treaty came about as an effort to fully integrate Europe into a closer political and economic union.

The treaty established the European Union. It also set the groundwork for creating the euro, the single currency of the EU. The Maastricht Treaty was subsequently amended by several other agreements. These included the Amsterdam, Nice, and Lisbon treaties.

This treaty represented a significant milestone in the process of integrating Europe. It modified other previously signed agreements like the treaties of Paris and Rome, as well as the Single European Act. These earlier arrangements had economic goals for the community. The original stated objective had been to create a common market for trading and investment.

With the Maastricht Treaty, the Europeans signed on to a spelled out vision of political union for the first time. After the treaty came into effect, the European project no longer went under the name of European Economic Community or EEC. Instead, it became known as the EU or European Union. Article 2 in this treaty called for "the process of creating an ever closer union among the peoples of Europe."

This Maastricht Treaty had a structural base of three pillars. The central pillar referred to the community dimension. It set out arrangements that pertained to common community policies, citizenship in the EU, and economic and monetary union. These were laid out in the Euratom, the ECSC, and the EC treaties. This pillar led to the eventual creation of the European Central Bank and the euro.

The second pillar concerned the CFSP Common foreign and security policy. Under this idea, the countries of the European Union would create a foreign minister for the EU to represent their single voice and policy objectives overseas. They also began working to come up with a common defensive policy with the intention of eventually creating an EU military force. This pillar also pertains to immigration and border control issues. It has suffered a serious challenge since the European refugee crisis has brought more than a million mostly Syrian and Iraqi refugees across the external borders of the E.U.

The third pillar of the Maastricht Treaty is the idea that there would be police and judicial cooperation. This pertained to criminal issues and concerns. It established a European Court of Justice whose decisions supersede those of the national country high courts.

The Maastricht Treaty also laid the grounds for the creation of the European Commission and the European Parliament. These bodies govern many budgetary and even political affairs within the block.

The Maastricht Treaty set in motion the discontent that led to the Brexit vote and the United Kingdom's decision to leave the EU. The pillars on common security and judicial cooperation turned out to major sore points with the British people. On the one hand, they despised the loss of control over their immigration policy and borders.

On the other they did not like the fact that they had also lost judicial control. A number of high profile court cases decided in the highest British court were subsequently overturned by the European Court of Justice. This all helped to explain why the majority of the British voted against the ever further political union which article two of the treaty established.

Financial Terms Dictionary - Laws & Regulations Explained

National Association of Securities Dealers (NASDAQ)

The NASDAQ is the acronym for the National Association of Securities Dealers Automated Quotation Systems, though the organization has dropped the Automated Quotation Systems part of the name as obsolete. This NASDAQ is the country's second largest stock exchange. It represents the principal rival to the NYSE, or New York Stock Exchange, which is the largest stock exchange in the country and only one larger than it.

The NASDAQ is also the largest equity securities trading market in the U.S. that is based on an electronic screen. When market capitalization, or the value of its stock per share multiplied by the number of outstanding shares, is considered, it is the fourth largest trading exchange in the world. The NASDAQ actually records a higher trading volume than does any competing electronic stock exchange on earth with its actively traded 2919 ticker symbols.

NASDAQ became established in 1971 by the NASD, or National Association of Securities Dealers. The system originally represented the successor to the OTC, or Over the Counter traded market. It later developed into an actual stock exchange of sorts. By 2000 and 2001, the NASD sold off the NASDAQ into the NASDAQ OMX Group, who presently own and operate it. Its stock is listed under the symbol of NDAQ since July 2 of 2002. The FINRA, or Financial Industry Regulatory Authority, oversees and regulates the NASDAQ stock market exchange.

The NASDAQ made major contributions to the world of electronic stock exchange trading as the first one of its kind on earth. When it began, it started out as a computer bulletin board system that did not literally put buyers and sellers in touch. Among its great achievements, the NASDAQ proved to be responsible for decreasing the spread, or the bid and the asking prices' difference for stocks. Many dealers disliked the NASDAQ in the early days, as they made enormous profits on these higher spreads.

In subsequent years, the NASDAQ evolved into a typical stock exchange through adding volume reporting and trade reporting to its new automated trading systems. This exchange became the first such stock market in America to advertise to the public. They would highlight companies that

Financial Terms Dictionary - Laws & Regulations Explained

traded on the NASDAQ, many of which were technology companies. Their commercials closed out with the motto the stock exchange for the nineties and beyond, that they eventually changed to NASDAQ, the stock market for the next one hundred years.

The NASDAQ is set to become a trans Atlantic stock exchange titan with its purchase of the Norway based OMX stock exchange. This will only enhance its European holdings that presently include eight other stock exchanges throughout Europe. Besides its NASDAQ stock exchange in New York City, the group possesses a one third stake in the Dubai Stock Exchange in the United Arab Emirates. With its double listing arrangement in place with the OMX exchange, the NASDAQ OMX is set to become the major competitor for NYSE Euronext in bringing in new listings.

Financial Terms Dictionary - Laws & Regulations Explained

National Bank Act

The National Bank Act refers to three different congressionally passed acts which set up a regime of national banks for the disparate state banks across the United States. These three Federal Banking Acts enabled the U.S. National Banking System to arise. The idea was to foster the creation of a nationwide currency which would be backed up by U.S. Treasury securities held by banks.

The Office of the Comptroller of the Currency under the umbrella of the U.S. Department of the Treasury wanted to be the sole issuer of American currency. To this effect, Treasury authorized the Comptroller of the Currency to start examining and regulating the nationally chartered U.S. banks. These series of acts were responsible for determining the system of national banks in place today and supporting a cohesive banking policy for the United States as a whole.

The first such effort to create a central bank since the First and Second Banks of the United States had failed began with the National Bank Act of 1863. This became the model which was used in the Federal Reserve Act of 1913 eventually. This first act permitted national banks to be created, gave the Federal government permission to sell securities and war bands, and established a plan for creating a unified national currency backed up by government securities.

The Federal government itself directly chartered these subsequent national banks which became subjected to tighter regulation than other banks were at the time. The national banks had to maintain larger capital requirements and could not loan out in excess of 10 percent of their total deposits. The government discovered they could discourage the competition by levying a burdensome tax on the state banks. It only took until 1865 for the majority of the state banks to apply for national charters or to fail altogether.

In 1864, the Federal government waded into the realm of active supervision of all commercial banks. They did this using the National Bank Act of 1864, which was itself based on a law from New York State. This important act created the Office of the Comptroller of the Currency. This office carried the responsibility for chartering, supervising, and examining every national bank.

Financial Terms Dictionary - Laws & Regulations Explained

A year later Congress added still more to this new legislation in the form of the Banking Act of 1865. This July 13, 1866 passed legislation expanded the law to more than simply mandating a 10 percent tax on all of their own state bank proprietary notes. It extended the tax from state banks, national banking associations, and state banking associations so that individuals who utilized such proprietary state bank notes would also be subjected to an additional 10 percent tax.

The act became challenged and subsequently strengthened as a result of the court case known as *Veazie* Bank versus *Fenno*, supra. Thanks to the Chief Justices of the Supreme Court electing to rule with Congress on the matter, all final resistance offered by the state banks to the National Bank Acts of 1865-1866 collapsed.

The 10 percent taxed proved to be so onerous that the majority of state banks chose to change their charters for national ones in order to sidestep the heavy handed tax. This led to the decline for a few years of state banks. In the 1870's and 1880's, state banks saw a resurgence once again as state bank created checks allowed them to get around the failing profitability and importance of their own proprietary bank notes.

Nonprofit Organizations

Nonprofit Organizations represent entities whose reason for being is to provide help or value to members or the community at large. These are also called not for profit organizations as well as non-business entities. There are many reasons why an agency would incorporate as a not for profit. They are often interested in promoting points of view or social and charitable causes. Such outfits utilize excess revenues they obtain in order to promote their mission and purpose. They do not ever distribute the so-called profits to stakeholders in the form of dividend payouts. This unique feature of nonprofits is called the non-distribution limitation.

When entities elect to become a Nonprofit Organization, there will typically be tax status ramifications involved. This is the case as not for profits generally seek out tax exemption because of their charitable or socially oriented nature. It is important to note that not all NPOs are charitable organizations, even though many individuals equate the two types of organizations. It is true that charities comprise the most visible component of the category, yet many other kinds of nonprofit organizations also exist.

Founders typically design other kinds of not for profits to serve their communities or members. Among the ones which serve their communities are organizations that concentrate on delivering services to the general community on a local, national, or global scale. These could be those that provide human development and aid, human service projects and programs, health and education services, medical research benefits, and others.

Member serving nonprofit organizations include such entities as cooperatives, mutual societies, credit and trade unions, industry associations, retired servicemen's clubs, sports clubs, and advocacy or lobby groups. All of these kinds of not for profit organizations actually benefit a certain group of individuals.

With many nonprofits, they are both member-serving and community-serving at the same time. Any grassroots-based support group for cancer victims would be such an example. It serves its members who have cancer by supporting them directly. It also benefits the community at large by providing much needed services to citizens who are also members of the general public.

Though the nonprofit organizations are allowed to create additional revenues beyond their expenses, they have to keep such profit surpluses and use them for ongoing future operations, plans, or expansion efforts. They can not distribute them to any board member or director, organization participant, or beneficiary of the group.

Not for profits have one thing in common with their for profit cousins. They both have boards of directors which exercise control over their respective organizations. Both will also typically have management and other staff which receive compensation for their efforts. Some NPOs utilize executives and volunteers who are not paid or who work for a token compensation. There are jurisdictions and nations that require a nominal fee be paid to directors and managers so that they can form a legally binding contract between organization and executive or board member.

It is interesting to remember that because an organization receives the nonprofit designation, this does not signify that it will not try to turn profits. Instead it means that the entity will not have any owners who benefit from the revenues and/or profits earned. In many cases, the amounts of surplus revenues that NPOs are able to generate, keep, and even deploy are restricted by government laws and regulations within their jurisdictions.

While many nonprofit organizations are service or charitably inclined, others organize and function like a trust or a cooperative. Supporting organizations are much like NPOs. They work as a foundation yet are more complex in their administration requirements. These supporting organizations also obtain a more advantageous tax treatment and commit to restrictions on the various public charities which they support. Such an organization's goals are not to amass wealth, but instead are to provide help for and meaning to the peoples they support.

Office of Financial Research (OFR)

OFR is an abbreviation and stands for the Office of Financial Research. This government organization that has its headquarter in the Treasury Building works to supply information in support of the Financial Stability Oversight Council.

The OFR strives to encourage financial stability throughout the United States. They do this by scanning throughout the American financial system in order to find, measure, and consider risks. They also engage in gathering critical research and then compile and homogenize the financial data so that it can be easily referenced, understood, and compared.

The Office of Financial Research says about itself that its job revolves around illuminating the darkest parts of the financial system. As they do this, they are looking to see where the risks to the system are heading. They then determine the level of threat such risks pose to the system and the economy. Finally, they deliver financial analysis, data, and insight on these threats along with an available policy tools' evaluation in order to effectively address and diffuse the threats.

Congress created this Office of Financial Research back in 2010 under the Dodd-Frank Wall Street Reform and Consumer Protection Act. They established this new organization in order to provide material support to the all important new super regulatory entity the Financial Stability Oversight Council.

The OFR was also to deliver useful information on the risks to the system to the member organizations of the Council as well as to any interested and concerned members of the public. The Director of the OFR is both appointed at the discretion of the President and must be confirmed by a majority vote of the Senate. In 2016, this Director was Richard Berner. The group was created to work around two offices of a Data Center and a Research and Analysis Center.

The mission of the Office of Financial Research is to encourage American financial system stability via providing high quality financial standards, data, and analysis of the information on behalf of the Financial Stability Oversight Council, its various member organizations, and the general public. To this effect, they maintain the vision of a financial system that is efficient, effective, stable, and transparent.

Every year, the Office of Financial Research produces several publications. Two of these that have become annual productions are the Annual Report to Congress on Human Capital Planning and the Annual Report to Congress. The Dodd-Frank Act itself requires that the OFR produces, compiles, and presents this general annual report once a year before Congress.

Every general annual report must include a complete analysis of the various threats to the American financial system and overall stability, the progress in their endeavors to meet the mission of the OFR, and the critical discoveries regarding threats from their research and analyzing of the whole United States' financial system.

The 2015 Office of Financial Research Annual Report to Congress is the fourth such yearly report since the office became established under the requirements of the Dodd-Frank Act. This particular report reviewed and analyzed the possible threats to American financial stability, reported on their important discoveries of risk, detailed their progress in meeting the OFR overall mission, and laid out the agenda of The Office for 2016.

The 2015 report stated that the various threats to United States' financial stability increased slightly from the prior year's report. They still consider the risks to be in the moderate to medium range. They did not change their threat assessment after the Federal Reserve FOMC raised the short term interest rates. A major portion of the 2016 agenda for the OFR is to affect a new programmatic approach in their work. They are striving to concentrate their initial efforts on the core areas of eight programs.

Financial Terms Dictionary - Laws & Regulations Explained

Office of Price Administration

The Office of Price Administration was a Federal agency created under the Office for Emergency Management within the U.S. Federal government. It was established by Executive Order number 8875 back on August 28th of 1941. The purposes of this OPA were initially to help keep a reign on the prices of rents and essential goods following the beginning of the American involvement in the Second World War.

It was then-President Franklin D. Roosevelt who dusted off the thirty year old Advisory Commission to World War I Council on National Defense beginning on May 29th of 1940. His goal was to involve both the divisions of Price Stabilization and Consumer Protection. These he merged together into the Office of Price Administration and Civilian Supply, known by its acronym OPACS under the auspices of the Office for Emergency Management utilizing Executive Order number 8734 on April 11th of 1941. As a result of this move, he transferred civil supply functions over to the Office of Production Management.

President Roosevelt's Office of Price Administration was intended to nip any wartime inflation in the bud before it appeared. His organization decreed a general maximum price rule which made any prices being charged as of March 1942 the maximum ceiling prices for the vast majority of commodities. At the same time, the OPA similarly imposed ceilings on all residential rents which consumers were forced to pay. Such regulations became modified and expanded as necessary under various administrators of the OPA, most especially Leon Henderson from 1941-1942, Prentiss H. Brown in 1943, and Chester B. Bowles from 1943-1946. By the time they had finished these tasks, nearly 90 percent of all retail food prices had been frozen through the end of the Second World War.

Despite these humanitarian aims and endeavors though, the prices kept creeping up steadily. The Office of Price Administration then initiated yet more attempts to force price and rent controls compliance on businesses and landlords. By the end of the war, the OPA was able to say with some satisfaction that it had mostly succeeded in maintaining generally stable prices throughout the second half of the war years for Americans.

The Office of Price Administration had a second function during the war.

Financial Terms Dictionary - Laws & Regulations Explained

This was to carefully ration hard to find consumer goods during the time of war. Rationing commenced with cars, tires, gasoline, sugar, coffee, fuel oil, meats, and even processed foods. By the conclusion of the war, the rationing gradually became abandoned. Price controls became abolished little by little. Ultimately the government disbanded the entire agency by 1947.

The majority of the Office of Price Administration functions then transferred over into the newly created OTC Office of Temporary Controls under Executive Order number 9809 on December 12th of 1946. The Financial Reporting Division became a part of the Federal Trade Commission at this point.

Eventually the OPA became entirely abolished as of May 29th of 1947. The March 14th of 1947 dated General Liquidation Order issued by the OPA Administrator was responsible for this closing up action. More important function of the ex-agency continued to be performed, albeit under the auspices of succeeding agencies.

Sugar and refined sugar products were still distributed under the Department of Agriculture's Sugar Rationing Administration thanks to the Sugar Control Extension Act of March 31st 1947. The Reconstruction Finance Corporation picked up the food subsidies from the war beginning on May 4th of 1947. The Office of the Housing Expediter assumed the rent controls policy beginning on May 4th of 1947. Any violations of price became litigated by the Department of Justice as of June 1st of 1947. Price controls on rice were assumed by the general Department of Agriculture as of May 4th of 1947 per Executive Order number 9841. Any other remaining OPA functions were assumed by the Department of Commerce's Division of Liquidation as of June 1st of 1947.

A number of important and famous individuals worked for the Office of Price Administration during the war. Among these were future President Richard Nixon, legal scholar William Prosser, and economist John Kenneth Galbraith.

Financial Terms Dictionary - Laws & Regulations Explained

Orderly Liquidation Authority

As part of the Dodd-Frank Act that Congress passed following the Financial Crisis and Great Recession of 2008, they accepted that there are financial firms that will ultimately fail. This is despite the fact that the new regulatory and supervisory framework scrutinizes banks and non banking financial entities more carefully than ever before now.

In the crisis and the years that followed, many policymakers decided that the U.S. Bankruptcy code and process did not quickly and effectively wind down institutions which were systemically important as they became insolvent.

The FDIC had the role of seizing such failing banks in order to resolve them. Their method for doing this has been seen as the best way to stop runs on banks and eliminate financial panics in the process. The FDIC maintains full discretion on which claims that are not deposits to pay and according to the priority that it sees fit. The FDIC generally subordinates debtors and creditors to the U.S. government and its interests.

Congress decided that a new way of winding down these failing institutions was in order to help regulators mitigate risks to the system. Because of this increasingly prevalent view in Washington, D.C. the Dodd-Frank Act set up a new mechanism mostly following the FDIC's existing process for resolving failing institutions. This new Orderly Liquidation Authority is designed to help liquidate financial firms that are systemically important and fail.

All entities that fall under the new regulation provided by the Financial Stability Oversight Council and the Federal Reserve will be resolved under this new mechanism. This includes not only companies who pose a systemic risk. It also covers financial entities whose failure can lead to negative consequences for the remainder of the United States' financial system. The Orderly Liquidation Authority is also known as simply the Liquidation Authority.

For the remainder of financial companies, the standard United States' Bankruptcy Code and judicial process continues to apply. Only in the cases where financial company failure threatens risk to the entire system as determined by the judgment of the Financial Stability Oversight Council will the Orderly Liquidation Authority mechanism supersede the traditional bankruptcy process.

Where the new Liquidation Authority takes precedence over the traditional bankruptcy rules and process, the FDIC is able to utilize this mechanism in order to seize a failing financial entity and move forward to liquidate it. This way, the company and its various creditors will not ponderously and slowly engage in typical restructuring agreements that the U.S. Bankruptcy Code envisions.

Because of these provisions contained in the Dodd-Frank legislation and now enforced by the Financial Stability Oversight Council, financial firms that may fail and threaten the system as a whole will be treated differently than other non-systemically important financial firms. This means that rating agencies, lenders, and various counterparties to financial firms should remember that there will be different results from companies wound down under the mechanism of the Liquidation Authority versus that of the standard United States' Bankruptcy Code.

In order for financial firms to be handled by the Orderly Liquidation Authority, the Treasury Secretary as head of the Financial Stability Oversight Council must intentionally designate these companies to be "covered financial companies." The secretary must first decide that the company will default or be at a substantial risk of default and that it also presents a risk to the financial system as a whole.

This authority gives the federal government the ability to put any financial entity under the auspices of the Liquidation Authority as they deem fit. Insurance companies that become insolvent will continue to fall under the authority of state regulators. Insured thrifts and banks will still be dealt with by the FDIC and its present system for winding down failed institutions.

OTC Bulletin Board (OTCBB)

The OTC Bulletin Board (OTCBB) proves to be a service for electronic trading that the NASD National Association of Securities Dealers maintains and provides to investors and dealers. It delivers live quotes on volume and pricing data to both investors and traders on stocks which trade OTC over the counter.

Every company which is listed on this backwater exchange has to be current in its filings of financial statements with regulatory oversight group the SEC Securities and Exchange Commission or some other applicable regulatory body. Other than this, there are no minimum listing requirements on the OTC Bulletin Board exchange; unlike with sister monster exchanges the NYSE New York Stock Exchange or the NASDAQ.

The OTCBB turns out to be a fairly young stock quoting system. It began in 1990 following the passage of the Penny Stock Reform Act of 1990. This legislation mandated that the SEC had to come up with some form of system for electronic quotes for those firms which were not able to qualify for listing on one of the rival major stock exchanges such as NYSE or NASDAQ. Those securities which trade on the over the counter basis does so between individuals who are utilizing either phones or computers to place trades. Every stock which trades on the OTCBB contains an ".OB" in its suffix.

It is important for potential investors in OTC Bulletin Board stocks to remember that this is not an extension of any major stock exchange. Instead, it is because these stocks are not well known, heavily traded, or largely capitalized that they are trading on the over the counter electronic quoting system basis in the first place.

These stocks are well known for their substantial risk and rampant instability and volatility. This is why the very few of the OTCBB stocks which enjoy great success eventually migrate over to the NASDAQ or even NYSE once they are able to meet the strict listing requirements of the relevant larger exchanges. The bid-ask spreads on OTCBB are commonly much higher since the volume is so much less.

OTC Bulletin Board serves a critically important role and fills a much-

Financial Terms Dictionary - Laws & Regulations Explained

needed vacuum with its existence and services. In truth there are many individual tiny companies which will never qualify for the stronger listing requirements so that their issues are allowed to trade on the major national stock exchanges.

The OTCBB gives them another avenue to float stock shares to a national investor audience so that they can obtain significant capital for their expansion needs. As long as investors recall that this is not a true exchange in any practical sense of the word, but merely an electronic quotation system, then investors will go into a potentially severely loss-making investment scenario with their eyes wide open. These securities which trade through the OTC Bulletin Board are actually a bunch of shares that exist in a tangled web of market makers who are trading them using the various quotes the system provides on a secure network computer which is only accessible by pay to play subscribers.

Another form of exchange network trading is via the so-called Pink Sheets. There are some parallels between the two systems. They are not at all related in fact though. Pink Sheets is an individually and privately held company which offers its own proprietary system of quotations. Companies whose securities trade as part of the Pink Sheets are not required to file any financials with the SEC. They also do not have to make any certain minimum docs available to members of the public or investing community at large. This is why some smaller firms prefer the simplicity and anonymity provided by the Pink Sheets operations and service.

Financial Terms Dictionary - Laws & Regulations Explained

Payroll Tax

Payroll tax refers to the specific withholding tax that employers take from their employees' checks. They do this for their employees so that they can pay it to the national (and sometimes also state or provincial and local) government. These tax amounts are deducted based upon the salaries or wages of the employees in question. In the majority of nations such as the U.S., the federal government (and many provincial or state governments as well) levy some kind of a payroll tax.

Such governing bodies deploy the revenues they gain from their payroll taxes in order to pay for specific government services and programs such as health care, retirement benefits (like Social Security income), workers compensation, and more. Besides these large scale national programs, local governments sometimes also levy smaller payroll taxes so that they can improve and maintain in good condition the area specific programs and infrastructure. This would includes such vital services and programs as road maintenance, first responders' emergency services, and parks and recreation programs, among others.

A payroll tax which is deducted is generally itemized out for the employees on their payroll stub. On such an specific breakdown as this, it usually denotes the amounts which Social Security and Medicare programs took from their pay, along with the municipal and/or state taxes held.

The Federal payroll taxes within the U.S. include contributions for Medicare and Social Security. In the year 2016, employers were required by law to hold back 6.2 percent of all employee earnings as a payroll tax. Besides this, the employers themselves are required to match these amounts from all employee payrolls and then turn in the two amounts to the IRS Internal Revenue Service.

As an example, for those employers who pay their workers $2,000, they will be required to hold back $124 in the federal component of payroll taxes. The employing company also must match this dollar amount. They send in an aggregate amount of $248 for the employee in this case directly to the IRS.

Employers only had to do withholding on payroll taxes for the initial

$118,500 of employee earnings as of 2015. On income amounts higher than this, they withhold another .9 percent of all net earnings. This is a special extra Medicare tax. Employers are not mandated to do their matching portion of this additional tax on employee income.

With all those who are self employed, the procedure is different. Self-employed individuals such as small business owners and independent contractors have no employer who can withhold and turn in their payroll tax for them. This means that they will have to be their own accountants and pay these taxes directly. These are known as self-employment taxes, even though they are basically the same as payroll taxes.

Because the self employed do not have any counter-party to match their payroll deductions, they have to pay a punishing 12.4 percent of all earnings to the Social Security Trust Fund and another 2.9 percent to the Medicare Trust Fund, as of 2015. These taxes are levied by the IRS on all earning up to $118,500. Beyond this dollar amount, the extra .9 percent Medicare tax still applies, as with the payroll taxes.

Payroll taxes should not be confused with income taxes. The main difference is that such payroll taxes cover particular programs. They are kept separate from the government primary revenues collected through the national income taxes that go instead into the government's general coffers. All employees have to pay their flat payroll tax, even though this is regressive. Income taxes are instead progressive, meaning that the rates increase along with higher earnings. Income taxes are never matched by employers either. Self-employed people will not pay higher income taxes than their employed counterparts as they must with the payroll tax.

Pension Benefit Guaranty Corporation (PBGC)

Pension Benefit Guaranty Corporation is also referred to many times by its government given acronym the PBGC. This federal agency arose as a result of the ERISA Employee Retirement Income Security Act of 1974. Its mission is to safeguard the benefits of pensions provided by private sector benefit plans that are defined. These plans commonly promise to pay out a fixed amount per month when retirement begins.

Should a plan end in the event of plan termination, and there not be enough money to pay out all of the promised benefits, then the insurance program of the Pension Benefit Guaranty Corporation will pay out the pension plan-provided benefit to the limits which the law establishes. This means that the majority of plan participants will actually still get the full benefit which they had already earned and been promised before termination of the plan occurred.

Some people have wondered where the money for the PBGC comes from so that they can cover failed plan benefits this way. The answer is that those firms whose plans the Pension Benefit Guaranty Corporation protects are required to pay insurance premiums for the insurance. PBGC similarly has investments as well as seized assets that they assume when they become trustee of a terminated pension plan. They also have assets from recoveries of firms which used to manage the plans. They do not derive any of this benefit-covering money from the general tax base. Even if a given employer does not pay its insurance premiums properly into the fund, the defined benefits pension plan will still be insured.

Employers may close out these defined benefit plans in what the PBGC calls a standard termination. They are only allowed to do this once they have demonstrated that the plan is sufficiently capitalized to pay out all owed benefits to the plan participants. To do this, the plan will be required to do one of two things. They might buy an annuity off of an insurance company. This annuity will pay out the promised lifelong benefits upon retirement of the participants.

Alternatively, they may provide one time single large payments that amount to the full benefit value amount. The PBGC provided guarantee of the plan will then cease to exist once the employer either buys this annuity or provides the beneficiaries of the plan with the one time, single payment.

Should the plan lack the money needed to cover all promised pension benefits to the participants of the plan while the employing firm finds itself in financial trouble, then the employers are able to request a distress termination from the PBGC fund. The plan will only be terminated under these scenarios when the employing firm proves to either a bankruptcy court or the PBGC itself that they will not be able to continue operating the firm if the plan does not become terminated. Once such an application request is approved, the PBGC typically becomes trustee and administrator of the plan. They would then pay out the promised plan benefits to the extent allowed by law.

The law similarly allows the Pension Benefit Guaranty Corporation to act alone in order to close out a pension plan where necessary to safeguard the participants' interests or that of the insurance program of the PBGC itself. As a standard procedural example, they will terminate any plan that is sure to be incapable of paying out the promised benefits when they become due.

The PBGC covers the overwhelming majority of defined benefit plans which private sector businesses provide. The lion's share pledge to pay out a set benefit (typically in a once per month distribution) upon commencement of the beneficiaries' retirement. Some pledge to deliver a single-value lump sum payment for their benefit. It is important to know that the PBGC will never insure any defined contribution plans that do not pledge to deliver a guaranteed benefit amount.

PBGC insures defined benefit plans offered by private-sector employers. Most promise to pay a specified benefit, usually a monthly amount, at retirement. Others, including cash-balance plans, may state the promised benefit as a single value. PBGC does not insure defined contribution plans, which are retirement plans that do not promise specific benefit amounts, such as profit-sharing or 401(k) plans.

PBGC does not commonly insure any plans that lawyers and doctors offer if they have under 25 active participants. They also do not cover the plans provided by local, state, or Federal governments. Finally, church group pension plans will not be covered.

Power of Attorney

A power of attorney is an agreement in writing that grants another individual the authority to make some choices if the grantor is not available. This person who receives the power does not have to be an attorney. Attorneys are typically only involved in drafting up or potentially witnessing such an agreement. The phrase comes from an individual receiving status as an agent or attorney in fact.

When people implement such a power of attorney they do not lose the ability to make their own decisions. Instead they are allowing another individual to act for them in matters specified within the written text. This can be very helpful if people are out of the country or in the hospital as an example. Someone else with this authority would be able to cash checks at the bank or pay bills on their behalf. It is simply a matter of sharing power with another person. The agent is only carrying out the grantor's wishes, not actually making choices for them, so long as they are coherent and mentally capable.

People who will be out of town for an extended period of time might find these arrangements particularly useful. With a power of attorney, the agent could carry out major decisions such as selling cars or other personal assets. The Internet has eliminated the need for some of these functions as computers and mobile devices make it possible for people to buy and sell stocks and handle many financial transactions from anywhere they have an online connection. There are still cases where a transaction will require an in person agent to handle them.

There is also a special kind of power of attorney that is used by individuals who lose their ability to handle decisions for their personal financial affairs. This is known as a durable power of attorney. In this case, the word durable refers to the ability of the agent to make the choices on the grantor's behalf when he or she can not mentally do them. This type of arrangement grants the agent the legal authority and responsibility to make the best possible physical and financial decisions for the grantor.

It means that the agent is able to spend the individual's money as appropriate, cash checks, deposit checks, and even withdraw money from the personal bank accounts. The agent further gains the authority to sign contracts, sell personal property, take legal actions, and file and follow up on insurance claims.

When people decide to enter a durable power of attorney arrangement, a notary public or lawyer should witness the document before they sign and execute it. If such individuals need to have a durable agreement established and are not mentally able to do it, courts can do this for them as they deem necessary.

Agents who become appointed to this position are expected to keep correct and segregated records on each transaction they perform. The records must also be easily available at all times. When the individual dies, his or her power of attorney becomes null and void. The will is responsible for the dispensation of the deceased person's estate.

Powers of attorney can be rescinded. If individuals feel unhappy in the ways that their agent is managing their personal affairs, they can simply revoke the authority back at any point. It is always wise for people to choose an individual to be agent whom they know and implicitly trust.

Financial Terms Dictionary - Laws & Regulations Explained

Promissory Note

Promissory notes are negotiable instruments that are called notes payable in accounting circles. In such promissory notes, an issuer writes an unlimited promise that he or she will pay a certain amount of money to the payee. This can be set up either on demand of the payee, or at a pre arranged future point in time. Specific terms are always arranged for the repayment of the debt in the promissory note.

Promissory notes are somewhat like IOU's and yet quite different. Unlike an IOU that only agrees that there is a debt in question, promissory notes are made up of a particular promise to pay the debt. In conversational vernacular, loan contract, loan agreement, or loan are often utilized in place of promissory note, even though such terms do not mean the same things legally. While a promissory note does provide proof of a loan in existence, it is not the loan contract. A loan contract instead has all of the conditions and terms of the particular loan arrangement within it.

Promissory notes contain a variety of term elements in them. Among these are the amount of principal, the rate of interest, the parties involved, the repayment terms, the date, and the date of maturity. From time to time, provisions may be included pertaining to the payee's rights should the issuer default. These rights could include the ability to foreclose on the issuer's assets.

A particular type of promissory note is a Demand Promissory note. This specific kind does not come with an exact date of maturity. Instead, it is due when the lender demands repayment. Generally, in these cases lenders only allow several days advance notice before the payment must be made.

Within the U.S., the Article 3 of the Uniform Commercial Code regulates most promissory notes. These negotiable forms of promissory notes are heavily used along with other documents in mortgages that involve financing purchases of real estate properties. When people make loans in between each other, the making and signing of promissory notes are commonly critical for the purposes of record keeping and paying taxes. Businesses also receive capital via the use of promissory notes that are sometimes referred to as commercial papers. These promissory notes became a finance source for the creditors of the firm receiving money.

Financial Terms Dictionary - Laws & Regulations Explained

Promissory notes have functioned like currency that proved to be privately issued in the past. Because of this, such promissory notes that are bearer negotiable have mostly been made illegal, since they represent an alternative to the officially sanctioned currency. Promissory notes go back to well before the 1500's in Western Europe. Tradition claims that the very first one ever signed existed in Milan in 1325. Reference is made to some being issued between Barcelona and Genoa back in 1384, even though we no longer have the promissory notes themselves. The first one that we still have dates back to 1553 where Ginaldo Giovanni Battista Stroxxi issued one that he created in Medina del Campo, Spain against the city of Besancon.

Protective Tariff

A protective tariff is a choice by a national government to create a financial barrier or tax on the imports of one or more nation's imports into the country. In many cases, such tariffs are not intended to raise additional national revenue as much as they are to artificially increase the prices of said imports. This helps to protect the sales and production of domestic goods and services so that they will continue to be manufactured and sold successfully in the host nation. Some critics argue that these types of tariffs are a real threat to free trade. Others argue that they provide two important benefits.

The first benefit is to trap domestic spending within the national economy rather than bleed it out to a foreign competing company and country. The second benefit lies in stopping cheap imports from crushing local business and industry. The import of oranges is a classic example of such a protective tariff. Not every place is able to grow citrus. South American countries are ideally situated and acclimated to grow huge amounts of citrus fruits to export.

While a nation may produce its own oranges but might instead simply import them from South American countries at a cheaper price than growing them internally, they could decide to apply a protective tariff to the price of foreign oranges and other citrus produce. Such a tariff is guaranteed to raise the price of the potentially imported oranges in order to level the playing field for domestic citrus producers. The tariff will make sure that these foreign oranges are similar to or more expensive than the prices of the locally grown variants.

Such a protective tariff proves to be a true tax on goods which a country chooses to import. These taxes make the prices of the foreign imports higher than the prices for typically more expensive goods and services. A piece or cloth might cost $5 in the United States and similarly $5 in Great Britain. If the American government wanted to encourage domestically-produced cloth over British manufactured cloth, they would need to set up a tariff on British cloth so that the cost was higher than locally produced cloth. They might add a $1 per piece tariff to the British cloth with a 20 percent rate. The ultimate goal of such a protective tariff is to protect the native industry from its foreign competition.

The very first American to suggest utilizing these protective tariffs to encourage American industrializing proved to be founding father and Treasury Secretary Alexander Hamilton. He wrote the important "Report on Manufacturers" to further this agenda. Hamilton believed that imposing a tariff on textile imports would help American industrial efforts to build up manufacturing facilities in order to one day compete effectively with the dominant in the world British companies.

Following the War of 1812, inexpensive British products began to flood the American markets. This undercut and even threatened to destroy the young industries in the U.S. Congress complied with Hamilton's wishes and established tariffs in 1816 so that they could deter British goods from dominating in the country. They followed this up with another tariff in 1824. The much debated Tariff of Abominations of 1828 culminated these early efforts. It was President John Quincy Adams who approved the final Tariff of Abominations following the majority vote approval of the House of Representatives.

The goal of this 1828 tariff actually lay in protecting both Western and Northern agricultural products from foreign competitors. The setting of this kicked off a national debate regarding how constitutional it was to slap tariffs on foreign imports unless the goal was to raise revenues from duties. Included in the case in question were molasses, iron, flax, distilled spirits, and various other completed goods.

Critics of these policies claim that tariffs are unethical. They argue that the expenses involved with shipping would be the only equitable cost to add on to a final good's price. Applying such protective tariffs threatens fair and free trade they correctly claim.

Financial Terms Dictionary - Laws & Regulations Explained

Public Company Accounting Oversight Board (PCAOB)

The Public Company Accounting Oversight Board turns out to be another regulatory group that Congress established to provide oversight on the auditing of public companies. This not for profit corporation is not a government agency. It does provide protection to the public and investors who are interested in the independent, accurate, and revealing audit reports that this group encourages. Besides this, the PCAOB oversees dealers and brokers' audits in order to foster protection for investors. This includes oversight of compliance reports that federal security laws require from public corporations.

This accounting oversight board arose as a result of the Sabanes-Oxley Act of 2002. It mandated that the firms which audit public companies in the United States endure independent and external oversight for the first time ever. Before Congress passed this 2002 regulatory law, auditors were completely self regulating.

The PCAOB Board and chairman of this board are made up of five members who receive appointments to five year terms each from the SEC Securities and Exchange Commission. They select these individuals after consulting first with both the Secretary of the U.S. Treasury and the Federal Reserve System Chairman of the Board of Governors. Given this SEC appointing role, it is not surprising that the SEC also maintains oversight responsibilities for the PCAOB. As part of this oversight, they must approve the Board's various standards, budget, and rules before they become final.

The SOX Act became amended by the Dodd-Frank Act. It created the necessary funding for all PCAOB pursued activities. This money mostly comes from the accounting support fees assessed annually on all publicly traded companies. These fees are actually figured from their average monthly market capitalization. Brokers and dealers are instead levied fees which are dependent on their quarterly average tentative net capital.

The mission of the PCAOB lies in providing oversight of public companies' audits. This ensures that they prepare and deliver reliable, honest, and unbiased audit reports for the benefit of both the interested investors and members of the public. Along with this oversight role, the PCAOB monitors the broker dealers and their audits to encourage protecting investors from

Financial Terms Dictionary - Laws & Regulations Explained

---

fraud. This includes monitoring their federal securities law required compliance reports filing.

PCAOB has a particular vision they seek to fulfill. Their overriding goal is to prove themselves a model for regulatory organizations everywhere. They seek to reduce the numbers of audit failures throughout the public securities markets in the United States, to improve the overall quality of audits, and to foster the public's trust of auditing as a profession and the process of financial reporting itself. They aim to do this while utilizing cost efficient and cutting edged tools.

The PCAOB maintains two special advisory groups as part of its mandate. The first of these is the PCAOB Investor Advisor Group, also known by its acronym IAG. It presents advice and viewpoints to the general board pertaining to investor concerns and regarding work related matters and important policy issues. The board is able to count on the IAG to deliver it expert and quality insight and advice for carrying out its important mandate to safeguard investors as outlined in the Sarbanes-Oxley Act.

The board also relies on its Standing Advisory Group, refereed to by its acronym SAG. The SAG advises the board regarding standards of professional practice and continuing developments within the world of auditing. Among the members of the Standing Advisory Group are investors, auditors, executives of publicly traded companies, and other individuals. This SAG group holds meetings between two and three times each year. They are chaired by the Chief Auditor and Director of Professional Standards of the PCAOB.

Repayment Penalty

A repayment penalty is commonly associated with paying back a loan before the end of its term. If you are contemplating paying off your loan balance in advance of its due date, then you should be aware that a number of loans come with these repayment penalties for liquidating the balance early. Different types of loans utilize different names for these same fees. Repayment penalties can also be called redemption charges, early redemption fees, prepayment penalties, or financial penalties.

The fees associated with repayment penalties vary depending on the loan in question. These repayment penalties are commonly stated as a percentage of the balance that is outstanding when prepayment is offered. Alternatively, they might be figured up as a certain number of months of interest charges. In general, when they are figured up using months of interest, they are comprised of one to two months' interest in fees. The sooner in the loan's life that you choose to repay the loan, the greater amount of charge you can expect to pay. This is because the anticipated interest portion of the loan comprises a great part of the repayment earlier in the loan's time frame. Early repayment penalties might increase the total cost of your loan significantly.

If you wish to avoid a repayment penalty in paying off your loan in advance of the term's end, then you will have to be aware of the loans that come with these fees and the ones that do not. Even if you change a currently existing loan into a loan for debt consolidation, you will have to cover the early repayment penalty if one is in the terms. The only way to avoid early repayment penalties is by selecting loans that specifically do not have ones attached to them. It is ironic that some of the least expensive loans out there do not include repayment penalties for early pay off actions.

Another factor of repayment penalties involves a gradual disappearance of the provision over time. With many mortgages, these repayment penalties gradually go down over the years of the mortgage. After the fifth year, the majority of repayment penalties no longer even apply. In many cases, repayments of as much as twenty percent of the original balance are permitted in a given year without you having to be penalized.

Besides this, there are different kinds of penalties for repayments. Penalties

Financial Terms Dictionary - Laws & Regulations Explained

that only apply to your refinancing of the mortgage are called soft penalties. Penalties that include the sale of the house and a refinancing are known as hard penalties.

Required Minimum Distribution (RMD)

The Required Minimum Distribution is a concept that pertains to retirement accounts and IRS rules which govern their distributions. Many individuals are not aware that they can not simply choose to hold retirement money in their retirement vehicle forever. They must begin accepting withdrawals from their traditional IRA, SEP IRA, Simple IRA, or other type of retirement plan and account after they turn age 70 ½. The notable exception to this rule is for Roth IRAs, which do not mandate disbursements while the owner is still alive.

The required minimum distribution is literally the minimum legal dollar amount that account holders have to take out of the retirement account every year. Naturally most people choose to withdraw a larger amount than this required minimum. Withdrawals that are received must be detailed in the individuals' taxable income. The exception to this is for any income that had been previously taxed as with Roth IRA contributions or any earnings which accrued on a tax free basis. This relates to distributions from Roth IRA accounts.

Figuring out the actual amount of the RMD is not so easy. The simplest way to do it is to work with the IRS published Uniform Lifetime Table. In this method, people figure their RMD in any given year by taking the balance from the end of the prior calendar year and dividing this amount by a distribution period taken from the Uniform Lifetime Table. There is also a different table to be utilized if the owner of the account's spouse is the only beneficiary and he or she is at least ten years younger than the owner.

The IRS provides worksheets on their website to help account holders figure up the mandated minimum amount. They also provide several tables to help with this. As mentioned, the Uniform Lifetime Table is for every IRA account owner who is figuring up his or her own withdrawal. The Joint Life and Last Survivor Expectancy Table is for those whose spouse is at least ten years younger and who is the only beneficiary.

The initial date for the first RMD on an IRA is figured out by taking the April 1st of the year that comes after the calendar year in which the account holder turns 70 ½. With a 401(k), 403(b), profit sharing plan, or similar defined contribution plan, either this same April 1st deadline applies or the

April 1st that follows the calendar year in which the owner actually retires.

The individual turns 70 ½ on the calendar date which falls 6 months following his or her 70th birthday. The plan terms themselves govern whether the individuals can wait until the year in which they actually retire to take the initial RMD. Other plans will require distributions begin on the April 1st following the year of turning 70 ½ whether or not the person has retired.

Once account holders have received the first RMD, they must take their subsequent ones on or before December 31st. It is possible to avoid having the first and second RMD's included in a single tax year. In the year individuals turn 70 ½ they can simply go ahead and take that first RMD by the end of the year to avoid the double distribution taxation in one calendar year.

People who do not take their full minimum required distribution will suffer an IRS penalty. Any amount which they do not take as the law requires will suffer a 50% excise tax that will be levied on it. This failure to take the RMD must be reported on a Form 5329, Additional Taxes on Qualified Plans.

Sarbanes-Oxley Act of 2002

The Sarbanes-Oxley Act of 2002 is also properly called the Public Company Accounting Reform and Investor Protection Act of 2002. It is more typically referred to by its abbreviation SarbOx or even SOX. Congress passed this much needed reforming federal law of the United States because of a variety of significant accounting and corporate scandals that successively rocked the nation. Among these were Enron, WorldCom, and Tyco International. Such scandals eroded the already low public trust Americans held in both accounting and reporting procedures.

The law became named after its two sponsors the democratic Senator Paul Sarbanes of Maryland and the republican Representative Michael Oxley of Ohio. The vote on the act proved to be nearly unanimous as the Senate passed it 99 – 0 while the House approved it 423 – 3. The legislation proved to be far reaching. As such it created improved or new standards for every publicly traded U.S. company management, board, and public accounting company.

Congress was also hoping to safeguard investors from fraudulent accounting practices that corporations had been increasingly engaging in over the years. The SOX decreed strict major structural changes that were intended to step up corporate financial disclosures and stop accounting fraud.

The numerous early 2000s years accounting scandals prompted Congress to act to improve the deteriorating situation. The failures at Enron, WorldCom, and Tyco had severely shattered investors' confidence in public financial statements. These led to a massive overhaul of the standards that regulated reporting in the industry.

The act itself is comprised of 11 sections or titles. These run the whole spectrum and range from criminal penalties to the responsibilities of Corporate Boards. The SEC Securities and Exchange Commission is charged with implementing the new rulings and requirements for compliance with the provisions in the new and improved corporate governance law.

Some observers felt the new legislation turned out to be important and

Financial Terms Dictionary - Laws & Regulations Explained

helpful. Others believed that it actually created more economic harm than it stopped. Still others claimed that the act itself was more modest in its scope and reach than the tough rhetoric that surrounded it proved to be.

The initial and most crucial ruling of the act set up a new semi-public agency. This Public Company Accounting Oversight Board was tasked with regulating, overseeing, inspecting, reprimanding, and disciplining any accounting firms who failed in their critical jobs as public company auditors.

The SOX Act also deals with important matters like corporate governing, auditor independence, and improved financial disclosure practices. Some analysts have called this among the most substantial changes to United States laws dealing with securities since President Franklin D. Roosevelt's New Deal in the 1930s.

These regulations and accompanying policies for enforcement, which the SarbOx laid out, changed and supplemented legislation that already existed and pertained to regulating securities. Two key provisions emerged from the SOX Act. In Section 302, a mandate was established requiring upper level management to personally certify and sign off on the accuracy of the financial statement as reported.

Section 404 provided a new requirement regarding internal controls and methods for reporting that auditors and corporate management were required to establish. The controls had to be determined to be sufficient enough to ensure accuracy. Publicly traded companies were less than pleased by this section. It implied costly changes would be required from companies which would have to create and build the necessary internal controls from the ground up. This proved to be expensive to implement.

Financial Terms Dictionary - Laws & Regulations Explained

Securities Exchange Act of 1933

The Securities Exchange Act of 1933 became sponsored and passed because of the devastating stock market crash which happened on and following Black Monday in 1929. The administration and Congress had two principle goals with this piece of legislation. These were to make certain a greater amount of transparency would exist with financial statements so that investors could engage in better informed choices on their investments. The other goal was to create laws which would crack down on fraud and misrepresentation of securities within the various securities markets.

This Securities Exchange Act of 1933 turned out to be the original piece of significant legislation that dealt with securities and their sales. Before this law became enacted, it was state laws which governed securities' sales principally. The laws dealt with the desperate need to have more effective and consistent disclosures from firms. It mandated that corporations must register their operations with the SEC Securities and Exchange Commission. This registration guaranteed that the corporations would deliver appropriate information to both possible investors and the SEC via both a registration statement and an official prospectus.

It was the Securities Exchange Act of 1933 which mandated that all investors deserve appropriate, fair, and free information on any securities the corporations are providing for sale to the public. Thanks to this act, before companies could launch an Initial Public Offering, they were required to provide information on the deal which was being freely disseminated to investors. Such a prospectus became not only required. It had to be shared with investors by the Securities and Exchange Commission on their own website.

This prospectus was required to deliver certain basic minimum information. Among this was a company business' and properties' description. They also had to offer a full description detailing the security which they were offering to investors. They had to divulge any and all relevant information concerning the management that operates the corporation. Finally, they had to provide certified financial statements which independent third party accountants signed off on before they could be released to the public domain.

Besides this, the Securities Exchange Act of 1933 was intended to outlaw any misrepresenting or deceiving throughout the process of securities sales. The framers of the act wanted to ensure that securities sales fraud could be not only reduced but eliminated.

This Securities Exchange Act of 1933 had an important legacy and set critical precedents for the financial world and American securities markets alike. As the first national laws which regulated and ruled on the stock markets, it seized this regulatory authority from the fifty states. The power of oversight for financial markets permanently evolved up to the federal government level. Most importantly, this act developed a universally acknowledged and clear body of regulations which helped to safeguard investors from fraudulent practices.

Today this act is generally referenced by the nickname the "Truth in Securities" law. Sometimes financial advisors and regulators will refer to it as "The Securities Act" or the "1933 Act." It was then-President Franklin D. Roosevelt who signed this important legislation into law. As such, it is often deemed to be part and parcel of the legendary New Deal package crafted personally by President Roosevelt.

There have been a range of important amendments to the Securities Exchange Act of 1933 which Congress passed into law over the years since the legislation became effective. Among these amendments which updated the regulations were those passed in 1934, 1954, 1959, 1960, 1970, 1980, 1982, 1987, 1996, 1998, 2000, 2010, and in 2012.

Securities Exchange Act of 1934

The Securities Exchange Act of 1934 is also known by its acronym of SEA. This piece of legislation was crafted in order to regulate transactions in securities which trade on the secondary market after they are already issued. The goal of this is to guarantee a higher level of financial transparency, better accuracy of trades, and a lower degree of manipulation and outright fraud.

This The Securities Exchange Act of 1934 laid the grounds for the SEC Securities Exchange Commission creation. In this way, the SEC became the SEA's regulatory body. Thanks to the act, the Securities Exchange Commission gained the authority to regulate securities like over the counter issues, stocks, and bonds. Thy also have regulatory oversight on the markets as a whole and the behavior of all financial professionals which includes dealers, brokers, and financial advisors. The SEC also reviews the financial reports of the various publically trading corporations, which they mandate be released.

Every company which chooses to be exchange listed has to adhere to the rules and regulations which The Securities Exchange Act of 1934 spells out for everyone. The principle requirements are disclosure, registration of all stock exchange listed securities, audit and margin requirements, and proxy solicitations. The reason for such requirements as these are to make sure that the playing field is level and fair. They also want to instill confidence in investors who participate in the various stock exchange markets.

It was then-President Franklin D. Roosevelt and his administration which arranged for The Securities Exchange Act of 1934 to come to Congress. They launched it as their official response to the generally accepted idea that poor financial market practices had been the primary perpetrator in the Black Monday stock market collapse of 1929.This act actually was not the first such legislation on the topic. The Securities Exchange Act of 1933 preceded it by a year. The 1933 piece of legislation mandated that all corporations had to publically disclose important and regulated financial information. This covered distribution and sales of stock shares. The 1934 act was more concerned with the behaviors of professionals in the financial advising and brokering industries.

The Roosevelt administration was not content with these two acts where regulation was concerned. They sponsored the Trust Indenture Act of 1934, the Public Utility Holding Company Act of 1935, The Investment Advisers Act of 1940, and finally the Investment Company Act of 1940. The numerous acts of legislation were passed in the wake of a devastated financial environment where the securities sales had little effective regulation. At the time, corporations could become controlled by a handful of investors while the public had no knowledge of these facts at all.

Thanks to this Securities Exchange Act of 1934, the SEC obtained broad and vast powers to oversee and police all corners of the securities business. To this effect, it is headed by five commissioners who lead the five divisions. The President of the United States appoints these commissioners. The divisions of the SEC are Division of Trading and Markets, Division of Corporation Finance, Division of Investment Management, Division of Economic and Risk Analysis, and Division of Enforcement.

They have both the authority and are the mandate to head up investigations into possible violations of The Securities Exchange Act of 1934. This covers a wide range of illegal and unscrupulous activities. Included in these are stealing the funds of clients, insider trading, selling unregistered stocks, manipulating the prices of the markets, and releasing falsified information or breaking the broker customer trust.

Besides this, the SEC is tasked with enforcing all corporate reporting they mandate for any company which possesses greater than $10 million of assets if their shares are owned by over 500 stake holders. The SEC has two tools for dealing with any and all matters which pertain to their areas of responsibility. They may settle any issue without it going to trial by dealing directly with the parties in question. They might also file a federal court case to resolve the problems.

Self Directed IRA

Self directed IRAs prove to be special kinds of individual retirement accounts. They are different from traditional IRAs because they provide the account holder with a significantly greater variety of investment choices and control over decisions on the account. With these types of IRAs, the owner or an investment advisor makes a variety of investment decisions. They then deliver these instructions to an IRA custodian who executes them.

Federal law allows these types of IRAs to invest in a tremendous range of investment vehicles. It is IRS section 408 that restricts the few categories that are not allowed. The IRS forbids investments of IRA funds in life insurance and collectibles such as rugs, art, gems, etc. It does allow a wide range of investment choices that cover most anything else.

Self directed IRAs may purchase real estate, mortgages and trust deeds, energy investments, gold and other precious metals in bullion form, privately held stock, privately owned LLCs and Limited Partnerships, and corporate debt or promissory notes. When accounts such as these are opened primarily to purchase precious metals bullion, they are typically known by the name of their primary metal in which they invest.

These Precious Metals IRAs can be called Gold IRAs, Silver IRAs, Platinum IRAs, and Palladium IRAs. Such self directed IRAs can even purchase franchises such as Subway or Timothy Horton. All of these different investment choices allow for superior and broad based asset diversification of investors' retirement funds.

These types of IRAs also provide all of the usual benefits which are commonly associated with Traditional IRAs. Money saved in these plans is contributed on a tax free or tax deferred basis. No taxes will be paid on either the money deposited, or the gains made on these investments within the account, until they are withdrawn at retirement or under early withdrawal rules and limitations. Self directed IRAs are still subject to the same yearly maximum contribution limits of $5,500 in 2016. They allow for larger contributions of $6,500 to be made as catch up once the account holders reach age 50.

Early withdrawals from these IRAs as with traditional ones are penalized. It

Financial Terms Dictionary - Laws & Regulations Explained

is often more advantageous to take a loan against the value of the IRA rather than suffer the financial consequences of early withdrawal. When loans are taken, there is no penalty. A repayment plan is established to put the borrowed funds back in the account in installments. Loans can be approved for a variety of expenses, such as home purchase, educational needs, or health care related expenses.

When an actual early withdrawal is taken, two penalties are assessed. First the money in the account is taxed as ordinarily earned income. Next a 10% penalty is levied by the IRS on all monies which the owner early withdraws.

These types of IRAs do have some limitations. The custodian must physically hold all assets in the account. This means that the account owners are not allowed to keep their real estate or mortgage deeds, stock certificates, or precious metals bullion at home in a safe. There have been offers made by some companies to help investors become their own IRA custodian by forming a special LLC company. This is a gray area which the IRS has not yet come down on with a hard ruling. In the future, they are likely to rule that investors absolutely can not be a custodian for their own gold, silver, platinum, or palladium bullion using either a safe deposit box or a home based safe.

The IRS requires that owners of these accounts begin taking distributions no later than at age 70. They can start withdrawing them as retirement funds at 59 ½ if they wish to begin using the money earlier.

Financial Terms Dictionary - Laws & Regulations Explained

SEP IRA

SEP IRAs are special simplified employee pensions that permit employers to contribute money to the retirement plans of their employees. If individuals are self employed, they may also set up and fund one of these accounts for their own benefit. These plans compare favorably to the more popular and utilized 401(k) plan. SEPs offer greater contribution amount limits. They are also much less complicated to establish and maintain than are the 401(k)s.

Any type of employer is allowed to create an SEP IRA. This means that businesses which are not incorporated, partnerships, and sole proprietorships can all work with and utilize them. Even self employed individuals who are employed elsewhere as well (with retirement plans at their other workplace) can make their own SEP.

SEP IRAs offer several advantages to owners and contributors. They provide significant tax benefits for employees and employers. Employer contributions give tax deductions to the employer during the tax year in which they make the contribution. Self employed individuals also can take this tax deduction for themselves. SEPs are also popular because they do not require any annual paperwork to be filed with the IRS. The paperwork that creates these accounts also offers the plus of being simple and minimal.

Individuals can make contributions for SEP IRAs in the year after the contribution applies. Deadlines for these contributions may also be stretched to the tax return due date. As far as establishing these accounts goes, deadlines are for the tax return due date and any extension that the IRS grants on the taxes.

In general, these accounts have to be opened and all contributions should be made by the April 15th that comes after the year in which the income was attained. Any taxpayers who take an extension on their tax returns to October 15th would receive a similar grace period for opening and funding the SEP IRA.

The contribution amounts for SEPs are quite flexible. No set percentage has to be contributed as with some of the rival retirement accounts like Keoghs. One could contribute nothing or as much as 25% of his or her income for the year (on as high as a $265,000 income amount). The full contribution for a single individual is not allowed to be greater than $53,000 in the year 2016. This amount contrasts with the typical standard IRA contribution limits of $5,500 for the year 2016.

The SEP limits are also substantially higher than the contribution limits on 401(k)s that come in at $18,000 for 2016 or at $24,000 for those who are at least 50 years old. SEPs do not have any provisions for catch up, as with other forms of IRAs or 401(k)s. Thanks to the higher contribution limits for every given year, this does not usually present a problem for those who are behind on their retirement accounts and want to put in more.

Employers are required to treat all employee contributions equally. This means that they must give the same contribution percentage for each employee who has made at least $600 in the year, who is 21 years or older, and who has worked for the company minimally three out of five prior years.

The only point where contributions to SEP IRAs get complicated centers on maximum contribution amounts. The 25% of income limit mentioned earlier is not figured out of gross revenue, but from net profits. Besides this, deductions on the half of self employment tax have to be first taken off of the net profit number before the limit for maximum contributions can be accurately determined off of the net profits.

Sherman Clayton Antitrust Acts

The Sherman Act and Clayton Act are two pieces of legislation which Congress designed to combat abusive trusts and monopolies. Over the years they have been utilized to break up certain large monopolistic enterprises. Their passage also led to the creation of the anti-trust division in the Department of Justice.

In 1890 Congress passed its Sherman Antitrust Act. Though it has been supplemented by other subsequent acts, analysts still consider it to be the most significant. The government felt that the act became necessary because of trusts and monopolies that were taking over major industries in the decades that followed the Civil War.

Trusts proved to be understandings where stockholders of a few companies would transfer over their shares to a group of trustees. The trustees would then give these stockholders certificates that provided shares of earnings from the companies that would then be jointly managed. This is how trusts became monopolies in a variety of significant industries. Among these were steel, railroads, sugar, tobacco, and meatpacking.

Trusts were bad for the economy and smaller competitors because of the means they utilized to eliminate their competition. They would undercut competitors' prices temporarily, make clients purchase products they did not want to get the ones they did, force their customers to agree to long term contracts, and buy out competitors. When none of these methods worked they would send out intimidators and use violence as necessary.

Farmers and other small businesses complaining about high costs of transport they had to pay for rail caused enough of a stir for Congress to take action. The public had become tired of the economic power that the big corporations had amassed and with the trusts. Sherman turned out to be a commerce regulation expert. As such he acted as main author for the Sherman Antitrust Act.

This measure proved to be the first such effort by Congress to outlaw trusts and monopolies of all kinds. A few states had passed their own laws, but these only applied to commerce passing within their own borders. This act used Congress' constitutionally held powers to regulate commerce

Financial Terms Dictionary - Laws & Regulations Explained

between states. It found almost no opposition in Congress. Only 1 member voted against it in the Senate and none in the House. President Benjamin Harrison signed it to make it the first such national antitrust law. The act granted the Federal government the authority it needed to dissolve these trusts.

Enforcing the law turned out to be another matter. The Supreme Court ruled against the government on the attempted enforcement of it against The American Sugar Refining Company in 1895. President William McKinley enacted an era of busting up trusts in 1898 by setting up the U.S. Industrial Commission. President Theodore Roosevelt at last managed to build on their report to break up the trusts. Subsequent action led to the breaking up of Standard Oil Company, among the most famous and powerful trusts of all time.

The Sherman act still needed more strengthening, so Congress acted again in 1914. This time they passed the Clayton Antitrust Act. This act laid out specifically illegal actions that monopolies were doing. It made it illegal for competitors to buy each other out without approval. Companies could not arbitrarily charge different prices to their customers. Board members could not sit on multiple companies' boards of directors. At the same time, Congress established the Federal Trade Commission to look into antitrust law violation and to stop practices that were not fair and competitive.

The Sherman Act most successfully applied to breaking up AT&T in 1984. The government attempted to use it against Microsoft for abusive anticompetitive practices in the late 1990s. A number of observers believe they failed to utilize the victory and sufficiently correct Microsoft.

Simple IRA

Among the stable of various types of IRAs American savers for retirement can take advantage of is a less common plan called the SIMPLE IRA. These kinds are a combination of traditional IRAs and employer offered plans like 401(k)s. The word SIMPLE in this case is actually an acronym that stands for Savings Incentive Match Plan for Employees. This is the most common name for the employer offered tax deferred retirement savings account.

SIMPLE IRAs were created to help smaller employers who have 100 or less employees. The idea was for them to offer their workers retirement plans. The IRS knew that the bigger packages of benefits all too often involved long and difficult opening procedures with mountains of complicated paperwork. Smaller employers simply did not have the time or resource capacity to complete and maintain these types of plans.

Among the advantages of SIMPLE IRAs is that they are not governed by ERISA, the Employee Retirement Income Security Act. This means that they are able to sidestep substantial expenses and significant amounts of paperwork in establishing them. The contributions to these kinds of IRA accounts are also fairly straightforward. Employers must make specific minimum amount contributions to the accounts of the employees.

They can accomplish this by establishing a match program at a minimum of 3% of their employee contributions. Alternatively they might set a 2% of his or her salary flat rate and offer it to every employee who participates.

When employees become part of a company SIMPLE plan, they are basically establishing a traditional IRA via their employing company. A significant disadvantage to these types of IRAs centers on their lower contribution limits. These are less than comparable 401(k) plans or other plans which employers sponsor. The limits amount to $12,500 for a single year in tax years 2015 and 2016.

Rolling over from these types of IRAs is also more complicated. They can not be started without a waiting period first being observed. Once employees start their participation with the plans, they can not do a rollover for generally two years on from their participation dates. The only exception

Financial Terms Dictionary - Laws & Regulations Explained

to this rule pertains to transfers between SIMPLE IRAs.

These can be done at any time since they are considered to be a tax free transfer from one trustee to another. In the even of any other type of transfer within the two years waiting period, these are deemed as distributions by the IRS. While most penalties for tax deferred plans are set at 10% withdrawal penalties, these particular IRAs carry a more punishing 25% withdrawal tax penalty.

After the conclusion of the two year time frame, individuals may then move their funds from the SIMPLE plan to a different kind of IRA. The only restriction is that they can not move them to a Roth IRA which is funded with pre-taxed dollars. The current SIMPLE plan as well as the new plan must also allow for the transfer to occur.

As with any kind of retirement plan, early withdrawal penalties apply. If any withdrawals occur before the official retirement age of 59 ½ is attained, the early withdrawal penalties of up to 25% will be assessed against the account withdrawals.

When rollovers are done, direct rollovers are much preferred to indirect rollovers. If account holders pursue indirect rollovers there are tax withholding requirements. It is also possible that the account owner will inadvertently fail to complete the transfer in time or at all and then suffer from the substantial early withdrawal tax penalties of up to 25%.

Solo 401(k) Plan

Solo 401(k) plans function much as their standard 401(k) plan cousins do, but display some important differences. These retirement savings plan vehicles for the self employed are also called One Participant 401(k)s, Self Employed 401(k)s, Individual 401(k)s, and Uni-Ks.

These particular 401(k)s provide business owners and spouses who do not have any employees beyond themselves with the ability to be a part of a 401(k) type of tax deferred plan. The plans are fairly new. Congress unveiled them as part of their 2001 Economic Growth and Tax Relief Reconciliation Act. At the time, these became the first specially tailored employer sponsored retirement plans intended for the self employed. Before their introduction, these self employed persons could only rely on such plans as IRAs, Keogh Plans, or Profit Sharing Plans.

These Solo 401(k)s possess practically identical requirements and rules as do the normal 401(k) plans. There are two important exceptions to this. The owner and the business do not find themselves governed by the expensive and complicated requirements of the ERISA Employee Retirement Income Security Act. Besides this, the company is not permitted to employ additional employees who are full time workers contributing 1,000 hours or more each year to the business.

Contributions also have their own particular rules with these Solo plans. The account owner is also both the employee and employer. For the 2016 tax year, employee contributions are limited to $18,000 (or $24,000 per year in the case of those who are fifty years of age or older). Other contributions can be put in as employer contributions. Whichever type a business owning participant wants to call these contributions, the limit for both employee and employer contributions may not be more than $53,000 for a given year.

One benefit that holders of these Solo 401(k) plans enjoy is that they do not have to employ a custodian as with IRAs. Instead they can work with practically any financial institution or bank as their account trustee. Assuming that the trustee will handle it, these plans are able to invest in a wide range of alternative asset types. This includes mutual funds, individual bonds and stocks, ETFs, CDs, real estate, life insurance, S corporations, and precious metals bullion such as gold or silver. Solo Plans are almost unique in their ability to invest in life insurance, which even the self directed IRA plans are not enabled to do.

This all makes the Solo 401(k)s practically unrivalled in their capability to provide retirement plans with low costs, that are easy to make transactions in, with great flexibility, and with generous contribution limits all at once. The downsides to the Solo 401(k) are two. Most workers are not allowed to participate with them. They also need a great deal of paperwork and account maintenance when measured up against numerous other types of retirement plans.

Rollovers are easy to do with these Solo plans. They are able to receive such transfers from other kinds of accounts and IRAs. Account holders may also transfer or roll them over to another kind of retirement account. It is important to check with the rules of an individual's particular plan, as some plans do not accept rollovers from the Solo 401(k)s. Besides this, there are Solo 401(k)s that specifically do not permit rollovers.

Business owners should take care when setting up these types of accounts. Rolling over these types of retirement vehicles will not incur any IRS tax penalties, so long as they are done according to the IRS rules and regulations. An individual has 60 days to finish the procedure and may only engage in it one time per year. Failing to abide by these rules will incur regular income taxes plus the 10% penalty for early withdrawals, unless the individual is older than the 59 ½ years retirement age.

Tariff Programs

Tariff programs are tariff regimes that apply to imports. Tariffs prove to be taxes that governments put on goods that are imported. Every nation has its own tariff programs and amounts. There are five principle tariff types in any tariff program. These are revenue, specific, ad valorem, protective, and prohibitive.

Revenue types of tariffs are those that boost government revenues. A revenue tariff would be one set up by a country that does not grow oranges but imposes tariffs on the import of oranges. This way, that government makes money when any business chooses to import and sell oranges.

Ad valorem tariffs are those that a government places as a percent of the value of imports. An example of such a tariff is fifteen cents for each dollar value. This contrasts with specific tariffs that do not revolve around the imported goods' estimated value. Instead, they are levied as a result of the specific quantity of the goods in question. Specific tariffs can be figured up based on the volume of the goods that are imported, on their weight, or on any other form of measurement applicable to goods.

Tariffs that are prohibitive in nature turn out to be the ones that stop a business from importing a good at all. These tariffs might be used on goods that a government does not wish brought into the country. This might be for safety, health, or moral reasons.

Protective tariffs are set by a government in order to ensure that the sale price of goods that are imported do not destroy a local industry. These are employed to protect domestic markets from foreign competition. Higher tariffs will permit local companies that may not be so efficient to compete effectively against the foreign competitors within the local domestic markets. While protective tariffs have their time and place in building up the local firms and economy, they can have unintended consequences. They might cause an item to be so costly that companies have to charge more for their related products.

A good example of this pertains to the prices of gasoline. As they rise excessively through tariffs, companies involved in shipping, like trucking companies, have no choice but to charge retail businesses higher prices for getting their products to them. The retail businesses will then respond by increasing the prices of their goods to compensate for the greater costs of transportation. They have to do this to make the same level of profit that they did in the past. The final result will be that consumers bear the brunt of the tariff by having to pay higher prices for their products and goods.

All countries employ tariff programs for one reason or another. They may not apply them evenly to every import or industry, but they will utilize them somewhere. Sometimes countries choose not to put tariffs on goods being imported. This is known as free trade in these cases. Free trade is believed by many economists to permit higher levels of economic growth. Critics say that without tariff programs, economies will be forced to rely on global markets instead of their own local markets.

Tax Sheltered Annuities 403(b)

Tax sheltered annuities are retirement savings programs and vehicles that the Internal Revenue Service allows for under the 403(b) section of their tax code. They were created for the benefit of employees who work for churches, educational institutions, and specific not for profit agencies.

They offer the advantage of permitting employees who are eligible to participate to contribute nearly all of their annual income towards retirement savings and investments in the plan. As an example of the generous limits with these particular plans, employers who choose to contribute can put in as much as $53,000 as of 2016 for any single tax year.

This supplemental program for retirement savings gives participating individuals a variety of ways in which they can choose to contribute funds. They may invest on an after tax basis, as with a Roth plan. They may also choose to contribute using funds that are pre-taxed. They can also opt to use a combination of the two methods. These plans and their participating contributions are entirely voluntary. Employees generally make the majority of these contributions as there is not always an employer match involved with them.

A variety of employees of eligible organizations may participate in these tax sheltered annuity plans. Employees of public schools, universities, and state colleges are allowed to participate. Many employees of churches are also allowed to become involved. Those who work for the school systems run by Indian tribes and their governments may participate. Not for profit 501(c)(3) churches' and organizations' ministers are included in them, as are ministers who are self employed who serve as part of a tax exempt organization. Chaplains are also usually qualified to participate.

There are several good reasons to become involved with these tax sheltered annuity plans. With automatic payroll deductions, it is a simple and relatively painless means of building up extra savings which individuals will require to increase their after retirement income.

They can get involved in a low cost program that is flexible enough to offer a good selection of investment choices. People can make contributions on a Roth after tax basis, a pre tax basis, or a combination of the two. Finally these plans are portable, meaning the owners can take their retirement vehicles with them when they move to a different job or another not for profit organization.

Thanks to these plans and vehicles, account holders are able to invest tax money that would otherwise go to the IRS. They can move money between the various funds in the plans without suffering from capital gains taxes or additional fees. This gives these TSA pre tax accounts a greater return than a taxable account would enjoy if it earned similar returns. For any individuals who use these account vehicles as Roth after tax accounts, all qualified distributions at retirement will be enjoyed completely tax free.

Money from these accounts can not be taken out without penalties until the individual reaches the government mandated minimum retirement age of 59 ½. They must begin taking distributions by the time they turn 70. An exception to the minimum retirement age is for individuals who stop working for their not for profit company before they reach retirement age. In this case, they are allowed to go ahead and begin receiving distributions without having to pay the extra 10% early withdrawal penalty tax. Only any taxes that were due for monies which had been contributed as pre tax dollars would apply in this particular case.

Term Auction Facility (TAF)

In response to the bank lending freeze that followed the outbreak of the banking and financial crisis in 2007, Ben Bernanke created and launched his Term Auction Facility TAF in December of 2007. The Fed was able to utilize its long mostly dormant discount window from December 2007 through to March 2010 as a creative new means of helping out struggling banks to access extra funds. They were then able to loan out these additional funds to consumers and businesses at their discretion. A primary new way of lending out such money to the banks lay in this Term Auction Facility.

Using the Term Auction Facility TAF, the Fed set up a system to auction out term funds to interested banking institutions. Any bank or credit union that already was able to borrow money via the primary credit program had eligibility to be a participant in these TAF Fed auctions.

The Fed was willing to accept bad loans as collateral for these funds. At every TAF auction, the Fed loaned out a set amount of money. They utilized the auction process starting with minimum bid rates in order to set the interest rates on these loan facilities. Banks could participate in the bidding process via phone through their local area Reserve Banks. The last of these TAF auctions occurred back on March 8 of 2010.

For the nearly three years that it ran, the Term Auction Facility worked according to a set out regular process. On a two weekly basis, the Federal Reserve would decide on the amount of money which it would then loan out on any given day. They would determine the minimum interest rate at which they would consent to loan out the funds. Banks which were interested in extra funds could then make bids for the dollar amount of money they wished to obtain at the interest rate they would agree to pay. Next the Federal Reserve sorted out the various competing bids by the level of interest rate that each participating bank offered them.

The Fed started with the greatest interest rate and then went on down from there, adding up the totals of money requested until they reached the maximum dollar amount which they were willing to lend out. Interest rates on each loan equaled the lowest interest rate which had been offered by the banks that had bids accepted.

The Fed was willing to do this so that there would not be funding shortfalls at a single institution which might cause the circular flow of credit and money in the whole American banking system to seize up and stop. In reality, most of the banks who borrowed from the Fed through the Term Auction Facility ended up leaving this money in their accounts with the Federal Reserve.

The Term Auction Facility served a useful purpose as the Federal Reserve Bank was willing to offer loans to member banks at rates that were lower than the associated market rates in exchange for putting up collateral in the form of bad loans that no one else would accept. On March 11, 2009, the banks had drawn total credit in the amount of $493.145 billion. The balance sheet of the Fed swelled to nearly a trillion dollars worth of collateral at its maximum extent.

In the end, the program proved to be successful for increasing confidence the banks had in each other, even though they did not loan out these borrowed funds generally. The TAF was originally intended to be more temporary than it turned out to be. Bernanke never envisioned it reaching the trillion dollar mark by June of 2008. All TAF funds have been repaid without taxpayers having to subsidize any of these loans which the Fed issued to the various banks.

Title Deed

Title deeds are a form of legal documents. They are utilized to demonstrate that a person owns a certain property. Title deeds are used most often to provide proof of home or vehicle ownership. Title deeds might also be given out on other kinds of property. Title deeds give owners privileges and legal rights. To transfer a property's ownership to another individual, a title deed is required.

Title deeds generally come with detailed descriptions of the property to which they are attached. They are made specific enough so that they can not be mixed up with other properties. They also include the individual's name who owns the piece of property. More than one person can be named as an owner on a title deed. Proof that the title deed is recorded with the appropriate office is provided by the presence of an official seal. Title deeds are commonly signed by the property owner and a person who witnesses the signature, such as a clerk or area government official.

Having a title deed does not mean that a person keeps the car in his or her possession. You can loan a car to a relative to use, even though they are not on the title. If you purchase a car using a loan, then the bank will have the title for its security, even though you would keep the car. You might purchase a house and rent it to a tenant. Although the tenant would not have the title deed, he or she would still possess and occupy the house. The title deed is useful for forcefully retaking possession in any of these scenarios.

When you sell a property, the old title deed is invalidated and a new one is given out that has the new owner's name on it. You might also add another person to a title deed by working with a title company for a property, or the Department of Motor Vehicles for vehicle titles. You have to fill in a request in writing before you receive a new title deed with the other names added to it. Once a person's name has been added to a title deed, they legally control the property along with the original title deed owner.

Title deeds have to be kept safe. As official legal documents, they are not easy to replace when stolen or lost. It is a smart idea to keep title deed copies separate from the original to have proof of ownership while an official replacement title deed is being issued. Physical possession of title

Financial Terms Dictionary - Laws & Regulations Explained

deeds allows a person to start a transfer of ownership, so they must be kept where they will not be stolen and then subsequently utilized to transfer your property to another individual.

Financial Terms Dictionary - Laws & Regulations Explained

Trans Pacific Partnership (TPP)

The Trans Pacific Partnership TPP represents a trade agreement that has been put together by twelve countries with borders on the Pacific Rim. Participants signed the final version of the deal in Auckland, New Zealand on February 4, 2016. This signing culminated the end of seven long years of negotiating the treaty. In order to enter into effect, the treaty must be ratified by the member states' legislatures. This includes the U.S. Congress, where opposition to the treaty has been intense and bipartisan from many members of both parties.

There are 30 different chapters to the Trans Pacific Partnership. Their goal is to encourage job creation and retention, economic growth, innovation, higher living standards, competitiveness and productivity, poverty reduction, better government and transparency, and better protection of the environment and labor. This TPP is made up of agreements that reduce tariff and non tariff barriers to trade. It also creates a means of resolving disputes through investor state settlement.

Originally the Trans Pacific Partnership was born from the Trans Pacific Strategic Economic Partnership Agreement that Singapore, New Zealand, Chile, and Brunei signed back in 2005. Starting in 2008, other nations on the Pacific Rim began to discuss a wider arrangement. This included The United States, Vietnam, Peru, Mexico, Malaysia, Japan, Canada, and Australia. This increased the nations who were a part of the trade negotiations to 12 countries.

Previously in force trade agreements of the countries participating will be amended to not conflict with the TPP. Deals that offer better free trade will still be in effect. The Obama administration looks at the TPP as a pair of treaties. Its twin is the still under discussion TTIP Transatlantic Trade and Investment Partnership between the European Union and the United States. The two deals are generally similar.

The original goal of the talks was to conclude negotiations in the year 2012. The final deal stretched on for another three years because of conflicts over difficult issues like intellectual property, agriculture, investments, and services. The 12 nations at last came to an agreement on October 5, 2015. The U.S. Obama administration has made implementing this TPP one of its principle goals for trade. On November 5, 2015, President Obama announced to Congress he would sign the deal and released a public version of the treaty for any interested American individuals and organizations to review. The U.S. President along with the other 11 leaders all signed the TPP February 4, 2016.

In order for the Trans Pacific Partnership to take effect, all of the signors have to ratify it within two years. In case it is not completely ratified by all parties in advance of the February 4, 2018 deadline, there is an alternative arrangement. It will become effective after minimally 6 signing countries with a combined GDP of greater than 85% of all the signing countries ratify it. This means that the U.S. must ratify if for it to ever take effect.

Other countries may be able to join the trade block in the future. Countries that have shown an interest in joining include South Korea, India, Bangladesh, Cambodia, Indonesia, Laos, Thailand, Colombia, the Philippines, and Taiwan. South Korea did not get involved with the original 2006 agreement. The U.S. invited it to join after South Korea and America concluded their own free trade agreements. South Korea is likely to be the first country to join in a next wave expansion of the group. First it will have to work through TPP treaty issues in agriculture and vehicle manufacturing.

Financial Terms Dictionary - Laws & Regulations Explained

Transatlantic Trade Investment Partnership (TTIP)

The Transatlantic Trade and Investment partnership represents a U.S. and European agreement for mutual trade and investment. In essence it is a free trade deal that the two economic superpowers are working to ratify. The two parties began the initiative in the June of 2013 G8 meeting. U.S. President Obama, European Commission President Barroso, and European Union Council President Van Rompuy introduced the idea and began working on the project.

The goal of the TTIP is to encourage both trade and investment. Governments on both sides believe that this will result in more economic growth and jobs for citizens of both sides of the Atlantic Ocean. Negotiations have been complex and mostly held in secret. The U.S. side is headed by the USTR, or Office of the United States Trade Representative. The Europeans are led by the European Commission. This EC handles negotiations for all 28 EU member countries.

TTIP turns out to be the largest and grandest vision for a trade agreement that has ever been attempted. This is because the United States and European Union economic blocks make up nearly fifty percent of the GDP of the entire world. The impacts on trade are expected to be substantial. Small to medium sized enterprises will gain several benefits in access to the new markets. They will have other countries to which they can export. They will also gain the ability to import input materials from other countries. It is anticipated they will have the ability to gain investments in their businesses at a cheaper, better price as well.

Consumers are supposed to benefit also. Lower prices are expected in both economic blocks because of the reduced tariffs and increased competition. This will improve the purchasing power of residents on both sides of the Atlantic and also help to create more jobs.

Twenty-four different chapters comprise the actual Transatlantic Trade and Investment Partnership. These have been divided into three principal topics. The topics are Market Access, Rules, and Regulatory Cooperation.

Market Access pertains to opening up markets. The goal is to allow for improved competition. Besides this, the architects of the agreement are trying to make it easier for products to flow back and forth across the Atlantic.

The rules section has to do with trade and investment. This area's goal is to increase the fairness and ease of importing, exporting, and investing for American businesses in Europe and European businesses in America. Rules cover a number of different important concepts. These include Energy and Raw Materials, Sustainable Development, Small and Medium Sized Enterprises, Customs and Trade Facilitation, Competition, Investment Protection, Geographical Indications, Intellectual Property, and the Government to Government Dispute Settlements.

The area of Regulatory Cooperation pertains to important regulation differences between the United States and the European Union. Both groups often have the same quality and safety levels that they insist on from specific goods. The problem is that each side employs its own procedures in considering the identical product. This imposes high costs on companies who produce the items. It can be prohibitively expensive for smaller to medium sized businesses.

There have been a number of objections raised by protestors to this free trade agreement, particularly in Europe. Many individuals on both sides of the Atlantic oppose the secrecy that surrounds the negotiations. The protesters have concerns that interest groups are creating special rules for larger companies.

The European labor markets are worried that their working conditions and benefits will suffer. Environmental groups are all concerned that environmental standards and safeties that are higher in Europe will be watered down as a result of the free trade initiative.

Financial Terms Dictionary - Laws & Regulations Explained

Treasury Inflation Protected Securities (TIPS)

Treasury Inflation Protected Securities (TIPS) are a unique and useful form of Treasury issued securities. What makes them special is their expressed and close linkage to inflation levels in their coupon payments. They are set up this way to safeguard investors from the interest destroying impacts of inflation.

TIPS prove to be lower risk investments because they enjoy the expressed and unlimited backing of the U.S. government. Besides this, their par value increases at the same pace as the official rate of inflation as depicted by the CPI Consumer Price Index. The interest rate itself stays fixed with these investments.

The interest earned by these Treasury Inflation Protected Securities pays out twice a year on the same fixed dates. TIPS may be bought directly off of the U.S. government by utilizing the Treasury Direct system. This allows for simple $100 increment purchases of the TIPS in a minimum of only $100 order size. They can be obtained from the site with 30 year, 10 year, and 5 year maturity date options.

Unfortunately for the Treasury Inflation Protected Securities holders, the inflation adjustments of the TIPS bonds fall under the IRS definition of taxable income. This is the case despite the fact that investors do not realize any of those inflation adjusted gains until the point where the bonds mature or they sell out their holdings. Because of this, some investors opt to obtain their TIPS exposure by utilizing a TIPS mutual fund or ETF. Otherwise, they could simply buy and hold them within tax deferred retirement accounts like IRAs. This would save them the tax headaches of having to pay the IRS now on money they will not obtain for possibly years or even decades.

On the other hand, buying TIPS directly means that investors sidestep the costs and fees applied by mutual funds and even ETFs. TIPS bought directly also feature complete exemption from the double or even triple taxation of local income and state income taxes which some investors must pay, depending on where they reside. Residents of Puerto Rico do not have to pay any federal income taxes on these inflation adjusted gains or interest payments because of the Commonwealth's completely unique status which it enjoys within the U.S.

If investors purchased $1,000 worth of TIPS and held them through year end and received one percent coupon rates while there was no CPI measured inflation within the United States, the investors could count on obtaining $10 payments for the entire year in interest payments. Assuming inflation increases by two percent, the principal of the bond would increase by two percent or in this specific instance by $20, to reach a total value of $1,020. The coupon rate would remain locked at one percent, yet it would apply to the entire new principal amount of $1,020 to help the holder receive interest payments of $10.20.

In the extremely unlikely event that deflation reared itself, the bonds would similarly decline in total face value. Should the CPI decline by three percent, the principle would drop by three percent, or $30, resulting in a new par face value of $970 on the formerly $1,000 Treasury bond. This would reduce that next year's interest coupon payments total to $9.70.

When the bonds mature, investors would then get the principal equity which equated either to the $1,000 original par face value, or an applicably higher adjusted principal based on the CPI adjustments higher. Interest payments throughout the life of the bond will be calculated from the principal amount as it rises or falls. This does not apply to the downside if the investors hold their TIPS until they reach maturity. Investors who do not wish to hold their TIPS until this interval can choose to receive a lower amount of principal than the par face value by selling their investment via the secondary bonds market if they so desire.

Value-Added Tax (VAT)

Value-Added Tax (VAT) turns out to be a kind of tax on consumption which governments place on all products. What makes this different from a sales tax is that whenever any value becomes added along the stages of production as well as at the final register, the VAT tax is applied.

These Value-Added Tax fees are commonly utilized within the European Union which is also the heaviest user of them in the world. The total VAT which end-users pay proves to be the difference between the product's cost minus the materials' cost which were utilized in making the product (which have already been taxed).

A good example to look at is a television set constructed by a manufacturer in Germany. The maker pays VAT on each of the various components it buys in order to produce the TV. After the set arrives in stores, the individuals who buy it must also pay the appropriate amount of Value-Added Tax.

Value-Added Tax is not based on income as with other forms of taxes. Rather it relies on the amount of goods which consumers purchase and consume. Over 160 different nations rely on VAT for at least partial funding of government budgets. The United States is strangely absent from this list of well over 75 percent of the countries on earth.

Advocates for implementing a VAT in the U.S. argue that by replacing the present inefficient income tax system in America with such a national VAT, this would offer numerous advantages. Among these are that it would lower the national deficit and debt, pay for critical social services, and boost government revenues.

Critics of the Value-Added Tax for the U.S. claim that such a tax is inherently regressive. This means that it would require the poor and low income workers to shoulder a greater economic burden and responsibility for funding the government outlays.

Both sides of the debate are in fact correct. In the advantages column, such a Value-Added Tax would bring in massive revenues on every product which traditional American stores, businesses, and Internet-based businesses sell. This would be a boon for government coffers that typically miss out on sales taxes which can not be levied on businesses that avoid sales taxes with customers (in those states where the businesses do not have any physical offices). It would collect presently unpaid billions in taxes from online sales that could be deployed then to pay for law enforcement, schools, and many other social services. Besides this, a VAT would ensure it is far harder to avoid paying taxes. It would further simplify the complicated and bureaucratic federal tax regulations so that the Internal Revenue Service could be massively downsized and made more efficient at the same time.

There are also a number of possible downsides to the VAT, per opponents of the concept. Business owners would suffer from higher costs all along the chain of goods production. A national VAT would also cause potential disputes between the Federal government and those many local and state governments which already charge sales tax rates set on local and statewide levels.

Critics also correctly point out that the consumers bear the ultimate brunt of the tax in the form of higher consumer goods prices, thanks to a VAT. The theory is that the burden of the tax spreads out through each phase of making goods from inputs to the ultimate product. The reality is that higher costs are nearly always passed off on the poor consumers.

As VAT applies equally to all purchases and for all types of salary and wage earners throughout the jurisdiction in which it applies, this would harm lower wage workers than higher ones. Higher wage earners are able to save massive percentages of their income, which would then not be taxed. Lower wage earners live from paycheck to paycheck. As they spend all of their earnings each month, their share of the VAT tax would be proportionally far higher than the wealthy Americans' share.

Financial Terms Dictionary - Laws & Regulations Explained

War Production Board (WPB)

The War Production Board, or WPB, proved to be a one time agency of the United States Federal Government which was established to order and oversee World War II production and materials procurement from January of 1942 by an executive order of the then-President Franklin D. Roosevelt.

The chairman of the board obtained broad and wide ranging powers over the economic output and production of the entire United States economy, factories, and facilities. Two different men served as chair of this important war effort board. Donald M. Nelson served from 1942 to 1944. He was succeeded by final Chair Julius A. Krug from 1944 to 1945.

The War Production Board expanded the national peace time economy and converted it to serve in the ultimate production of weapons of war to assist the young men who fought in Europe and the Pacific theaters. Controls were established that gave priority of production to such scarce materials delivery and which prohibited industrial activities that were then deemed to be less significant or unimportant to the war efforts.

The board may only have existed and operated effectively for three years, but in this span of time, it directed or oversaw the production of an astonishing $185 billion in supplies and weapons. This represented fully 40 percent of all munitions and ammunition production in the world during the years of the Second World War. By way of comparison, Great Britain, Russia, and all the other allies combined produced 30 percent of all war materials while all of the Axis powers including the Nazis and Japanese only managed to produce 30 percent of war time materials.

It was on January 16, 1942 that President Franklin D. Roosevelt created the War Production Board by implementing an Executive Order numbered 9024. This new WPB then replaced the Supply Priorities and Allocation Board as well as the Office of Production Management. It started by rationing important and limited commodities such as heating oil, gasoline, rubber, metals like copper and aluminum, steel, plastics, and paper.

As such the WPB was converting industries from peacetime production to wartime output, creating important national priorities in distributing services and goods, and stopping all non important production nationwide. The board became dissolved at the conclusion of the war with the final defeat of the Japanese in 1945. The Civilian Production Administration then replaced it in an effort to reconvert production back to a normal market forces controlled peace time economy in late 1945.

Thanks to the efficiency of this board, the war effort in both Europe and the Pacific proved to be ultimately successful. The chairman and his council decided to channel production into a set military hardware production and distribution. This led to a quarter of all national output going into the production of warplanes, while another quarter became allocated to naval warships. Other munitions and civilian needs comprised the balance 50 percent of national production and output.

The War Production Board proved to be so effective on a national and local scale because it operated through 12 regional offices as well as over 120 field offices scattered throughout the country. There were also statewide war production boards that worked hand in glove with the federal board. The state boards kept critical records on state levels of war production facilities and factories. They assisted state based businesses in obtaining loans and war production contracts.

This board also engaged in patriotic propaganda efforts to rally American citizens around the war effort. They had slogans such as "Give us your scrap metal to help the Oklahoma boys save our way of life." It created important national efforts like nationwide scrap metal drives that happened on local levels all throughout the United States with impressive results. As an example, the national scrap metal drive from October of 1942 produced so much metal that it amounted to almost 82 pounds of scrap metal on average per American.

World Trade Organization (WTO)

The World Trade Organization, or WTO, proves to be an organization that is intergovernmental in scope and signatories. Its ultimate purpose is to regulate international trade. This WTO began in 1995 on January 1 under the auspices of the Marrakesh Agreement that 123 different nations signed on April 15th of 1994. It then replaced the preexisting General Agreement on Tariffs and Trade, or GATT that had begun functioning from 1948.

The World Trade Organization handles the legal regulating of trade between those nations that participate. It does this via a framework that helps to negotiate trade agreements and resolve disputes, all the while enforcing the obedience of participating members to the agreements of the WTO (which member nation governmental representatives have previously signed). Their parliaments or congresses had to ratify the signatories as well. The majority of the issues which the WTO itself concentrates on come from prior trading negotiations, particularly from the lengthy Uruguay Round which went on from the years of 1986 through 1994.

The World Trade Organization has long struggled to finalize negotiations on what is now referred to as the Doha Development Round. They launched this latest endeavor back in 2001 to concentrate on the developing nations of the world. Its future remained uncertain as the 21 subjects whose deadline expired in 2005 continued to stymie participants of the trade regulating organization.

Among the major obstacles were the arguments between free trading of industrial goods and associated services while still keeping farm subsidies for the agricultural sector (which developed nations insisted on), as well as the fleshing out of fair trade rules on agricultural products (insisted on by developing nations). These obstacles ensured that no further negotiations or initiatives could be launched to go beyond the Doha Development Round.

The present day Director General of the World Trade Organization turns out to be Roberto Azevedo. He heads a staff of more than 600 individuals based in Geneva, Switzerland. The first comprehensive arrangement which the member states agreed upon was the Bali Package, a facilitation of trade agreement. They finally signed off on this on December 7th of 2013.

The immediate predecessor to the World Trade Organization was the GATT General Agreement on Tariffs and Trade. The member states of the world established this group following the conclusion of the Second World War. This occurred as part of the marathon cooperation efforts of the victors of the world war. They were dedicated to expanding the cooperation in spheres of international economics to help rebuild the devastated world.

Among these organizations which have stood the test of time are both the International Monetary Fund, or IMF, and the World Bank. The negotiators attempted to set up a similar international group to focus on trade and trading rules called the ITO International Trade Organization at that time. It never got off the ground effectively since the United States and several other signatories never approved it. This left the GATT to gradually evolve into the eventual de facto world trade organization.

By the 1980s, the GATT was struggling to adapt to the increasingly globalizing and expanding world economy. The member states came to the conclusion that the existing system would not suffice to deal with problems of this brave new world order. This was the reason they launched the eighth GATT round of talks which eventually became famous under the name of the Uruguay Round. These were held in Punta del Este, Uruguay.

It represented the largest mandate to negotiate trade in the history of the world (which actually was mutually agreed upon and signed). It covered an expansion of trade system ideals into intellectual property and services trade. The Marrakesh Agreement finally emerged from the last ministerial meeting held in Marrakesh, Morocco. Fully 60 different agreements, decisions, annexes, and understanding became adopted as a result. This led to the eventual creation of the WTO.

Financial Terms Dictionary - Laws & Regulations Explained

Zoning Laws

Zoning laws are statutes that mandate the ways that you are able to utilize your property holdings. Townships, counties, cities, and alternative local governments affect zoning laws so that they are able to create standards for development that benefit all residents in common.

It does not matter how big or how small a property is; it will be impacted by zoning laws. If you contemplate improving your property or purchasing another piece of property, you should be certain that you are fully aware of zoning restrictions that will affect you in advance of making any kind of commitment.

As an example, properties can be zoned according to residential or commercial restrictions. Commercial buildings will never be permitted to be constructed in a residential area, while residential dwellings can not be put up in commercial zones, unless the zoning laws of the area are changed.

Getting the zoning laws for a property altered proves to be extremely difficult. You would first have to give out public notice before getting an approved variance from the responsible government agencies in charge of zoning plans. Many times, neighbors will stalwartly resist your proposed zoning changes.

Zoning laws allow for a variety of different zoning designations and uses. Among these are commercial zoning, residential zoning, industrial zoning, recreational zoning, and agricultural zoning. These categories are generally further subdivided into other categories. Residential zoning might have sub zoning categories under it including multiple family use, for condominiums or apartments, or single family houses.

Zoning laws include a number of limitations to the property and potential improvements. The total size and height of buildings on the property is commonly restricted. The buildings can only be placed so close to each other. There will be limits to the total area percentage that is allowed to have buildings on it. Perhaps most importantly, the types of buildings that can be built on a given land's zone will be mandated.

You can learn about the zoning laws and ordinances simply by getting in touch with the area planning agency. Alternatively, you might go on the Internet to the local and state search engine to learn about your county and city zoning rules. Local planning organizations will tell you what must be done to get a variance to the area zoning.

Financial Terms Dictionary - Laws & Regulations Explained

American Bankers Association (ABA)

The American Bankers Association, or ABA, is a trade association of the U.S. banks large and small conveniently located in Washington, D.C. This powerful lobbying organization hails back to 1875 when it was established by several bankers.

Today, the ABA has grown to represent banks of all stripes and sizes and encompasses more than 95% of all bank assets in the nation. This means that money center banks, regional banks, community thrift banks, mutual savings banks, savings and loans associations, trust companies, and large commercial banks all count the ABA as their voice before the federal government. The typical sized member bank boasts around $250 million in assets.

This trade and industry group proves to be the biggest banking trade association by far within the U.S. today. It is also known as the biggest financial trade group anywhere in the United States. The American Bankers Association thrives and prospers because of its impressive range of both services and products it delivers to member institutions. This includes help in such diverse industry segments as insurance, staff training and education, asset management, capital management, consulting, and risk-compliance endeavors.

Probably the most famous creation of the American Bankers Association remains the all important nine digit routing numbers which designate all banks everywhere within the U.S. These routing numbers are pictured on every single check and are also necessary identification for wire transfer transactions. The ABA can truthfully boast that it created this system over a hundred years ago, way back in 1910.

Today's American Bankers Association keeps extremely busy lobbying with Congress for its banking members and their common interests. The group has concentrated its efforts in the last several years on banning the so-called unfair tax exempt status enjoyed by credit unions. Credit unions originally catered to selective and tiny targeted memberships, as with a particular company's own employees. This did not threaten commercial banks and other similar financial institutions.

More recently though, to bank's undying enmity and impotency in the face of this real and rising threat, credit unions found the means to vastly expand their roles of membership and possible pools of customers. It is no exaggeration to state that numerous credit unions can boast over $1 billion in assets nowadays. This makes them as big as some of the larger and even too big to fail banks.

The ABA strenuously maintains that such credit unions have morphed into a structure and operations which are so similar to the traditional commercial banks that they no longer deserve this special favor of tax exempt status. It was actually the infamous Panic of 1873 that gave rise to the initial founding of the American Bankers Association. A banker James Howenstein of St. Louis, Missouri, one day discovered that he was up against a proverbial wall in his bank. He only possessed several hundred dollars in cash against his millions of deposits he needed to return back to panicking depositors.

By falling back on assistance and knowledge willingly provided by his peers in the banking business via rapid and frequent correspondence, Mr. Howenstein escaped from his business-threatening dilemma to survive. He then knew that he had been saved by this informal network and fraternal organization of fellow bankers and wanted to expand on this successful construct.

To this effect, Mr. Hownestein convened his first meeting of 17 different bankers on May 24, 1875 in New York City. Together they made plans for an initial American Bankers Association convention that did successfully take place on July 20, 1875 in Saratoga Springs, New York. Fully 349 different bankers who hailed from 31 states as well as the nation's capital attended.

Chief among the first endeavors of the ABA proved to be setting up the American Institute of Banking. They founded this in 1903 in order to offer certificates and examinations as professional banking education in their local branch chapters. This AIB offered interested participants a different way to pursue a banking career than by going to university for a degree in law and finance.

American Stock Exchange (AMEX)

The AMEX is the acronym for the American Stock Exchange. This exchange proves to be the third biggest such stock market in all of the United States when trading volume is considered, after the NYSE and the NASDAQ national exchanges. Located in the American financial center of New York, the AMEX carries around ten percent of every security that is listed within the United States. In the past, it had a much larger market share of traded securities.

The origins of the AMEX lie before it was called the American Stock Exchange. In 1953, the New York Curb Exchange became known as the AMEX. This exchange proved to be a mutual organization that the members owned. In decades past, the American Stock Exchange had an important position as a major competitor for the New York Stock Exchange. This role gradually fell to the rising NASDAQ stock exchange.

Back on the seventeenth of January in 2008, the NYSE Euronext exchange announced its intentions to buy out the American Stock Exchange in consideration of $260 million in NYSE stock. They completed the transaction on the first of October in 2008. NYSE originally intended to integrate the AMEX exchange into its Alternext European small cap exchange. They first renamed it the NYSE Alternext U.S. By March of 2009, NYSE had scrapped this plan and renamed it the NYSE Amex Equities exchange.

The overwhelming majority of AMEX trading these days is done in small cap company stocks, derivatives, and exchange traded funds. These are niches that the AMEX exchange carved out and maintained for itself despite the rising allure of the newer NASDAQ in the 1990's. The AMEX observes regular trading session hours running from 9:30 in the morning to 4:00 in the afternoon on Monday through Friday. The exchange is closed on Saturdays, Sundays, and all holidays that the exchange announces in advance.

Appraised Value

Appraised Value refers to the property value evaluation from a certain frozen moment in time. Professional appraisers perform these appraisals when the origination process of the mortgage is underway. Lenders themselves typically select specific property appraisers to do them. It is the borrowers who are expected to pay for getting the appraisal.

Home appraised value proves to be a critical factor in getting through the process of loan underwriting. It enjoys a special place in deciding the amount of money that buyers can borrow and according to what terms. As a key example, the LTV Loan to Value ratio is determined utilizing the appraised value. When the LTV proves to be higher than 80 percent, the lender will insist that the borrowers purchase PMI private mortgage insurance. Once the LTV declines to 78 percent or lower with an appraisal, the need for expensive PMI payments can be excused.

This appraised value should not be confused with market value. The two are both important in residential home transactions, for retail buildings, commercial property, land, and farms. Yet real distinctions between the appraised value and market value of real estate exist. The market values will be driven by consumers and their demand versus available home supply in a given city, county, or even region. The experts make the appraised values.

Appraised values of given properties relay the information in the form of a precise number on the value of the home or other property in question. These appraised values come from both the professional opinion of the appraiser as well as the data they gather from similar home sales on the same street, in the neighborhood, and in that section of the city. Market values on the other hand vary more dramatically. Buyers have great influence on the property's market value. This is because any home is ultimately truly worth as much as a buyer will actually pay for it.

Sometimes people also confuse the idea of assessed value and appraised value. Assessed values are those which the city or town assessor's office will put on a given property. They do this so that they can decide what amount of taxes should be levied and collected for the property tax. Whole towns and cities become assessed in a particular (from four months to twelve months) period. Qualified assistants will actually determine the final values once they interview the owners and examine the properties in question. Municipalities then combine all of the assessed values for all properties within their jurisdiction to determine how much the tax rate should be for the year in question. It is possible for the town or city to revalue its tax rate every year in order to gather the revenues they require to run the municipality. This means that while assessments do not typically change on a yearly basis, tax rates could.

It is only in cases where the city or town's assessed values are deemed to be outdated that they will reassess the properties in the jurisdiction. This happens as dramatic inequities arise between one property and the next. It would require a sufficient reason to spend the money on conducting a new assessment of all properties within the municipality. There are states which have standard regulations that each home must be reassessed on an individual basis whenever it becomes sold or transferred. It is also true that rarely will the assessed values versus the appraised values for a given property be precisely the same dollar amount. This is because while assessed values are not impacted by market activity in a certain time period, the appraised values will inevitably be influenced by them due to actual market activity of homes selling in the area.

Capital Gains

Capital gains refer to profits that arise when you sell a capital asset like real estate, stocks, and bonds. These proceeds must be above the purchase price to qualify as capital gains. A capital gain is also the resulting difference between a low buying price and a high selling price that leads to a financial gain for investors. The opposite of capital gains are capital losses, which result from selling such a capital asset at a price lower than for what you purchased it. Capital gains can pertain to investment income that is associated with tangible assets like financial investments of bonds and stocks and real estate. They may also result from the sale of intangible assets that include goodwill.

Capital gains are also one of the two principal types of investor income. The other is passive income. With capital gains' forms of income, large, one time amounts are realized on an asset or investment. There is no chance for the income to be continuous or periodic, as with passive income. In order to realize another capital gain, another asset must be purchased and acquired. As its value rises, it can also be sold to lock in another capital gain. Capital gain investments are generally larger amounts, though they only pay one time.

Capital gains have to be reported to the Internal Revenue Service, whether they belong to a business or an individual. These capital gains have to be designated as either short term gains or long term gains. This is decided by how long you hold the asset before choosing to sell it. When an asset with a gain is held longer than a year, the capital gain is long term. If it is held for a year or less time frame, such a capital gain proves to be short term.

When an individual or business' long term capital gains are greater than long term capital losses, net capital gains exist. This is true to the point that these gains are greater than net short term capital losses. Tax rates on these capital gains are lower than on other forms of income. Up to 2010's conclusion, the highest capital gains tax rates for the majority of investors proves to be fifteen percent. Those whose incomes are lower are taxed at a zero percent rate on their net capital gains.

When capital gains are negative, or are actually capital losses, the losses may be deducted form your tax return. This reduces other forms of income

Financial Terms Dictionary - Laws & Regulations Explained

by as much as the yearly limit of $3,000. Additional capital losses can be carried over to future years when they exceed $3,000 in any given year, reducing income for tax purposes in the future. These capital gains and losses should be reported on the IRS' Schedule D for capital gains and losses.

Capital Loss

Capital Loss refers to a type of loss that companies or individuals experience as one of their capital assets decreases by value. This includes a real estate or investment asset. The loss only becomes realized when the asset itself sells for less than the price for which it was originally purchased. Another way of looking at these capital losses is that they represent the difference from the asset's purchase price and the asset's selling price. In other words, for it to be a loss the selling price must be less than the original price. As an example, when investors purchase a home for $300,000 and then sell the same home six years later for only $260,000, they have taken a capital loss amounting to $40,000.

Where income taxes are concerned, capital losses often offset capital gains. Capital losses in fact reduce the personal or business income in a like dollar for dollar amount. When net losses are higher than $3,000, then the overage amount can not be applied. Instead, this amount higher than net $3,000 simply carries over against any other gains or taxable income to the following year when they will similarly offset capital gains and income. When losses are multiple thousands, they continue to carry forward as many years as it takes for them to be fully exhausted.

Both capital losses and capital gains will be reported using a Form 8949. This form helps taxpayers to determine if the sale dates allow for the transactions to be counted as long term or short term losses or gains. When such transactions are deemed to be short term gains, they become taxable by the individual's ordinary income tax rates. These ranged from only 10 percent to 39.6 percent as of 2015. This is why the shorter term losses when paired off against shorter term gains give significant tax advantages to higher income earning individuals. It benefits them when they have earned profits by selling off any asset or assets in under a year from original purchase point.

With longer term capital gains, investors become taxed by rates of zero percent, 15 percent, or 20 percent. This occurs when they take a gain which results from a position they possessed for over a year. Such capital gains also can only be offset by capital losses which they realize after holding the investments for over a year. It is also on form 8949 that these assets become reportable. Here investors list out both the gross proceeds from the sales and assets' cost basis. The two figures are compared to determine if the total sales equate to a loss, gain, or wash. Such losses become reported on Schedule D. Here the taxpayer is able to ascertain the amount that may be utilized to lower overall taxable income.

These wash sale rules can be confusing to individuals without an example. Consider an investor who dumps his IBM stock on the last day of November in order to realize a loss. The taxing authority of the Internal Revenue Service will disallow such a capital loss if the exact stock was bought again on the day of December 30th or before this. This is because investors have to wait at least 31 days before such a security can be repurchased then sold off once more in order to realize another loss.

Yet the regulation does not affect sales and re-buys of different mutual funds that possess similar positions and holdings. As an example, $10,000 worth of Vanguard Energy Fund shares may be entirely reinvested in the Fidelity Select Energy Portfolio at any point. This would not forfeit the investors' ability to recognize another loss even as they continue to own an equity portfolio (through the mutual fund) that is similar to their earlier mutual fund holdings.

Corporation

A corporation refers to a business entity where it is distinctive and separated from the owners. Such corporations may take on many responsibilities similar to individuals. They can borrow and loan out money, make and execute contracts, hire and terminate employees, sue or become sued, pay taxes, and own cash and assets. This is why corporations are many times referred to by the phrase of legal person.

A corporation is a legal construct that controls and runs businesses of all types all over the globe. There may be differing legal arrangements from one government jurisdiction to the next, but they all have the attribute of a limited liability. With this protection, shareholders enjoy important rights like benefitting from dividends as a result of profits and price appreciation from successful business endeavors. While enjoying these advantages, limited liability means that they do not carry any of the personal responsibility for payment of the company's debts.

Practically every famous business and brand in the world is a part of a corporation. This includes such internationally recognized entities as Coca-Cola, McDonalds, Microsoft, and Toyota Motors. Corporations can also do business under a different name. A classic example of this is Alphabet Inc. that runs Google.

Corporations are established as a group of stock holders choose to incorporate. They pursue this follow up after a common goal in their ownership of the business. Such corporations may be charitable as well as for profit. The overwhelming majority of such companies are founded with the ambition of earning positive returns for the stock holders. These shareholders own some percentage of the corporation in exchange for paying for their shares. If they obtain them directly from the company, then their payments remit to the treasury of the company itself.

Corporations sometimes possess thousands of shareholders, especially when they are publicly traded companies. These entities could also have only a few or even one shareholder. The most common corporations within the United States are called "C Corporations."

Shareholders use their one vote per share to vote for the company board of directors every year. This group is responsible for naming the management which they oversee. The managers run the daily activities of the company. It is the corporation's board of directors which must carry out the business plan of the entity. They also do not bear responsibility for the company's debts, but have a fiduciary responsibility to care for the corporation. If they do not fulfill the duty faithfully, they may become personally liable for mistakes. There are tax statutes that allow for board of directors members to be personally liable.

As these corporations fulfill their goals, they can be wound down through a process also known as liquidation. In this process, they appoint a liquidator to sell off the company assets, pay the creditors, and share out all cash assets which remain among the stockholders. This can be done as a result of an involuntary or a voluntary procedure. Creditors can force liquidation when a company can no longer pay its debts. This often leads to corporate bankruptcy.

Economic Embargo

An Economic Embargo is a type of government-mandated order. They limit the exchange of goods and commerce to a country which they specify. Sometimes they affect only particular goods which represent a threat to the importing nation's vital economic or security interests.

Such embargoes are typically established because two nations find themselves in a political spat or economic disagreement or because of a combination of the two. The idea behind such an economic punishment and restriction is to economically isolate a nation. The enforcer hopes to make life difficult for the people and ultimately government of the nation so that it will have no choice but to carry out the desired actions of the embargo issuer.

There are two different main forms of economic embargoes. A strategic embargo will stop the trade in any type of military hardware, equipment, or goods with the victim nation. Trade embargoes are far more restrictive. They stop any individual or company from exporting given goods (or sometimes all goods) to the nation which is targeted. In today's world, a large number of countries depend on global trade to function and prosper. This is why an economic embargo can prove to be such a potent weapon to influence the behavior of a nation without having to go to war.

A trade embargo may lead to severe negative consequences for the victim nation and its economy. The U.S. often relies on the mandates issued by the United Nations in deciding which countries to inflict economic and trade embargoes against. In many cases, allied nations will combine their collective economic and trade powers to issue joint economic embargoes. This restricts trade with the targeted countries in an effort to force them to make strategic changes for world peace or to engage in better humanitarian behaviors.

The United States has become famous for its imposition of a few long-lasting economic embargoes against other sovereign states. Among these are ones which have been in place on nations that include Iran, North Korea, and Cuba. Back in the decade of the 80's, a number of countries with the U.S. enforced a trade embargo against the once-prosperous nation of South Africa. They did this because of several issues the combined

Financial Terms Dictionary - Laws & Regulations Explained

governments opposed, including apartheid (segregation and official discrimination against the native African black population by a ruling white minority) and a drive for nuclear technology and weapons capability within the country.

America- enforced embargoes leveled against some of these and other nations particularly leave out the trade of certain goods, such as necessary items. In these cases, they focus more exclusively on weapons, ammunition, and weapon systems or luxury item goods. Other forms of trade they leave in place. Comprehensive forms of economic embargoes are more devastating to the victim nations since they stop all types of trade between the victim nation and the inflictors.

After the terrorist attacks which began with September 11, 2001, American-led embargoes have increasingly tended to focus on threatening nations like the Sudan. This country and others such as Iran are well-known for their historic and present-day ties to terrorists and their funding around the globe. This makes them a direct threat to American national security interests and those of its allies and friends around the world.

The U.S. has occasionally also been the recipient of such economic embargoes. During the 1970s, the American economy suffered great harm because of the infamous Arab Oil Embargo. The Organization of the Petroleum Exporting Countries, or OPEC, enforced this oil embargo and created misery through skyrocketing gas prices, fuel rationing, and even gasoline shortages at the pump.

In the United States, it is the American President who has full authority to inflict embargoes in war times. This he can do under the existing Trading with the Enemy Act. Besides this, the President may also rely on the existing International Emergency Economic Powers Act to enforce national emergency based commercial restrictions. Such embargoes become administered by the Office of Foreign Assets Control within the U.S. This is a division of the Department of the Treasury that helps to find and freeze the ultimate sources of funds for both terrorist operations and drug businesses.

Economic Sanctions

Economic sanctions turn out to be both financial and commercial penalties which a nation or several nations level against a targeted nation, organization, or individual. Such sanctions can cover different types of punishments. Among these are tariffs, trade barriers, or financial transacting restrictions.

What is interesting about these is that they are not always applied thanks to an economic dispute. In fact they can be forced on other countries, organizations, or individuals because of several different types of military, political, or even social concerns. Such sanctions are often utilized to realize international and sometimes domestic policies or goals.

These economic sanctions may be deployed as an extension of international foreign policy. They are typically forced on smaller and weaker nations by one or more larger and richer ones because of two different reasons. It might be the weaker nation is actually a threat to the greater nation's security, as with Iran's aggressive nuclear weapons program versus the United Nations. It might also be that the more powerful country feels the weaker state is practicing human rights violations on its own people, as with Syria versus much of the rest of the world's countries.

This is why economic sanctions might be employed as a means of forcing the stronger countries' wills on the lesser one. Some of these policies pertain to achieving more open and fair free trade or for punishing and stopping violations of basic human freedoms and rights. In modern times, these forms of sanctions have often been utilized in lieu of waging actual military conflicts in order to reach desirable end results and outcomes without actual loss of human life.

The problem with these sanctions according to many analysts and economists is that they mostly harm the ordinary citizens of a nation rather than its government or military-industrial complex. Besides this, these kinds of sanctions are not always effective in achieving their hoped for results. Regime change is a classic example of this type of foreign policy. Though it is the most common basis for such sanctions, it is rarely successful.

Haufbauer et al. have studied these types of sanction policies and determined that in only 34 percent of the relevant instances did they work out successfully. An analysis of this study by Robert A. Pape ended with the conclusion that in only five out of the forty claimed successes did the results really stand out, which dropped the successful rate down to only four percent.

The reason for this is governments have a wide range of choices for trading partners and even financial conduits which they may go through. Consider the case of Iran and its frightening nuclear weapons program. For most of a decade the democratic nations of the world united to force a range of restrictive economic sanctions via the United Nations on the Islamic Republic. The sanctions were never one hundred percent effective, as countries including North Korea, Cuba, and Venezuela still continued to trade freely and openly with Iran. Some multinational companies and even a few countries secretly conducted trade with Iran as well.

The world's largest international bank (according to balance sheet) British multinational giant HSBC is the best known example of a company cheating on these specific economic sanctions. The United States' justice department found the banking giant with significant operations in 71 countries and territories guilty of helping the Iranian government to circumvent the international sanctions regime. While HSBC received several billion dollars in penalties, this did not reverse the damage to the sanctions' policy that they had already done.

These economic sanctions similarly impact the national economy of the country which imposes them to a lesser degree. When they erect restrictions on imports, the country imposing them will find its consumers suffer from less selection of goods. As export restrictions occur, the companies from the imposing nation(s) lose their access to and investment opportunities in the victim country. Other rival companies from foreign nations will take over these opportunities instead.

Equifax

Equifax today is an agency that reports consumer credit within the U.S. Analysts number it among the big three American credit bureau agencies alongside rivals Trans Union and Experian. The company proves to be the oldest of the three main credit bureaus in the country as it became established back in 1899.

The firm gathers and keeps information on more than 800 million consumers and over 88 million businesses around the globe. They are headquartered in Atlanta, Georgia and remain a worldwide data services provider that has annual revenues of $2.7 billion. They have over 7,000 staff operating in 14 different countries. The company is listed on the NYSE New York Stock Exchange. One of their many divisions (Equifax Workforce Solutions) is among the 55 national contractors which the United States Department of Health and Human Services hired to help develop the federal government's HealthCare.gov website.

The original company which later became Equifax was Retail Credit Company founded in 1899. The firm rapidly expanded and already counted offices around both the United States and Canada by 1920. In the 1960s, this Retail Credit Company represented among the largest of the credit bureaus. It contained files for millions of American and Canadian citizens.

While the firm engaged in some credit reporting at the time, the main part of their business came from providing reports to the many insurance companies throughout the U.S. and Canada as consumers applied for insurance policies such as auto, life, medical, and fire insurance lines. Back in the day, every one of the significant insurance firms relied on Retail Credit Company to gather their information on health, morals, habits, finances, and the utilization of cars and vehicles. Besides this, the firm investigated various insurance claims and also gave employment reports out to companies as consumers sought new jobs. The majority of their credit reporting work at that time they delegated to a subsidiary company called Retailers Commercial Agency.

In 1975, the company changed its name to be Equifax because of image problems they had earned by keeping shady and intimate personal details on all American's lives and selling them to anyone willing to pay. It was

Financial Terms Dictionary - Laws & Regulations Explained

after this that the new company Equifax expanded its operations into commercial credit reporting on firms located in the United States, the United Kingdom, and Canada. Here it engaged in competition against such firms as Experian and Dun & Bradstreet. In the 1990s, they began to phase out their insurance reporting operations and spun off their division which gathered and sold specialist credit information to insurance companies. Among this was the CLUE Comprehensive Loss Underwriting Exchange database they had developed, which they included in the Choice Point spinoff back in 1997.

Throughout the vast majority of its company history, the firm engaged mostly in the B2B sector. They sold insurance and consumer credit reports and associated analytics to businesses which operated in a variety of industries and segments. Among these were insurance firms, retailers, utilities, healthcare providers, banks, credit unions, government agencies, specialty finance companies, personal finance operations, and various other kinds of financial institutions.

Since they divested from their insurance reporting primary operation, the company sells information which includes business credit and consumer credit reports, demographic information, analytics, and software. Their credit reports offer a wide and detailed profile on the payment history and personal creditworthiness of individuals and businesses. This reveals how well these groups have honored their various financial obligations, including paying back loans and bills.

Starting in 1999, Equifax started offering its vast services into the consumer credit sector. They also began consumer operations with such important services as protection from identity theft and from credit fraud. The company along with its other two main rivals is required to offer American residents a single free credit file report once per year. The data from the U.S. Equifax credit records becomes incorporated into the Annual Credit Report.com website.

European Central Bank (ECB)

The European Central Bank is responsible for the European Union's monetary system and for maintaining the euro currency. The EU created this central bank of European central banks in June of 1998. It works alongside the various national banks of the EU member states to come up with unified monetary policy. This policy is intended to help achieve price stability throughout the countries in the EU.

The ECB became responsible for the EU's monetary police on January 1 of 1999. This was the point in time when the euro currency became adopted by the various EU nations. This landmark event was the culmination of 20 years of steps towards a currency union.

In 1979, eight of the EU nations created the EMS European Monetary System. It effectively fixed the exchange rates between the eight participating nations. By 2002, the ECB had become more entrenched. Twelve EU nations signed on to a common monetary policy and formed the European Economic and Monetary Union that year.

The European Central Bank is independent of political groups in the various institutions of the EU such as the European Commission, European Parliament, and European Council. It handles all EU monetary issues and policies. Maintaining price stability is the first goal of the central bank. It also sets the important interest rates for the Eurozone and area.

Besides creating monetary policy for the Eurozone block, the ECB also engages in foreign exchange, holds reserve currencies, and authorizes euro bank note issues. Euro currency is actually created, printed, and maintained by the European System of Central Banks, also known as the ESCB.

The ECB has become involved in some controversial activities which were beyond the scope of its original role. It has further expanded its mandate in recent years by buying up bonds of financial companies like banks and also sovereign countries whose bonds are not finding enough interested subscribers at competitive low rates.

They have been practicing this quantitative easing and injecting money into euro area economies in an effort to encourage growth and to increase financial liquidity in the banking system. Keeping the interest rates down on sovereign national bonds also improves the budgets and balance sheets of the euro area countries which are struggling. The result of these activities has led to negative real interest rates in Europe.

Individual EU countries collect their own taxes. They also determine their own national budgets. The ECB has nothing to do with these activities. National governments work together at the EU level to come up with uniform rules on public finances. This helps them to cooperate better on policies for employment, growth, and financial stability.

The financial crisis that broke out around the globe in 2008 hit some European countries especially hard. It created a need for the ECB to work closely with the European Commission and the national governments of the EU and Eurozone members in a series of coordinated, sustained actions.

These groups are continuing to strive together to promote employment and growth, keep credit flowing to consumers and businesses at affordable prices, safeguard savings, and to guarantee inter-European financial stability. This has led to the accusation of critics of the European institutions that they only work effective when there are crises, as in a management by crisis style.

Despite these ongoing and best efforts of the ECB and other European institutions, severe imbalances and problems remain in several Eurozone countries. As of 2016, unemployment in Spain still sat at over 25% and Greece teetered on the brink of yet another recession and potential insolvency.

Federal Reserve Bank

Twelve different Federal Reserve Banks make up the Federal Reserve System that functions as the central bank for the U.S. Federal reserve banks are also utilized to sub-divide up the country into the twelve Federal Reserve Districts.

Every Federal Reserve Bank bears the responsibility for individually regulating the various commercial banks that are found in such a bank's geographical district. Ensuring the continuation of the financial system and all of the member banks is among the primary responsibilities of the Federal Reserve System.

Each Federal Reserve Bank also issues its own stock shares that can only be acquired by participating member banks. The banks are required to obtain these shares by law. While the shares may not be traded, pledged as a loan security, or sold, they do pay dividends that run as high as six percent each year.

American banks are required by law to keep certain fractional reserves of their actual deposits. These are mostly held by the regional Federal Reserve Banks. Although in years past, the Federal Reserve did not pay member banks interest on these funds kept on reserve, as of 2008 Congress passed the EESA that permits them to pay the participating banks interest.

The twelve Federal Reserve Banks and districts are found geographically spread out around the nation. They include the Federal Reserve Banks of Boston, New York, Philadelphia, Cleveland, Richmond, Atlanta, Chicago, St. Louis, Minneapolis, Kansas City, Dallas, and San Francisco.

The largest and still most important of the individual Federal Reserve Banks proves to be the Federal Reserve Bank of New York. Not only does this bank have the greatest asset base of all the twelve branches, valued at over a trillion dollars and representing four times the asset base of the next largest Federal Reserve Bank, but it also boasts the biggest gold depository on earth, valued at in excess of $25 billion. The gold kept in the New York Federal Reserve Bank vaults belongs to other nations who store it there for safe keeping. Saudi Arabia and Kuwait both keep their significant holdings here.

Among the various states that have Federal Reserve Banks headquartered there, a few of them contain more than one branch within their state. California, Missouri, and Tennessee are the ones that make this claim. Tennessee actually contains two branches from two different districts within its state boundaries. The only state that has two Federal Reserve Banks headquartered within it is Missouri. For the largest geographical areas covered by the districts, San Francisco is the largest, Kansas City is second biggest, and Minneapolis is the third largest.

FICO Score

FICO Score refers to the overwhelmingly most popular and heavily utilized credit score in the United States. The company which created, owns, and manages it to this day is Fair Isaac Corporation. Financial institutions that loan out money employ this FICO score for an individual to assess any credit risk and decide whether or not they will offer the person credit. Sometimes they also consider specific information on the credit report of the borrower, but this is increasingly uncommon.

The reason for this is that the FICO score contemplates a well-rounded set of risk parameters for the would-be borrowers. These five areas it considers and draws upon to issue a credit score for credit worthiness include the individual's payment history, present amount of debts, types of credit utilized, amount of credit history, and new credit inquiries and issued accounts.

Ninety percent of financial institutions in the United States that offer loans rely on the FICO score for assessing the creditworthiness of an individual. These scores vary from as low as 300 to as high as 850. Generally speaking, scores over 650 represent desirable credit history. Individuals who boast less than 620 conversely typically find it hard to get decent financing offers approved at reasonable interest rates. Financial institutions claim that they also consider various other details besides FICO scores. These include history of time at a job, applicant's income, and the kind of credit they are seeking.

It is interesting and illuminating to understand how the three main credit bureaus calculate this FICO Score. Fair Isaac Corporation has its proprietary model in which they weigh all categories differently for every individual. This makes it more difficult to say with certainty what percentages in each of the five categories they consider.

Yet generally speaking, payment history represents 35 percent of the total. Amount owed on accounts comprises 30 percent generally. Amount of years of credit history equals approximately 15 percent. Credit mix equates to around 10 percent. New credit inquiries and accounts represent about 10 percent.

Payment history is the simple answer to the question, "does the individual borrower pay the accounts in a timely fashion?" Thanks to the exhaustive nature of credit history, the bureaus clearly demonstrate the payments which have been made for every single line of credit. The reports make special note if any of the payments came in 30, 60, 90, 120, or still more days later than due.

Amounts owed on accounts pertains to the dollar amounts individuals owe on their various accounts as a percentage of the total available credit. This does not mean that possessing a great amount of debt ruins a credit score. What the Fair Isaac Company is considering is the ratio of amount owed to amount available. A clear example shows that when Ringo owed $100,000 yet was not near his limits on any of the accounts, he had a higher credit score than George who only owed $25,000 yet had nearly maxed out his credit card accounts.

Credit history length is a complex category. FICO considers the age of the oldest account as well as the age of the most recent one. They then compile the average account age and come up with a value for this category. Those with shorter credit histories can still get a good credit score.

Credit mix pertains to the variety in types of credit accounts. Higher category credit scores go to those people who have a strong and varied mix of credit cards, retail accounts, and installment loans like mortgages, vehicle loans, and signature loans.

Finally, the Fair Isaac Company does not like recently opened accounts in much of any quantity. When borrowers take out a range of new credit lines and accounts in only a brief amount of time, this tells them that the person is becoming a credit risk and thus decreases the total FICO score.

Fiscal Policy

Fiscal policy is a government policy for managing the economy. In these actions, a government changes its tax rates and spending amounts. They do this to influence the national economy in a certain way. Fiscal policy's sister strategy is called monetary policy. In this complementary series of government actions the central bank adjusts the country's money supply. They do this to pursue the national economic goals.

Governments adjust their fiscal policy by altering the government spending and tax levels. They do this to impact the amount of economic activity in the country. It is an attempt to change the aggregate demand to boost consumer and business spending. Aggregate demand proves to be the complete amount of spending in the economy. This is the total combination of consumer spending, business spending, and government spending.

There are a number of reasons that a government uses fiscal policy. They are to affect growth and inflation rates. Fiscal policy can effectively boost and encourage economic growth when the economy is suffering in a recession. It can also be used keep inflation under control at a targeted level. This is accomplished by cutting government spending levels. Ultimately the purpose of this type of policy is to stabilize the nation's economic growth. Governments hope to avoid the common boom and bust cycles in the economy this way.

Many times governments will use this fiscal policy alongside monetary policy. Much of the time governments prefer to utilize monetary policy in their efforts to stabilize the economy. Monetary policy is easier to change. It also makes less of a dramatic and potentially disruptive impact on an economy.

Expansionary fiscal policy is the type a government employs when the economy slows down. This is also known as loose fiscal policy. To engage in it the government must increase the aggregate demand. They will do this by one of three methods. They may increase the government spending to create more demand and jobs. They can cut taxes to put more money in consumer's and business' hands. This will increase consumer spending as they effectively receive a greater amount of disposable income. In some cases governments may choose to both boost spending and reduce taxes.

There are side effects of this expansionary policy. The government budget shortfall, or deficit, will worsen. As a result, the government must increase the amount of money it will borrow to finance the spending.

Deflationary fiscal policy is the opposite of expansionary policy. In deflationary policy the government becomes concerned about how fast the economy is growing. They attempt to slow it down. This is also known as tight fiscal policy. For a government to pursue this policy they must reduce the amount of aggregate demand. They will do this in one of three ways. They might reduce the government spending. Governments could also raise taxes. A higher level of taxes forces consumers to reduce their spending. The government might also both cut its spending and raise taxes in conjunction.

While this slows economic growth, it does have a positive side effect. The government budget deficit improves as a result of cutting government spending and raising taxes. The government can choose to reduce borrowing and pay down national debt.

Fiscal policy arose from the economic theory of John Maynard Keynes the British economist. He argued that government is able to affect change on macroeconomic levels of productivity. They could do this by raising or lowering public spending amounts and tax levels. According to Keynes, they are able to reduce inflation, keep the currency value healthy, and boost employment with this tool. These ideas are also called Keynesian economics in honor of his work.

Financial Terms Dictionary - Laws & Regulations Explained

Foreclosure

Foreclosures represent houses or commercial properties that have been seized by a bank or other mortgage lender. These properties are then sold to recoup mortgage loan losses after an owner and borrower has not made the payments as promised in the mortgage agreement.

Foreclosure is also the legal procedure in which the lender gets a court order for the termination of the mortgagor's right of redemption. This is the case since most lenders have security interests in the house from the borrower. The borrower will secure the mortgage using the house as the collateral.

Borrowers fall into home foreclosure for several reasons, most of which could not be predicted in advance. Owner might have been let go from their job or forced to take a job transfer to another state. They might have suffered from medical problems that prevented them from working. They might have gone through a divorce and split up assets. They could have been overwhelmed by too many bills. Whatever the reason, they are no longer able to make their promised monthly mortgage payments.

Foreclosures represent potential opportunities for investors. They may be purchased directly with a seller in advance of a bank completing foreclosure proceedings. Many investors who concentrate on foreclosures prefer to deal with the owners directly. They have to be aware of many laws pertaining to foreclosures, which are different in every state. For example, while in some states home owners can stay in their properties for a full year after defaulting on payments, while in others, they have fewer than four months in advance of the trustee sale.

Practically all states also allow a redemption period for the delinquent homeowner. This simply means that a seller possesses an irrevocable ability to catch up on back payments and interest in order to retain ownership of the house. The owner will likely be required to pay any foreclosure costs experienced by the bank up to that point.

Another means of purchasing a foreclosure home is to buy it at the Trustee's Sale. When this means is pursued, it is better to bid on a house that allows you to look it over in advance of putting up an offer. This is helpful so that you can determine how many repairs will be needed to make it salable and even possibly habitable. It is also worth knowing if the occupants are still living in the house and will have to be forcefully evicted. The process of going through an eviction can be both expensive and time consuming.

Many Trustee Sales will have certain rules in common that have to be followed for a foreclosure house to be purchased. They may demand sealed bids. They could require you to demonstrate your proof of financial qualifications. They might similarly insist on you putting up a significant earnest money deposit. Many of them will state that the property is being purchased in its present condition, or as is.

Fractional Banking System

The fractional banking system is also known as the fractional reserve banking system. This system is the way that virtually all modern day banks around the world operate. In a fractional reserve banking system, banks actually only maintain a small amount of their deposited funds in reserve forms of cash and other easily liquid assets.

The rest of the deposits they loan out, even though all of their deposits are allowed to be withdrawn at the customers' demand. Fractional banking happens any time that banks loan out money that they bring in from deposits.

Fractional banking systems are ones where banks constantly expand the money supply beyond the levels at which they exist. Because of this, total money supplies are commonly a multiple bigger than simply the currency created by the nation's central bank. The multiple is also known as the money multiplier. Its amount is determined by a reserve requirement that the financial overseers set.

This fractional reserve system is managed ultimately by central banks and these reserve requirements that they enforce. On the one hand, it sets a limit on the quantity of money that is created by the commercial banks. The other purpose of it is to make certain that banks keep enough readily available cash in order to keep up with typical withdrawal demands of customers. Even though this is the case, there can be problems. Should many depositors at once attempt to take out their money, then a run on the bank might occur. If this happens on a large national or regional scale, the possibility of a banking systemic crisis emerges.

Central banks attempt to reduce these problems. They keep a close eye on commercial banks through regulations and oversight. Besides that, they promise to help out banks that fall into difficulties by acting as their ultimate lender of last resort. Finally, central banks instill confidence in the fractional reserve banking system by guaranteeing the deposits of the customers of the commercial banks.

A significant amount of criticism has been leveled against this fractional reserve banking system. Mainstream critics have complained that because money is only created as individuals borrow from the banking system, the system itself forces people to take on debt in order for money to actually be created. They say that this debases the currency. The biggest problem that they have with the commercial banking system growing the money supply is that it is literally creating money from nothing.

Other critics associate fractional banking with fiat currencies, or money that is only valuable because the governments say that they are. They decry these as negative aspects of current money systems. They dislike that fractional banking systems and fiat money together do not place any limits on how much a money supply can ultimately grow. This can lead to bubbles in both capital markets and assets, such as real estate, stock markets, and commodities. All of these can be victims of speculation, which is made easier by the creation of money through debt in the fractional reserve system.

Franchise

A franchise can be defined in many ways. The definition from the International Franchise Association describes franchising as a means to expand a business so that goods and services can be distributed more effectively via a licensing relationship. The word itself legally means a specific kind of license. Ultimately, franchising refers to the personal relationship which a franchisor maintains with its franchisees.

In this arrangement, the franchisor licenses out its trade name as well as its operating methods, or systematic way of doing business, to a particular franchisee. In exchange for this arrangement, the franchisee pledges to run the business as per the terms of this license. The operating method here refers to the franchisor's system and way of doing business.

Franchisors guarantee their franchisees will have their support and help. They also maintain a certain level of control over specific parts of the franchisee business. This is critical for the franchise owner to safeguard its intellectual property rights as well as to be certain that the franchisee keeps to the guidelines of the brand itself. The quid pro quo of this is that the franchisee typically delivers a one time start up fee (known as the franchise fee) to the franchisor. The franchisees also pay a royalty fee to the franchisor, which is periodic and continuous. This enables the franchisee to utilize the franchisor's operating system and trade name.

The franchisor itself carries little responsibility for involvement in the daily management of the business of the franchisee. This is because franchisees exist as independent operators. Neither are they joint employers with their franchisors. This gives the franchisees a free hand in hiring employees, paying them according to their wishes, scheduling their shifts as they see fit, arranging their employment rules and practices, and even disciplining their own employees, all without requiring any approval from their franchisor. However, the uniforms which the employees wear will be stipulated by the brand and operating system of the franchisor.

Franchising is about a contractually defined relationship between the two parties. The franchisees and franchisor will share the brand in common. Despite this, both are distinctly separate businesses in both real terms and legally. The role of the franchisor is simply to build up its business and brand as part of supporting the various franchisees. The part which the franchisees play is to operate and manage their own business according to the specific terms of the franchise agreements.

It is interesting that definitions of franchises range from one state to the next according to the various laws which different states enforce. Some states include among the various elements of franchising the responsibilities of the franchisor to deliver a marketing plan to its franchisees. Others insist that the franchisor maintain an interested community of the business jointly with the franchisee.

Business Format Franchises are the most readily recognizable types of these arrangements for the everyday individual. These relationships typically cover the whole of the business and its format, not only the products, services, and trade name of the franchisor in question. In this common type, franchisors are expected to give their franchisees training, operating manuals, standards for the brand, a marketing plan and strategy to carry it out, quality control monitoring, and more.

Examples of the idea make these distinctions clear. Pizza Hut does not license out pizzas or breadsticks. Burger King does not license out hamburgers or chicken sandwiches. The two mega franchise operations instead license out components of their intellectual property. In this case it includes both their business systems and their trade marks, or their ways of producing these food items and company-described premises and atmosphere.

The history of these and other brands demonstrates that both services and products have changed significantly over the decades. Among the various advantages to these types of business format franchises and their arrangements is that they have the flexibility to do so effectively.

Today there exist numerous kinds of franchises throughout a constantly expanding array of industries and market segments in not only the United States and Canada but around the globe. Estimates state that more than 120 separate industries utilize the concept and practices of franchising now. The greatest share of franchising by far is still the food and restaurants businesses. Nowadays even medical services and home based health care rely on franchising though.

Intellectual Property

Intellectual property, also known by its acronym of IP, is the concept having to do with creations from a person's mind. The ownerships of such property are recognized as rights that can be possessed, bought, and sold. As such, they have also given rise to relevant fields of law.

As a result of this intellectual property rights and law, creators and owners of many intangible assets obtain exclusive rights to them. This includes literary, musical, and art works; inventions and discoveries; and also phrases, designs, symbols, and words. The most prevalent forms of intellectual property are then trademarks, copyrights, trade secrets, patents, and industrial design rights.

Intellectual property rights go back to the 1600 and 1700's in early modern Great Britain. The Statute of Monopolies from 1623 is viewed as the origin of patent law, while the Statute of Anne from 1710 is looked at as the basis for copyright laws. The phrase intellectual property arose in the 1800's. It finally became common in the U.S. in the late 1900's.

Intellectual property rights are believed to create economic growth and a flourishing free enterprise system. This is because such rights of exclusivity permit the creators and owners of these intellectual properties to realize financial benefit from their creation. It gives individuals and businesses motive to develop and invest in intellectual property. With patents, such businesses are willing to come out of pocket for the development and research costs because of this incentive.

Because of this, the creation and maintenance of these intellectual property laws are given the credit for major contributions made to great economic growth in the Western World like the United States and Great Britain. Many economists point out that around two thirds of big businesses' value lies in intangible assets. It is also said that industries that use intellectual property intensively create as much as seventy-two percent more added value for every employee than do those industries that do not use intellectual property intensively. This is to say that a great deal of economic growth is generated by intellectual property rights and associated industries.

Critics of intellectual property rights do exist. Those in the free culture movement hold up intellectual monopolies as examples of things that hold back progress, damage health, and concentrate ownership to the disadvantage of the common people. They argue that the public good is hurt by monopolies that constantly grow out of software patents, extensions of copyrights, and business method patents.

Besides this, some claim that intellectual property rights that are strictly enforced slow down the transfer of technological advances and scientific break through to poor countries. Still, developing nations are beneficiaries of developed nation technologies like vaccines, the Internet, mobile phones, and higher yielding crops. Critics claim that patent laws come down too hard in favor of the people who develop innovations versus those who employ them.

IRA Custodian

An IRA custodian is commonly represented by some form of a financial institution. This would likely be a brokerage or a bank. These Individual Retirement Accounts' custodians have the job of protecting your assets in your IRA.

Per the rules of the Internal Revenue Service, such IRA custodians have to be financial institutions that are approved. People can not choose to perform the role of an IRA custodian. In order for institutions that are not financial in nature to perform the responsibilities of such IRA custodians, they have to receive a special approval issued to them by the Internal Revenue Service.

These IRA Custodians actually carry out the transactions that the clients request of them. They also file any and all reports, maintain all required records of anything done on the account as a custodian, and send out statements and notices for taxes, either of which may be mandated by law or the agreement for custodianship.

They sometimes will disburse the assets found in the IRA as per the wishes of the client, as well as file all necessary and relevant paper work with this action. One thing that IRA custodians do not have to do is to offer legal or investment advice to you, the IRA holder. This means that you have to provide the custodian of your IRA with clear and accurate instructions which follow the code established by the IRS.

IRA custodians can be responsible for overseeing a great range of investment securities and financial instruments. While IRS rules restrict IRA money being invested into collectibles like rare coins and artworks, or even life insurance, the custodian is able to work with various different investments like franchises, real estate, tax liens, and mortgages.

Still, a great number of financial institutions acting as IRA custodians will choose to restrict the kinds of investments that they will allow to be held in one of their IRA's under custodianship. It is important for owners of IRA's who wish to have their funds placed into investments that are not traditional for IRA's, such as real estate or franchises, to seek out and choose an IRA custodian who will allow and work with these kinds of investments. This is the particular reason that a real estate management firm might choose to attain IRS certification in order to obtain the permission for overseeing real estate investment IRA's.

Much of the time, IRA customers will just deposit their retirement money and assets into their account that the custodian holds and will supply them with overall guidelines for their investments. The IRS mandates fiduciary responsibility for IRA custodians. They have to place clients' interests first. This translates to practical requirements, such as not being allowed to put the IRA money into investments and projects that come with a great amount of risk, unless they have the customer's expressed consent.

IRA custodians are also involved with self directed IRA's. Self directed IRA's contain investments that are actively managed directly by the customer. The custodian only performs the actions that the customer requests in these cases.

Land Law

Land law represents the type of law discipline that pertains to the various inherent rights of individuals to utilize (or restrict others from) owned land. There are many jurisdictions of the world that employ the words real property or real estate to describe such privately, corporately, or government owned land. Land utilization agreements such as renting prove to be a critical intersecting point where land law and contract law meet.

Water rights and mineral rights to a piece of property are closely connected to and interrelated with land law. Such land rights turn out to be so important that this form of law always develops one way or another, regardless of whether or not a country, kingdom, or empire exists to enforce it. A classic example of this phenomenon is the American West and its claim clubs. These institutions came about on their own as a means for land owners to enforce the rules which surrounded staking claims and mines' ownership.

When people occupy land without owning it, this is called squatting. This problem was not limited to the old American West, but is in fact universally practiced by the poor or disenfranchised throughout the world. Practically all nations and territories of the world maintain some form of a system for land registration. With this system there is also a process for land claims utilized in order to work out any disputes surrounding land ownership and access.

International land law recognizes the territorial land rights of indigenous peoples. Besides this, country's legal systems also acknowledge such land rights, calling them aboriginal title in many regions. In societies which still utilize customary law, land ownership is primarily exercised by customary land holding traditions.

Land rights also pertain to the inalienable abilities for individuals to freely purchase, use, and hold land according to their wishes. Naturally this assumes that their various endeavors on the property do not interfere with the rights of other members of society.

This should never be confused with the concepts of land access. Land access means that individuals have the rights to use a piece of property economically, as with farming or mining activities. Such access is considered to be far less secure than ownership of the land itself, since a person only using the property can be evicted from it at the whim of the land owner.

Land law also deals with the statutes which a nation sets out regarding the ownership of land. This can be difficult to reconcile in some countries as they have the more traditional customary land ideas such as group or individual land rights as part of their culture instead of legal understandings. This is why the various laws between land rights and land ownership have to be harmonious to prevent bitter disputes, fighting, and indigenous territorial standoffs.

Around the world, a growing focus on such land rights and the way these intersect with traditional laws on the land has emerged. Land ownership represents an important and often necessary for survival (in many cultures) source for food, water, resources, shelter, financial security, and even capital. This is why the United Nations Global Land Tool organization links landlessness in rural areas with both poverty and malnutrition.

It led to the Millennium Development Goal 7D which works to better the lives and livelihoods of around 100 million individual slum dwellers. This project is working to promote land rights and land ownership for poor people the world over in hopes that this will finally lead them to a higher quality of life and more stable and secure existence.

Legal Tender

Legal tender proves to be official forms of payment that the nation's government recognizes for paying either private or public debts or for meeting any number of financial obligations. In nearly all nations, national currency is the one and only legal tender. Creditors have no choice but to receive this currency for repaying of debts owed to them. It is only the appropriately endowed national institutions which are permitted to issue such legal tender. In the United States, this means the U.S. Treasury. In Canada, it refers to the Royal Canadian Mint.

Any type of payment which must be taken for a debt is legal tender. The laws of the land determine which payments are such currencies. This term mostly pertains to money in cash form like coins and bills. It does not include credit cards, bank cards, checks, or lines of credit. Laws which pertain to legal tender are the bedrock in the forming of a country's fiscal policy for a great number of states.

In the days of the American federalist debates, individuals who sought to restrict the powers of the new central government attempted to force rules restricting the creation of a national central bank and to ensure that the national government could not issue currency. Such positions as those espoused by the anti-federalists were mostly defeated. The U.S. Constitution does in fact forbid individual states from issuing their own currencies, meaning they obtained at least a partial state-level victory.

Following the American war for independence, the fledgling nation utilized a wide range of foreign silver and gold coins in trade. Throughout the American Civil War, these policies had to be altered because of the enormous levels of government debt issued and assumed. Because of these expenditures, the American government chose to start producing paper bills for money. With its landmark ruling in 1965, the U.S. Supreme Court affirmed that all American government issued money, including coins and bills, was legal tender. This meant that it had to be taken in payment of debts by every party within the U.S. They similarly ruled that foreign-issued money is not acceptable for forms of payments.

This Supreme Court ruling did not completely settle the issue once and for all. In 2002, the long simmering topic on the issue of currency rose to the forefront of policy debate once again. It was the introducing of the Legal Tender Modernization Act within the U.S. House of Representatives that set it off once again. Besides various other provisos, the act insisted on the termination in circulation of the penny.

Those in favor of the bill under discussion argued that pennies were worthless as a currency since they could not be utilized in most purchases or with vending machines. They cost significantly more than their face value to make and circulate and depend on heavy metal polluting industries in mining both zinc and copper. Despite its public interest, this bill never moved forward into the Congress. Rather it died a slow death for lack of interest and sponsors following the termination of that year's lawmaking session.

Among the great debates for the early years of the 21st century, the Europeans adopting the Euro took monetary center stage. A great number of nations had century's long association with their proprietary and historical national currencies. The switch over to such a common currency format angered the fearful nationalists living within Europe. Around 20 nations eventually joined this new Euro zone and replaced their beloved old currencies with the euro. Most significantly, the U.K., Sweden, and Denmark refused to join and gained exemptions from the common currency requirements and mandate, electing to hold on to their own national currencies instead.

Lien

A lien is a claim on one individual's property by another person or entity. The party that holds the lien is able to recover the property if a debtor will not follow through with making payments. There are also other circumstances in which liens would allow the lien holder to take the property. Mortgages on houses or buildings prove to be one kind these. Vehicle loans for a business or individual represent other types that are put on the value of the vehicle. When the obligation is paid off, the lien becomes discharged.

Before individuals are able to receive their money after the sale of an asset like a car or house, the lien must be paid off first. With a vehicle, this means that the lender will not send out the title until they receive complete repayment of the principal.

The majority of liens allow for the individuals or businesses to utilize the property as they are paying it. There are scenarios where the lender or creditor physically holds the property while the borrower is making payments. These are a part of bankruptcy procedures as well because they are secured loans with debt repayment rules that have to be addressed in a case.

While there are a number of different types of liens, the most typical one is on a vehicle. Individuals buy a car from the dealer. The bank loans the money and secures the loan. They do this by placing a vehicle lien which allows them to hold on to the automobile's title. The lender files a UCC-1 form to record this. So long as the debtor continues to make payments, the loan will be paid off finally. The bank would then release to the individual the title.

If the individuals stop making their payments, the bank is able to take possession of the vehicle back while still holding the title. If the vehicle owners choose to sell the automobile when they still owe principal, they must clear the bank loan in order to obtain the title. Without the title, a person can not sell the vehicle.

There are a variety of different types of liens in the world. Consensual ones are those which individuals voluntarily accept when they buy something.

Non consensual ones are also known as statutory. These come from a court process where an entity places a lien on assets because bills have not been paid. Three of these are fairly common.

A tax lien occurs when individuals do not pay local, state, or federal income taxes. These are put on the offender's property. A judgment lien comes as a result of a case in a small claims court. When a court gives a judgment to one party, the offending party might refuse to pay. In this case the court will place a judgment lien on the offender's property.

A mechanic or contractor lien happens when a contractor performs a job for a home owner. If the owner refuses to pay, the contractor can ask a court to place a lien on the property in question. This would have to be paid off along with other security interests before the property owner is able to sell.

Financial Terms Dictionary - Laws & Regulations Explained

Money Laundering

Money laundering refers to the methods for taking income from corruption and crime and turning them into legal assets. Many countries and jurisdictions have re-defined the term to focus on financial or business crime, often used to support drug dealing empires or terrorism financing. The phrase can also refer to improperly utilizing the financial system for a variety of reasons. In these cases, it might involve digital currencies, traditional currency, credit cards, and even securities.

In recent years money laundering has become associated with international sanction avoidance and financing of terrorist acts. The pursuit of this focuses on the source of money while that of terrorism financing is worried about the destination of this money.

Throughout history, countries, kingdoms, and rules created regulations designed to seize wealth from their citizens. This eventually caused the formation of tax evasion and offshore banking. Though these are not crimes in all countries, the ones that do penalize and pursue it consider it to be a form of money laundering.

In the early years of the 1900s, wealth began to be seized as a means of stopping crime. This began in earnest during the American Prohibition of the 1930s. Law enforcement agencies and the government became concerned with tracking down and seizing money involved in illegal alcohol sales. Organized crime had obtained an enormous boost because of the major new source of funds illegal alcohol vending provided.

The emphasis for fighting money laundering shifted in the 1980s to drug dealers and empires in the American led war on drugs. Governments and law enforcement became concerned with seizing the financial rewards from drug related crime as they pursued the drug empire founders, managers, and dealers. These laws required individuals to demonstrate that their seized funds were from legitimate sources in order to get them back.

The most recent focus of this illegal activities pursuit centered around terrorism empires that began with the 9/11 attacks in 2001. The Patriot Act in America and comparable legislation passed around the developed world gave a new motivation for such rules which would help fight terrorism and its financing.

The G7 Group of Seven wealthy nations created its Financial Action Task Force on Money Laundering to pressure other governments around the globe. They wanted greater observation and monitoring for financial transactions with information sharing between nations. This resulted in improved monitoring systems for financial transactions and stronger anti-laundering laws from 2002.

These regulations have created a far heavier burden for international banks. Enforcement of perceived money laundering breaches has led to severe investigations and steep fines against major international financial institutions. British banking giant HSBC received a hefty $1.9 billion fine from the U.S. in December of 2012. French bank BNP Paribas reeled from a steep $8.9 billion fine from the U.S. government in July of 2014.

A number of nations have also instituted stricter rules on the amount of currency which is allowed to be physically carried across borders. Governments have set up central transaction reporting systems to make all of the financial institutions report every electronic financial transaction. The American Department of the Treasury established its Office of Terrorism and Financial Intelligence to seek out and exploit weaknesses in the networks of money laundering operations through national and international financial systems.

Oversight

Oversight is a critical regulatory concept. Thanks to the Congressional act the Sarbanes-Oxley Act of 2002, independent oversight became a major new requirement for occupations pertaining to accounting at public companies. This act and trend in government regulating led to the creation of the PCAOB. PCAOB stands for the Public Company Accounting Oversight Board.

This organization proves to be a not for profit entity which oversees the auditors at publicly traded corporations. The aim of the board lies in safeguarding both stakeholders and investors in public firms. They do this by making certain that the company financial statements and auditor statements follow a rigorous set of guidelines.

The PCAOB also has borne the responsibility since 2010 of overseeing broker-dealer audits. This means that any compliance reports which auditors file according to the requirements of the federal securities laws must foster protection of investors. It is up to the United States SEC Securities and Exchange Commission to approve all standards and rules of this particular regulatory entity. This organization has brought about the historical first time oversight (via both independent and external means) of American public company auditors. Before this Sarbanes-Oxley Act passed in 2002, the profession and industry was self-regulated from within its own ranks.

There are four main functions of the Public Company Accounting Oversight Board. These include overseeing auditors in the specific capacities of standard setting, inspection, registration, and enforcement. They do this to ensure that there will be accurate, highly informative, and completely independent audit reports prepared for the good of the investing and buying public.

Today's Public Company Accounting Oversight Board counts five members on its continuously standing board. The Chairman is the head of this governing and steering body. They receive appointments for five year terms of service which are staggered for continuity in and stability of the board composition. It is the SEC Securities and Exchange Commission who appoints the board members. They do this after consulting with the

Secretary of the U.S. Treasury and the Board of Governors for the Federal Reserve System's Chairperson. Besides approving the composition of the board members for the PCAOB, the SEC has other important functions. They must also sign off on the board's budget as well as their standards and rules.

The PCAOB activities are paid for through means provided in the Dodd-Frank Wall Street Reform and Consumer Protection Act. This provided a means of funding for all of their functions. The money mostly is derived from annually assessed accounting support fees. Public companies are required to pay these fees. The amounts are set by the size of their average monthly market capitalization relative to other publicly traded firms. Broker dealers are also now assessed fees (since 2010) that go to the PCAOB's support. These are determined by the firms' average quarterly tentative net capital on a relative basis to the other broker-dealers in the industry.

The vision for this Public Company Accounting Oversight Board is to establish itself in the tradition of a model organization for regulation. They do this by employing cost-effective means and tools which are innovative. They seek to better the quality of audits overall and to lessen the dangers of auditing failures for the United States' public markets. They are also working towards improving public trust surrounding the auditing profession in particular and the process of financial reporting in general.

This Public Company Accounting Oversight Board arose because of a constantly increasing series of restatements from the accounting filings of American public firms during the 1990s. There were especially a number of embarrassing and highly damaging accounting scandals that decade which led to horrific and record-making bankruptcies of huge public firms. Among these were the two major scandal examples of Enron and WorldCom. Arthur Andersen was the big five accounting firm that was incriminated in helping to make these scandals possible. They became complicit in signing off on the financial statements and filings of the two companies in question.

Before the PCAOB became founded, it was up to the AICPA American Institute of Certified Public Accountants to self-regulate the industry. The board became dissolved officially on March 31st of 2002. SEC Chairman Harvey Pitt appointed William H. Webster as official first chair of the

PCAOB.

Ponzi Scheme

Ponzi Schemes prove to be frauds surrounding investments that are related to the pay out of returns to investors in the scheme that are covered using contributions from new investors. The individuals who run Ponzi schemes are able to attract newer investors through boasting of tremendous opportunities that will guarantee terrific investment returns, typically with little to no risk.

With a great number of these Ponzi Schemes, the managers of the scheme concentrate their efforts on constantly bringing in new sums of money in order to be capable of giving out the payments that they promised investors from earlier time periods. Besides this, they utilize the new money for their own personal expenses. Rarely does any energy actually go into real investment opportunities and strategies.

Ponzi schemes always fail at some point in time. This eventually happens since there are no real earnings to distribute. Because of this problem, Ponzi schemes need constant money flowing into them from newer investors in order to survive. As attracting newer investors becomes more challenging, or if a great number of currently involved investors request their money back, then the Ponzi Scheme will likely fall apart.

Ponzi Schemes actually earned their name from a famed early con artist Charles Ponzi. He became famous after he tricked literally thousands of well to do New Englanders into pouring their money into his speculation in postage stamps in the 1920's. The allure of his scheme proved to be hard to resist, since bank accounts were paying only five percent annual returns while he offered investors incredible returns of fifty percent in only ninety days. In the early days, Charles Ponzi really did purchase a small quantity of international mail coupons to support his investment scheme. Before long, he decided to employ the money that came in to cash out earlier investors.

The most successful Ponzi Scheme of all time proved to be the one run by Bernie Madoff. Madoff ran an over thirty year, over thirty billion dollar investment scheme that tricked thousands of investors out of their money. Madoff proved to have a different angle on his Ponzi scheme in that he did not offer his investors who were short term amazing returns. Rather than this, he sent out fake account statements that constantly demonstrated moderate but always positive gains, no matter how turbulent the market proved to be.

Bernie Madoff is presently undergoing a one hundred and fifty year sentence in federal prison for his activities. His investment advisory company began back in 1960 and did not come down until the end of 2008. All during the years that his scheme ran, he served as Vice Chairman of the National Association of Securities Dealers, and even as a member of the board of governors and chairman for the NASDAQ stock market.

The Securities Exchange Commission is ultimately responsible for discovering and prosecuting Ponzi Schemes. They typically utilize emergency actions to freeze assets while they break up the schemes. In 2009 as an example, the SEC actually pursued sixty different Ponzi schemes, the highest profile one of which turned out to be Robert Allen Stanford's $8 billion Ponzi scheme.

Financial Terms Dictionary - Laws & Regulations Explained

Price Controls

Price Controls turn out to be government decreed standards for maximum or minimum prices which they set on specific goods. These are typically put into place in order to intervene directly in an economy so they can arrange for essential goods to be made affordable. Governments are interested in affecting these controls on staple goods. These include such critical things as foodstuffs and energy. Within these types of controls, price ceilings are those which decree maximum prices which can be charged, at the same time as price floors are such controls which determine minimum prices.

Governments have a lengthy sordid history with attempting to implement price controls. Their attempts have demonstrated that the effects of these measures work only effectively for short time frames. In the long run, such controls always cause great difficulties like rationing, shortages, poor quality product declines, and black market transactions which become popular as an alternative means of providing the goods which are price controlled via unofficial distribution systems.

As prices are alternatively set by free market forces of supply and demand, the prices naturally rise and fall in order to maintain the equilibrium between such demand and supply. There has never been a successful effort by governments over the long term to defeat the all powerful forces of supply and demand. Governments which impose their controls end of creating either too much demand when price ceilings are established or too much supply when price floors are enacted. As a method of government intervention, these controls have been proven to never work in practice, even when governments have established them with the very best of end goals.

Examples of failed and botched efforts at price controls abound in the United States. Rent controls are a classic example of these and how ineffective they usually are. New York City widely implemented such rent controls to try to enable a sufficient supply of housing which is affordable. The real world impact has actually been to lower the total supply of rental units. This has caused still higher costs for rental in the rental housing market.

The true net effect of such rent controls has been that they discouraged entrepreneurs in real estate from getting into the landlord business. It has led to a supply crisis which means that a significantly lower amount of rental housing is now available than would have been the case if they had simply left the free market forces to work out the fair prices. Another problem that has arisen from these rent controls is that landlords do not have the necessary motivation to improve the rental properties or even to properly maintain them to an acceptable standard for the tenants. This has caused a significant deterioration in the quality of the available rental housing stock as well.

The U.S. also implemented price controls in the wake of the Japanese bombing of Pearl Harbor, Hawaii, which led to the outbreak of World War II in America. The feds began to expand existing controls and to establish new ones to preserve the critical elements of the economy. President Franklin D. Roosevelt on January 6, 1942 detailed his new production goals which were necessary to support the war effort he claimed. Practically all of the national economic industries were placed ever increasingly under direct control of the government.

Economists are typically dead set against these types of controls, but everyone agreed this was a national state of emergency at the time. To do this more effectively, the Federal Government created the agencies like the Office of Price Administration (OPA) and the War Production Board (WPB) in 1942 to help boost overall production output and to control prices and wages as well.

The National War Labor Board arose as the result of President Roosevelt's executive order on January 12, 1942. This implemented price and wage controls along with the firing and hiring of employees. This agency approved increases to wages and adopted what became known as the Little Steel formula to make wartime changes because of the increasing cost of living.

A final recent example of such botched price controls centered on the Nixon administration implementation of controls on gasoline products. This finally caused massive supply shortages, rationing of fuel, and lengthy, tedious lines at gas stations.

Price Gouging

Price gouging involves businesses charging higher prices than those that are considered to be fair or normal. It is most often done when there are crises or natural disasters strike. This gouging could also result from temporary boosts in demand that are not matched by supply. If suppliers' expenses rises, this is not considered to be a form of gouging when they pass it along to customers.

Because price gouging is usually considered to be unethical, it is generally treated as strictly illegal in a great number of places. Interestingly though, this gouging originates from what many economists call an efficient market outcome.

As demand goes up for a given product, this signifies that consumers will and are able to pay more to purchase an additional quantity of the good at the fair market price. Increases in a good's demand generally lead to short term product shortages. Suppliers are tempted when they see extended lines of people forming (to purchase their product) to both raise their prices and to increase the amount of their product that is available. Suppliers who are retailers will attempt to bring in more product into their stores. Supply and demand return to balance at a higher price in many examples.

When demand increases, everyone can not have the amount that they want for the initial market price. This means that if the price does not go up, shortages will occur. It is because the supplier needs an incentive to provide a greater amount of the goods in question. As supply and demand return to balance, all people who are capable of paying the market price can obtain as much as they need.

The supply and demand balance proves to be efficient economically. The goods go to all individuals who want the product for a greater price than they cost to make. Companies can maximize their profits as well. With shortages, there is no set way that the goods become rationed. Though usually this is on a first come, first serve basis, it might be resolved through bribes to the owner of the store. Such a bribe would amount to raising the price anyway.

It is critical to realize that in times of excessive demand, everyone can not

Financial Terms Dictionary - Laws & Regulations Explained

obtain their full demand for the product at the original price. Higher prices will generally increase the amount of good supplied so that those who wish most to have them can. This should not be confused with price gouging per se.

There are many critics of price gouging, including most governments. These critic argue that short term supply can not be adequately resolved by higher prices. Demand increase in cases like natural disasters do not allow for suppliers to provide more of the product. They only lead to increases in the price or shortages. This is because supplies in these cases are limited to the inventory a store has on hand.

The critics say that such short term shortages and accompanying price gauging only leads to suppliers realizing excessive profits at the consumer's expense. Though higher prices are often illegal in such cases, these prices serve a purpose. They distribute the goods more efficiently than prices which prove to be artificially low will since they lead to shortages.

As a classic example, when there is an increased demand, higher prices will reduce hoarding by the people who arrive first at the store. This means that there should be more of the demanded good remaining for others who arrive later and are willing to pay more than the original price.

Progressive Taxes

Progressive taxes exact a larger pound of flesh from the income of higher income earners than they do from lower income contemporaries. The idea is a tax system which is based upon the ability of an income earner to pay. In other words, the system demands a bigger percentage and absolute amount in taxes from the larger earners than from the lower income workers.

The American income tax system has long been considered to be progressive in practice. For the taxing year 2016, those persons who possess under $9,275 in income pay only 10 percent in income tax. The taxpayers who bring in over the benchmark highest income level of $415,050 are grouped in the maximum tax system bracket. These people will pay rates as high as 39.6 percent of their income to the tax man.

These progressive taxes gouge the higher income groups for a substantially higher tax rate percentage and absolute amount than they do the lower income earners. It is based more on the ability of the earner to pay than a simple flat percentage tax would be. Progressive tax systems could hit the lower earners at 10 percent, while assessing middle income earners at 15 percent and higher income workers for over 30 percent. This is the basis of the United States taxing model and system.

A tax structure's actual progressivity is dependent on how fast the rate rises in correlation with the income increases of the earner in question. A tax code with a lowest rate of 10 percent and a highest bracket of 30 percent would be less progressive than one that offers rates of income taxes which vary from a low of 10 percent to a high of 80 percent. These kinds of radically progressive tax systems are most famous in the countries of Scandinavia and Northern Europe.

There are some obvious advantages to progressive taxes. They lower the relevant tax burden on those working poor and the families which can not afford to pay them at all. This is why such taxing systems leave as much money in the lower wage earners' accounts as possible. These people will in fact spend all they make from their paychecks and stimulate the economic activity of the country.

Such progressive taxes also possess the unique ability to bring in a greater amount of tax income to the governments than do the regressive or flat income tax plans. This is because the tax rates climb as does the relevant earned income. With a progressive tax system, those wage earners who have the highest possible resources to contribute will fund a larger share of the public services and goods which all citizens equally enjoy and utilize. This includes snow and debris removal, national park usage, first responder activity, and roads and other forms of national infrastructure.

There are also some disadvantages to progressive taxes as well. The critics of this form of taxing system say that they unfairly discriminate against earners based on how much they earn or if they are wealthy through business, investments, or inheritance. Such critics feel that the U.S. progressive system of income taxes is actually a sneaky and covert way of redistributing income. This is based on the incorrect notion that the majority of taxes go to pay for social welfare programs in America. In truth, only a tiny proportion of actual government spending is directed at welfare programs and their income redistributing payments.

Financial Terms Dictionary - Laws & Regulations Explained

Proportional Taxes

Proportional Taxes are a type of income tax system. In this taxation system, the identical percentage of taxes is applied to all taxpayers in an economy. It does not matter how much or how little they earn. This type of tax simply levies the same rate on all high income, middle income, and low income workers as well as businesses.

This stands in direct contrast to a more widely utilized progressive tax system. In this competing type of tax plan, those taxpayers who enjoy greater income levels pay at higher income tax rates than the unfortunate bottom income earning citizens. Proportional taxes are also often known as the flat tax since it is a one tax plan fits all sizes means of collecting revenues for a government.

Besides proportional taxes and progressive taxes, there are also regressive taxes. A regressive tax takes a larger share of income from the lower classes than they can afford. Sometimes flat taxes are considered to be regressive in nature. The difference between these three types of tax structures comes down to the way the tax addresses the tax base (of a business income or household income) as the income level is significantly different.

In these proportional taxes systems, every tax payer, regardless of income level or job, will pay the identical percentage of their earnings in taxes. If this given proportional rate is set up at 20 percent, then the earner at $10,000 gives $2,000 of income to the taxing authorities, while the worker making $50,000 will pay in $10,000. At the same time, the higher earner with $1 million in annual income will pay the same rate for a grand total of tax payment amounting to $200,000. This system is so much simpler and eliminates the needs for large, wasteful, and bureaucratic taxing agencies.

Sales taxes are another example of proportional taxes. This is the case because every consumer, regardless of the amount of money which he or she makes, will pay the sales tax at the identical fixed sales tax rate. It is almost a given that sales taxes will be proportional. Since all goods and services are affected by them, a government can not simply alter the rate based on a person's actual income. Buying a good does not factor in the income of the buyer in the transaction, and so far there is no known way to change this to a more progressive form of tax.

Many economists and analysts consider these proportional taxes to be a form of regressive tax by accident. Since the rate never goes up regardless of how high the income of the person in question goes, the higher burden remains on the lower income earners. They can least afford to pay the flat rate tax, while a high income earner has the ability to pay his or her elevated but still same percentage share. With the same example from above, the earner who garners $10,000 only has $8,000 left on which to live after paying his or her share of taxes. The worker bringing down $50,000 gets to keep fully $40,000 after taxes. The million dollar stunner holds on to $800,000 after paying his or her share. The percentage of the tax is the same in every scenario.

Many people call this the epitome of truly fair. The problem is that the low income earner suffers from a severe after-tax hangover effect because the burden makes it impossible for him or her to live on what remains. This is how the critics of such a flat tax are able to insist that higher income people should be forced to pony up a larger percentage in income taxes than the poorer workers who outnumber them so vastly anymore.

Those in favor of proportional taxes insist that they are more fair since they encourage workers to go for greater earnings without punishing their results with higher income tax brackets and rates, as a progressive tax system inherently would. They argue that when everyone receives the same treatment, this is the ideal definition of the concept of fair. Proportional tax systems have the additional advantage of being simple for everyone to grasp and to practice. This is because there is no room for debate on the tax rate in question for any business, individual, or family.

Regressive Taxes

Regressive taxes are those which exact a greater percentage in income off of the lower income wage earners than they do from the fortunate higher income earners. This stands in direct contrast to a progressive tax that instead grabs a bigger percentage of taxes from the higher and highest income wage earners. A regressive tax is typically one which is equally applied to all residents in whatever their situation may be. It does not matter what the financial condition of the payer turns out to be.

The problem with a regressive tax is that it most harshly impacts those who can least afford to bear it, the lower income segment of society. The higher income individuals do not mind such taxes, as they can most easily afford to pay the flat rate percentages which are common in regressive taxes. It might actually be fairer for all people to pay in the identical tax rate, yet this proves to be most unjust in some scenarios. The majority of developed nations' tax systems actually utilize a more progressive schedule which over taxes the higher income persons more than the lower wage earners.

Some other kinds of tax are more equally levied. There are many examples of real world regressive taxes. Among these are sales taxes, property taxes, and user fee taxes.

Sales taxes are nearly always equally levied on all consumers in a given economy. Their ability to pay is not a factor so much as is the amount of money which they spend on taxed items. The tax is equitable as a flat rate for all consumers, yet it remains a fact that those lower income earners are most dramatically impacted and even materially harmed by it.

Take the case of two separate individuals who both buy $200 in groceries every week. They will each pay $14 in sales tax on their grocery bills. The first person in this example makes $2,000 every week, translating to a sales tax rate for the groceries of .35 percent of all income. The other worker only brings home $320 each week. This amounts to a grocery sales tax of a whopping 2.2 percent of actual income. While the literal tax rate may be the same in the two scenarios, the individual with the significantly lesser income is paying a far greater share of his or her income on the regressive sales tax.

Financial Terms Dictionary - Laws & Regulations Explained

Property taxes are another classic example of regressive taxes in theory. Assuming two property owners reside in the same taxing jurisdiction and own similar properties with identical values, they will both pay the identical dollars in property taxes to the local taxing administration. This is the case no matter how much they make. The lower wage earner would pay a substantially greater share of his or her income on the property taxes in this case. One caveat is that different wage earners do not usually have identically valued properties. The poorer people and families typically live in cheaper homes, which help to index property taxes to relevant income. This is why property taxes are not purely regressive in practice.

User fees taxes are those which the government assesses in a regressive tax form. These might cover admissions to government-owned and -operated state parks, national parks, and museums. They might also include tolls on bridges and roads and drivers' license and identification cards fees. As an example, when two families go to the Grand Canyon National Park, they each pay the same $30 fee for admission to the nature park. The higher income family is actually paying in a significantly lower percentage of total income than is the poorer family. The fee may be identical literally, yet it represents a substantially greater burden for the family which has the lesser income.

Printed in Great Britain
by Amazon